Spanish Conversational Review Grammar
Third Edition

Spanish Conversational Review Grammar

Third Edition

Everett W. Hesse

University of Maryland

Héctor H. Orjuela

University of California, Irvine

VAN NOSTRAND REINHOLD COMPANY

New York   Cincinnati   Toronto   London   Melbourne

Van Nostrand Reinhold Company Regional Offices:
Cincinnati   New York   Chicago   Millbrae   Dallas

Van Nostrand Reinhold Company Foreign Offices:
London   Toronto   Melbourne

Manufactured in the United States of America

Published by Van Nostrand Reinhold Company
450 West 33rd Street, New York, N.Y. 10001

Published simultaneously in Canada by
D. Van Nostrand Company (Canada), Ltd.

10 9 8 7 6 5 4 3

Preface

The Third Edition of *Spanish Conversational Review Grammar* continues the major objectives of the previous editions: To present a comprehensive but concise review of grammatical principles, verbs, and idioms while promoting the basic language skills, with special emphasis on audio-lingual practice.

In the new edition we have modified the lesson organization so as to follow explanations of structure directly with appropriate practice, and we have expanded the exercises with pattern and verb drills. We have divided the initial lesson of the previous editions into two lessons to provide more gradual review and practice of verb forms. To improve the student's writing skill, we have, as before, included *Práctica escrita* and *Composición* in each lesson.

Each lesson consists of eight sections:

I. *Diálogo:* The dialog involves the basic vocabulary, idioms, verbs, and grammatical points with which the student will work in the remaining sections of the lesson. The language of the dialogs is up to date, using current vocabulary and common idioms close to the student's level of experience. The *diálogo* is to be assigned for home study; it may be committed to memory and dramatized in class.

II, III. *Modismos y expresiones* and *Práctica sobre modismos y expresiones:* The idioms and expressions are essentially nongrammatical items for special study intended to sharpen the student's sense of discrimination between Spanish idioms and equivalent English. The idioms and expressions are listed for handy reference and review and then drilled in several types of exercises.

IV. *Repaso de verbos:* The verb review gives practice in using verb forms in complete sentences involving variations in number, person, and tense.

V. *Gramática y ejercicios:* Brief explanations of grammatical principles are arranged topically and numbered consecutively through the book for easy reference. The grammatical explanations for the lesson on personal pronouns have been completely rewritten in this edition to aim for greater clarity and precision of meaning. In line with modern techniques, model sentences precede descriptions.

The exercises have been integrated into the grammatical section in order to furnish immediate drill within close proximity of the explanation. They proceed from the easy to the more difficult. For the most part, they are of the structural type designed, through repetition and reinforcement, to establish correct responses until mastery of the structural elements involved becomes automatic.

VI. *Práctica escrita:* The exercises in this section combine structural manipulation with practice in writing, using grammar, vocabulary, and idioms previously learned.

VII. *Práctica oral:* This section, in three parts, provides additional oral practice and review. A *diálogo complementario* contains previous vocabulary, expressions, and grammatical points in a new context. *Expresión oral* suggests ideas for self-expression within a range of topics, expressions, and vocabulary featured in the dialogs. *Plática espontánea* asks questions of a general nature designed to make the student talk about persons, places, things, and ideas with which he should be familiar. The *plática* affords the student an opportunity to draw upon his cumulative knowledge of Spanish and his imagination to express himself "freely."

VIII. *Composición:* The final section in each lesson offers suggestions for written composition.

The eight sections may be taken up on two or three class days, supplemented by practice in the language laboratory. Three class periods may well be spent on each lesson, as follows:

First Day: Sections I, II, III.
Second Day: Sections IV, V.
Third Day: Sections VI, VII, VIII.

Information about the comprehensive tapes accompanying *Spanish Conversational Review Grammar, Third Edition,* appears inside the front cover of this book. The tapes are available from the publisher.

Contents

In each lesson:

I. Diálogo
II. Modismos y expresiones
III. Práctica sobre modismos y expresiones
IV. Repaso de verbos
V. Gramática y ejercicios orales
VI. Práctica escrita
VII. Práctica oral
    A. Diálogo complementario
    B. Expresión oral
    C. Plática espontánea
VIII. Composición

Lección primera   *2*

1. Present   2. Imperfect   3. Preterit

Lección segunda   *20*

4. Future   5. Conditional   6. Present Perfect   7. Pluperfect
8. Preterit Perfect   9. Future Perfect   10. Conditional Perfect
11. **Saber** and **conocer**

Lección tercera   *36*

12. Gender of Nouns   13. Plural of Nouns   14. Definite Article
15. Contractions of Definite Article   16. Indefinite Article
17. Neuter Article **lo**

Lección cuarta   *52*

18. **Ser**   19. **Estar**

Lección quinta   *68*

20. Personal **a**   21. Personal Pronouns   22. Subject Pronouns

23. Direct Object Pronouns   24. Indirect Object Pronouns
25. Indirect Object with Intransitive Verbs   26. Indirect Object
after Special Verbs   27. Prepositional Pronouns   28. Two
Pronouns as Objects of the Verb

Lección sexta 88

29. Affirmative and Negative Words   30. Uses of Affirmative
and Negative Words   31. Numerals   32. Use of Ordinals
33. Time of Day   34. Seasons   35. Days of the Week
36. Months of the Year

Lección séptima 104

37. Possessive Adjectives   38. Possessive Pronouns   39. Demonstrative Adjectives   40. Demonstrative Pronouns   41. Fourth
Demonstrative   42. Neuter Demonstrative Pronouns

Lección octava 120

43. Adjectives   44. Position of Adjectives   45. Shortened Form
of Adjectives   46. Special Uses of Adjectives   47. Adverbs

Lección novena 134

48. Comparison of Adjectives and Adverbs   49. Irregular
Comparison   50. Comparison of Equality   51. "Than"
52. Absolute Superlative

Lección décima 146

53. Interrogatives   54. Interrogatives as Exclamations
55. Relative Pronouns, Adjectives, and Adverbs

Lección once 162

56. Reflexive Verbs   57. Reflexive Pronouns   58. The Reflexive
in Fortuitous Events   59. Passive Voice   60. Substitute
Constructions for the Passive

Lección doce 178

61. Subjunctive in Independent Clauses   62. Subjunctive in
Dependent Clauses with Main Verbs Suppressed   63. Imperative

Lección trece 192

64. Subjunctive in Dependent Clauses   65. Clauses Introduced
by the Conjunction **que**   66. Clauses Introduced by a Relative

Pronoun   67. Sequence of Tenses in the Subjunctive
68. Table of Tense Sequence

Lección catorce   208

69. Subjunctive in Dependent Clauses   70. Conditional
Sentences   71. **Como si** Clauses

Lección quince   224

72. Infinitive   73. Participles   74. Present Participles   75. Past
Participles

Lección diez y seis   238

76. Conjunctions   77. Prepositions   78. Uses of the Preposition
por   79. Uses of the Preposition **para**   80. Infinitive after Verbs
81. Verbs Which Include the Preposition   82. Adverbs
83. Diminutives and Augmentatives

Appendix   254

Regular Verbs
Simple Tenses
Compound Tenses
Radical-Changing Verbs
Orthographic-Changing Verbs
Irregular Verbs

Vocabularies   270

Spanish-English
English-Spanish

Index   298

Spanish Conversational Review Grammar
Third Edition

Lección primera

I • DIALOGO

(En la fraternidad.)

PEDRO　El otro día mi padre y yo hablábamos de las fraternidades y de cómo han cambiado en los últimos años.

CARLOS　Sí, tienes razón. Hace poco mis hermanos dieron sangre a la Cruz Roja.

PEDRO　Mañana que es sábado, yo y dos neófitos de la fraternidad vamos a recoger juguetes y ropa vieja para los niños pobres del barrio.

CARLOS　Yo estoy encargado de un comité que visitará el hospital infantil el mes que viene con el fin de entretener a los niños con música, canciones y regalos.

PEDRO　Aquí viene Jorge. ¿Qué hay?

(Sale Jorge.)

JORGE　Acabo de ver a las muchachas de la sororidad y me he enterado de que están preparando un baile en beneficio de una fundación que ayuda a los jóvenes pobres que quieren asistir a la universidad. Venden boletos a cinco dólares la pareja.

PEDRO　Magnífico. Creo que todas las fraternidades y sororidades de la universidad deben cooperar en este plan.

CARLOS　¿En dónde tendrá lugar el baile?

JORGE　En el gran salón de fiestas del Hotel Victoria.

PEDRO　¿Habrá una orquesta de renombre?

JORGE　Sí, la de Carlos Martínez y sus gauchos.

CARLOS　He oído decir que una de las fraternidades va a llevar un grupo de niños pobres a Disneylandia.

JORGE　Sí, lo sé. Dicen que los llevarán en sus propios coches y que van a pagarles los gastos de entrada, el almuerzo y los refrescos.

PEDRO　¡Ojalá fuera pobre otra vez! Durante los primeros años de vida estudiantil tuve que trabajar en una gasolinera.

Nadie me llevó a Disneylandia. En las vacaciones traba-
jaba en un hotel para pagar los gastos de mi educación.

CARLOS Has sido muy afortunado porque no todos pueden trabajar y estudiar a la vez. Tú eres muy inteligente y tienes
mucho ingenio y entusiasmo.

PEDRO Gracias. ¿Cuánto te debo por la flor?

II • MODISMOS Y EXPRESIONES

a más no poder	*to the utmost*
a ver	*let's see*
¡cómo no!	*of course!*

By Fujihira from Monkmeyer
Estudiantes de Lima, Perú

echar piropos, flores	*to flatter, toss bouquets*
oír decir	*to hear it said*
¿qué tal?	*how are you?*
tener lugar	*to take place*
tener razón	*to be right*
una vez por semana	*once a week*
ya caigo	*now I understand*

III • PRACTICA SOBRE MODISMOS Y EXPRESIONES

A CONTESTE EN ESPAÑOL:

1 ¿Qué ha oído decir Ud. de la situación política?
2 ¿Dónde va a tener lugar la fiesta?
3 ¿Qué tal?
4 ¿Quién tiene razón, usted o su padre?
5 ¿Por qué le echa piropos a su amiga?

B USE EN FRASE COMPLETA:

1 ¡cómo no!
2 una vez por semana
3 a más no poder
4 a ver
5 oír decir

IV • REPASO DE VERBOS

A REPASE LA FORMACIÓN DE LOS TIEMPOS DE LOS VERBOS REGULARES DEL INDICATIVO EN EL APÉNDICE Y HAGA LOS EJERCICIOS ORALES QUE SIGUEN:

B PONGA EL VERBO EN EL PRESENTE, USANDO LOS SUJETOS INDICADOS:

1 Yo no necesito coche.
(nosotros, tú, ellas, usted, ustedes)
2 Nosotros bebemos leche.
(ellas, yo, usted, tú, él)
3 Ellos reciben cartas.
(nosotras, tú, usted, yo)

C PONGA LOS VERBOS DE B EN EL IMPERFECTO:

D PONGA LOS VERBOS DE B EN EL PRETÉRITO:

E VERBOS IRREGULARES EN EL PRESENTE:

caber	(to fit)	**quepo**
caer	(to fall)	**caigo**
decir	(to say)	**digo**
hacer	(to do, make)	**hago**
oír	(to hear)	**oigo**
poner	(to put, place)	**pongo**
salir	(to leave)	**salgo**
tener	(to have)	**tengo**
traer	(to bring)	**traigo**
venir	(to come)	**vengo**
dar	(to give)	**doy**
estar	(to be)	**estoy**
ir	(to go)	**voy**
ser	(to be)	**soy**
poder	(to be able)	**puedo**
querer	(to wish, want)	**quiero**
saber	(to know)	**sé**

F PREGUNTELE A UN ESTUDIANTE SI VA AL CINE HOY:

Modelo ¿Vas al cine hoy?
      Sí, voy al cine hoy.

1 si habla portugués en casa
2 si come mucho
3 si bebe leche
4 si ve a su tía todos los días
5 si sabe cuándo llegan
6 si cabe en un VW
7 si quiere estudiar
8 si hace la cama
9 si oye lo que cantan
10 si tiene dinero
11 si viene esta noche
12 si va al laboratorio
13 si puede ver la pizarra
14 si da dinero a los pobres

G CONTESTE LAS PREGUNTAS:

Modelo —Juan y Anita traen plata. ¿Y usted?
      —Yo también traigo plata.

1 Nosotros salimos del pueblo. ¿Y usted?
2 Hablan español en casa. ¿Y usted?
3 Ella quiere estudiar. ¿Y usted?
4 Ellos caben en el coche. ¿Y usted?
5 Tenemos que leer la novela. ¿Y usted?
6 Anita siempre dice la verdad. ¿Y usted?
7 Ponemos la mesa. ¿Y usted?
8 Oyen lo que gritan. ¿Y usted?
9 Alberto viene mañana. ¿Y usted?
10 Sabemos la lección. ¿Y usted?
11 El ve muy bien. ¿Y usted?

H CONTESTE:

1 ¿Cuántos años tienes?
2 ¿Cuándo vas a la fiesta?
3 ¿Por qué no puedes volver a casa?
4 ¿Qué dices?
5 ¿De dónde vienes?
6 ¿De dónde sales?
7 ¿Qué me traes?
8 ¿Cuándo quieres ir a la biblioteca?
9 ¿En dónde pones el libro?
10 ¿Sabes la lección?
11 ¿Qué me das?
12 ¿Cabes en el coche?
13 ¿Oyes lo que te digo?
14 ¿Por qué no te caes cuando corres?

V • GRAMATICA Y EJERCICIOS ORALES

1 PRESENT (EL PRESENTE)

a **Hablo.** *I speak. I'm speaking. I do speak.*

The present is equivalent to three different forms in English.

b Lo **hago** ahora.
I will do it now.
Esta noche **vamos** al cine.
Tonight we're going (will go) to the movies.

The present may be used to express a definite action in the immediate future.

EJERCICIO **A**

Conteste según el modelo:

Modelo ¿Estudian ahora?
No, estudiamos después.

1 comen
2 escriben
3 charlan
4 deciden
5 preguntan

EJERCICIO **B**

Conteste según el modelo:

Modelo ¿Cuándo vas a estudiar?
Mañana estudio.

1 nadar
2 trabajar
3 decidir
4 entrar
5 comer

EJERCICIO **C**

Conteste según el modelo:

Modelo ¿Vas a leerlo?
Sí, lo leo en seguida.

1 escribirlo
2 decirlo
3 hacerlo
4 abrirlo
5 traerlo
6 verlo
7 beberlo
8 escucharlo
9 recibirlo
10 tomarlo

c **Estudiamos** español **hace un año.**
Hace un año **que estudiamos** español.
We have been studying Spanish for a year.

The present is used with the idiom **hace . . . (que)** to express an action that began in the past and is continuing in the present.

EJERCICIO **D**

Repita las frases. Luego repítalas nuevamente cambiando el orden:

Modelo   Hace un mes que estoy aquí.
            Estoy aquí hace un mes.

1   Hablo español hace dos años.
2   Yo escucho la radio hace poco tiempo.
3   Vivo en la ciudad hace diez semanas.
4   Asisten a la universidad hace un año.
5   Se siente enfermo hace un rato.
6   Me levanto a las siete hace tres meses.
7   Enseña español hace tiempo.
8   Compro este pan hace mucho tiempo.
9   Llevo esta ropa hace dos días.
10 Pablo lee esta novela hace una semana.

EJERCICIO **E**

Haga preguntas:

Modelo   Hace dos años que estudio español.
            ¿Cuánto tiempo hace que estudia usted español?

1   Hace mucho tiempo que vive aquí Marta.
2   Hace un año que preparan las comidas.
3   Hace cinco semanas que estoy aquí.
4   Hace diez minutos que escribo la carta.
5   Hace tres semanas que viajamos por el campo.
6   Hace muchos meses que escriben la historia.
7   Hace poco tiempo que escucha Juan la radio.
8   Hace cuatro horas que nos paseamos por el parque.
9   Hace seis años que juegan al béisbol.
10 Hace media hora que jugamos.

d   Le hablé **hace** dos minutos.
       Hace dos minutos **que** le hablé.
       I spoke to him two minutes ago.

The present is used in the idiom **hace . . . (que)** to express the
idea of "ago". The main verb is in the preterit.

EJERCICIO **F**

Repita las frases. Luego repítalas nuevamente cambiando el orden:

Modelo   Hace un minuto que estuvimos aquí.
            Estuvimos aquí hace un minuto.

1   Hace unos días que estuve aquí.
2   Hace un año que viviste en México.

3 Hace ocho días que se lo prometí.
4 Hace mucho que leyó el libro.
5 Hace un rato que ella se sintió enferma.
6 Hace poco que salieron de California.
7 Hace años que existió este problema.
8 Hace quince días que partieron para Guatemala.
9 Hace varios días que estuvo aquí.
10 Hace mucho que estudió español.

2 IMPERFECT (EL IMPERFECTO)

a Mientras **llovía, estudiábamos.**
While it was raining, we were studying.
Escribía una carta cuando entró mi padre.
I was writing a letter when my father entered.

The imperfect expresses an incomplete past action, an action that was going on in the past without indication as to when it began or ended, or an action that was interrupted by another action.

b **Llegábamos** a la universidad a las ocho.
We used to arrive (we would arrive) at the university at eight.
Se levantaba a las seis todas las mañanas.
He used to get up (he would get up) every morning at six.

The imperfect expresses repeated, habitual, or customary past action.

c La muchacha **era** bonita.
The girl was beautiful.

The imperfect is used in description.

d **Eran** las diez de la mañana.
It was 10 a.m.

The imperfect is used to express past time.

e Tres verbos irregulares en el imperfecto:

ir	**iba**
ser	**era**
ver	**veía**

EJERCICIO G

Cambie los verbos al imperfecto:

1 La mañana es bonita.
2 Todos los días comemos en casa.
3 Me acuesto a las once.
4 ¿A qué hora llega usted a la universidad?
5 Tenemos mucho dinero.
6 Mientras nieva, hablan.
7 No beben café.
8 Yo no vivo en la residencia.
9 No vamos a los partidos de fútbol.
10 La ven todas las tardes.
11 Ya es la una.
12 Son las nueve de la noche.
13 Vamos al parque todos los días.
14 Visitamos a mi abuela todos los domingos.
15 Traen plata.

f **Hacía** dos años **que estudiábamos** español cuando decidimos
   ir a México.
   *We had been studying Spanish for two years when we decided to
   go to Mexico.*

The imperfect is used with the idiom **hacía . . . (que)** to express
an action that had begun in the past and continued up to a
point in the past.

EJERCICIO H

Cambie al pasado:

Modelo Hace dos años que estudio español.
        Hacía dos años que estudiaba español.

1 Hace poco tiempo que come Juan aquí.
2 Hace nueve años que preparan las comidas.
3 Hace una semana que estoy en Los Angeles.
4 Hace cinco minutos que escribe la carta.
5 Hace diez semanas que viajamos por el país.
6 Hace muchos meses que escriben la novela.
7 Hace poco tiempo que escucha Juan el disco.
8 Hace cuatro horas que nos paseamos por la calle.
9 Hace doce años que juegan al fútbol.
10 Hace hora y media que jugamos al tenis.

3 PRETERIT (EL PRETERITO)

a **Llegó** ayer.
He arrived yesterday.
Me levanté tarde esta mañana.
I got up late this morning.

The preterit expresses a completed past action, a state, or a mere fact.

b Me **vio** tres veces el mes pasado.
He saw me three times last month.

The preterit expresses repeated past action if such repeated action is considered as a complete unit.

c **Salí** de la residencia a las seis con mis amigos.
Era una mañana fresca. Andábamos lentamente.
De repente **nos detuvimos.**
I left the dormitory at six with my friends.
It was a cool morning. We were walking slowly.
Suddenly we stopped.

The preterit is used in narration in contrast to the descriptive imperfect.

d Lo **conocí** en España.
I met him in Spain.
Lo **supo** ayer.
He found it out (learned it) yesterday.
Quise hacerlo.
I tried to do it.
No **quise** hacerlo.
I refused to do it.
Al fin **pude** hacerlo.
I finally managed to do it.

The preterit expresses special meanings with certain verbs.

EJERCICIO I

Cambie los verbos al pretérito:

1 Llegan temprano.
2 Juan nada en la tarde.
3 No bebemos café.
4 María me ve a menudo.
5 El año pasado yo no asistía a la Universidad.
6 Sale Alberto de casa a las ocho.

7 No lo estudian.
8 Ella no cantaba muy bien.
9 El avión bajaba lentamente.
10 Subimos al tren.

e Verbos irregulares en el pretérito:

andar	(to walk)	**anduve**
estar	(to be)	**estuve**
tener	(to have)	**tuve**
caber	(to fit)	**cupe**
saber	(to know)	**supe**
decir	(to tell, say)	**dije**
traer	(to bring)	**traje**
hacer	(to do, make)	**hice**
venir	(to come)	**vine**
querer	(to wish, want)	**quise**

ser (to be), ir (to go): **fui, fuiste, fue, fuimos, fuisteis, fueron**
caer (to fall): **caí, caíste, cayó, caímos, cayeron**
oír (to hear): **oí, oíste, oyó, oímos, oyeron**
dar (to give): **di, diste, dio, dimos, dieron**
ver (to see): **vi, viste, vio, vimos, vieron**

EJERCICIO J

Use las palabras indicadas como sujetos del verbo:

1 Lo supe la semana pasada.
   (nosotras, tú, ella, ellos)
2 Quisimos levantarlo.
   (Juan y Marta, yo, ella, tú)
3 No quisieron venir.
   (tú, nosotros, yo, él)
4 Al fin pudo abrirla.
   (yo, María, Marta y María, nosotros)
5 Le hicieron reír.
   (yo, nosotros, tú, ella)

EJERCICIO K

Conteste:

1 ¿Qué pudieron abrir al fin Jorge y Carlos?
2 ¿Por qué no quisieron entrar en la casa?
3 ¿Cuándo lo supieron Uds.?
4 ¿A dónde quisieron ir?
5 ¿En dónde la conoció Ud.?

6 ¿Por qué no vino usted ayer?
7 ¿Quién se lo dijo a usted?
8 ¿A dónde fue usted ayer?
9 ¿Por qué se cayó el niño?
10 ¿Qué ruido oyó usted?

EJERCICIO **L**

Cambie los verbos al pretérito:

1 Yo nunca me caía en el hielo.
2 Veníamos tarde a la fiesta.
3 Yo no podía nadar porque no traía traje.
4 No oigo lo que me dicen.
5 Elena hace la cama.
6 Las gallinas ponían huevos.
7 ¿Sabe usted la verdad?
8 Juan va al garaje.
9 No me dan dinero.
10 No tenemos tiempo.
11 ¿Ves a las muchachas?
12 ¿A dónde vas?
13 No queríamos cantar.
14 ¿Qué me dices?
15 ¿No puede usted decirme la hora?
16 ¿Qué pone usted en la mesa?

EJERCICIO **M**

Repita las frases. Luego dígalas en el pretérito:

Modelo Siempre comían en este restaurante.
Ayer comieron en este restaurante.

1 Todos los días veía a mis amigos.
Ayer _____.
2 Todos los viernes íbamos al mercado de Toluca.
Hace pocos días _____.
3 No hacía sol.
_____ anteayer.
4 Nos levantábamos tarde.
_____ la semana pasada.
5 Ellos lo sabían.
_____ el lunes pasado.
6 El tren llegaba a las cinco todos los días.
_____ ayer.
7 Los jueves yo recibía una carta de mi padre.
El otro día _____.

8 A menudo yo iba al cine.
   Esta mañana _____.
9 Muchas veces leíamos en la biblioteca.
   Anteayer _____.
10 Cada semana hablaba con mi tía.
   La semana pasada _____.

EJERCICIO N

Ponga el verbo en el imperfecto:

Modelo Ayer fueron al mercado.
          Todos los sábados iban al mercado.

1 Anteayer mi primo fue a la montaña.
   Muchas veces _____.
2 El viernes pasado salimos a las ocho para la Universidad.
   Todas las mañanas _____.
3 Hace unos días me invitaron a tomar té.
   De ordinario _____.
4 Anoche fue al teatro.
   Siempre _____.
5 El año pasado no dije mentiras.
   En esos días _____.
6 Después de un rato me dio un regalo.
   Muchas veces _____.
7 Yo hablé delante de la clase una vez.
   _____ como de costumbre.
8 Ella trabajó en la biblioteca por un rato.
   _____ en esa época.
9 Escribieron mucho ese invierno.
   _____ por regla general.
10 Juan nadó ese verano.
   _____ en los veranos.

VI • PRACTICA ESCRITA

1 I have been studying here for ten years.
2 We have been eating here for five months.
3 They have been reading there for a long while.
4 They have been talking for an hour.
5 You have been saying that for years.
6 I read the book a week ago.
7 They wrote the lesson an hour ago.

8   She taught the lesson two days ago.
9   We left the house fifteen minutes ago.
10 He studied French three years ago.
11 They met us in Madrid last year.
12 We found it out last week.
13 I tried to lift the stone but I couldn't.
14 Finally I managed to lift it.
15 Did you see the man who entered the house?

VII • PRACTICA ORAL

A   DIALOGO COMPLEMENTARIO

(En la sororidad.)

MATILDE   Oí decir que preparas algo para el certamen de poesía. ¿Qué es?

EVELIA   Unos versos de Bécquer que voy a recitar la semana que viene. Mi profesor de español, el Dr. Guerra, está encargado del certamen para todas las clases de español. Estoy en el grupo «B» que es para estudiantes de segundo año. ¿Quieres oír los versos del poema?

MATILDE   ¡Cómo no! A ver.

EVELIA   «Volverán las oscuras golondrinas
en tu balcón sus nidos a colgar,
y otra vez con el ala a sus cristales
   jugando llamarán;
pero aquéllas que el vuelo refrenaban
tu hermosura y mi dicha al contemplar,
aquéllas que aprendieron nuestros nombres . . .
ésas . . . ¡no volverán!»

MATILDE   Bravo. Espero que ganes el primer premio.

EVELIA   Gracias. Me dicen que tú enseñas español por la tarde.

MATILDE   Sí, enseño español de primer año en la escuela secundaria.

EVELIA   ¿En dónde se reúnen las clases?

MATILDE   En la misma escuela. Tengo que ir allá una vez por semana.

EVELIA   ¿No son clases regulares?

MATILDE   No, son especiales para los estudiantes que necesitan práctica adicional.

EVELIA   ¿Cuánto te pagan?

MATILDE   Nada. Pero los grupos son pequeños y como espero ser profesora de español así adquiero la experiencia necesaria.

EVELIA   Ya caigo. Los alumnos son de familias pobres que no pueden pagar nada.

MATILDE   Sí, y en esta forma espero hacer algo por la sociedad en general.

EVELIA   ¡Qué altruista eres! Aquí viene Lupe.

LUPE   Buenos días, chicas. ¿Qué tal?

MATILDE Y EVELIA   Bien gracias.

LUPE   ¿Saben ustedes lo que estoy organizando?

LAS DOS   No, ¿qué?

LUPE   Un baile en el Hotel Victoria. Es en beneficio de la fundación que otorgará una beca a un estudiante en cualquier universidad del país.

MATILDE   ¿Cuáles son los requisitos de la beca?

LUPE   Que el estudiante sea pobre y no pueda pagar los gastos de su educación y que merezca la ayuda. Es decir, que tenga notas sobresalientes en sus estudios.

EVELIA   Yo ayudo a mis amigos de una fraternidad en otro proyecto de servicio social.

LUPE   ¿Qué proyecto es ése?

EVELIA   El primer sábado de octubre llevaremos un grupo de jóvenes pobres a Disneylandia. Al mismo tiempo que participamos en un proyecto valioso, nos divertiremos mucho.

B   EXPRESION ORAL

Pregunte a un amigo:

1   si vive en una fraternidad
2   cuánto tiene que pagar a la semana
3   por qué decidió ingresar en la fraternidad
4   cuándo se reúne la fraternidad
5   qué pasa en la fraternidad los fines de semana
6   si la fraternidad participa en proyectos de servicio social
7   si él participa en las actividades de la fraternidad
8   qué actividades hay

C PLATICA ESPONTANEA

1 ¿Cuántos miembros hay en su fraternidad o sororidad?
2 ¿Quién es el presidente de la fraternidad?
3 ¿Cuánto tiempo hace que usted es miembro de la fraternidad?
4 ¿Qué piensan sus padres de las organizaciones sociales universitarias?
5 ¿Cuáles son los planes de la fraternidad para el año escolar?
6 ¿Por qué vale la pena ser miembro de una fraternidad?
7 ¿Dónde está la casa?
8 ¿Es cómoda la casa?
9 ¿Cómo está organizada la fraternidad?
10 ¿Por qué no se interesan más los estudiantes en las organizaciones sociales universitarias?

VIII • COMPOSICION

Sugerencias para escribir una carta a un amigo (o amiga) informándole sobre un proyecto especial de su fraternidad (o sororidad):

1 un baile
2 un festival
3 planes para el «Homecoming»
4 la donación de sangre a la Cruz Roja
5 una beca para un joven en la universidad
6 contribución de la fraternidad para ayudar a los pobres del barrio

Lección segunda

I • DIALOGO

DIEGO   Hola, Enrique. ¿En dónde te has metido?

ENRIQUE   Hace tiempo que estoy con mi padre en Nueva York. ¿Qué haces por aquí?

DIEGO   Salgo mañana por la mañana para España. Voy a pasar todo el año en la Universidad de Madrid. Quisiera presentarte a María Contreras y a Marta Sánchez.

LAS DOS   Mucho gusto en conocerte.

ENRIQUE   El gusto es mío. Si no tienen inconveniente, quisiera invitarlos a todos a cenar conmigo. Vamos al restaurante «La Playa». Marta, ¿de dónde eres?

MARTA   Soy de Chicago y asisto allí a la Universidad.

MARÍA   Y yo estudio en la Universidad de California en Berkeley. Tengo interés en hacer un viaje a España para aprender a hablar español.

ENRIQUE   Aquí está el restaurante, señoritas. Favor de pasar.

LAS DOS   Con mucho gusto.

MARTA   Tengo mucha hambre.

MARÍA   Cuidado, Marta, o engordarás demasiado.

ENRIQUE   (aparte) Tengo dolor de cabeza. Después de la comida me iré al hotel a descansar un rato.

II • MODISMOS Y EXPRESIONES

anteayer	*day before yesterday*
ayer	*yesterday*
cerca de	*near*
con mucho gusto	*with much pleasure, gladly*
dejar	*to leave something or someone somewhere*
despedirse de	*to take leave of someone (say good-by to)*
después de	*after*
detenerse, parar	*to stop*

dolor de cabeza	*headache*
encontrarse con	*to meet*
hacer un viaje	*to take a trip*
mañana por la mañana	*tomorrow morning*
pensar (más infinitivo)	*to intend*
salir (de)	*to leave*
tener interés en	*to be interested in*
vestirse de	*to be dressed in*

III • PRACTICA SOBRE MODISMOS Y EXPRESIONES

A LEA EN EL TIEMPO INDICADO:

1 (futuro) Mañana nosotros _____ (hacer un viaje) a México.

2 (presente perfecto) Usted _____ (despedirse) de sus amigos.

3 (pretérito) Enrique _____ (encontrarse con) su prima.

4 (pretérito) Yo _____ (dejar) el mapa en el rincón.

5 (presente) La muchacha _____ (vestirse de) azul.

6 (imperfecto) Tú _____ (tener interés en) ir a España, ¿verdad?

7 (pluscuamperfecto) Ellos _____ (salir de) casa.

8 (presente) ¿Qué _____ (pensar) ustedes estudiar en Venezuela?

9 (presente) El ómnibus no _____ (parar) en la esquina.

10 (pretérito) ¿Por qué _____ (detenerse) ellos delante del escaparate?

B USE LOS MODISMOS SIGUIENTES EN FRASES COMPLETAS Y LUEGO DÍGALAS EN INGLÉS:

1 anteayer
2 cerca de
3 mañana por la mañana
4 con mucho gusto
5 dolor de cabeza

IV • REPASO DE VERBOS

A REPASE LA FORMACIÓN DEL FUTURO, CONDICIONAL Y LOS TIEMPOS COMPUESTOS EN EL APÉNDICE Y HAGA LOS SIGUIENTES EJERCICIOS ORALES:

B PONGA LOS VERBOS EN LOS TIEMPOS INDICADOS: FUTURO, CON-
DICIONAL, PERFECTO Y PLUSCUAMPERFECTO:

1 Usted no necesita coche.
2 Tú no bebes leche.
3 Yo recibo cartas.

C USE LOS SUSTANTIVOS Y PRONOMBRES COMO SUJETOS DEL VERBO.
(REPASE LOS VERBOS **andar** Y **caer** EN EL APÉNDICE.):

1 Nosotros andamos por la Quinta Avenida.
   (Juan, Juan y María, tú, yo, usted)
2 Ellos caen al suelo.
   (yo, nosotros, tú, ella)
3 Tú andabas en el jardín.
   (ellos, nosotros, usted, yo)
4 Ayer yo me caí en la casa.
   (nosotros, ella, usted, tú)
5 La semana pasada nosotros anduvimos mucho.
   (yo, ellas, tú, usted)

D CAMBIE LA FRASE:

AL SINGULAR:

1 No anduvimos lejos.
2 No caigan.
3 Andarían despacio.
4 Cayeron al suelo.
5 Habrán caído al océano.

AL PLURAL:

6 Ella cayó del tejado.
7 Yo habré andado mil millas.
8 Caeré si no me ayuda usted.
9 He andado todo el día.
10 Que no cayera él.

E CAMBIE LOS VERBOS AL TIEMPO INDICADO:

1 Anduve toda la noche. (futuro)
2 Caigo al mar. (perfecto)
3 Andamos lentamente. (imperfecto)
4 Cayó en la piscina. (presente)
5 El coche no anda mal. (pretérito)
6 Ojalá que no cayesen. (presente de subjuntivo)
7 Desea que anden más rápido. (condicional)
8 Caíamos en la acera. (pretérito)
9 Yo andaba allá a menudo. (pretérito)
10 Que no caigan desde arriba. (imperfecto de subjuntivo)

F DÉ UNA SINOPSIS EN TODOS LOS TIEMPOS DEL VERBO:

   1 El coche no anda bien.

   2 Yo caigo al agua.

V • GRAMATICA Y EJERCICIOS ORALES

4 FUTURE (EL FUTURO)

a **Llegará** el año que viene.

    He will arrive next year.[1]

The future is generally used as in English.

EJERCICIO **A**

Use los sujetos indicados:

   1 Irán el mes que viene.
      (yo, nosotros, usted, tú)

   2 Visitaremos el museo pronto.
      (ellos, tú, yo, ella)

   3 Ya escribiré la novela.
      (nosotros, tú, usted, yo, ellas)

   4 Marta no tomará la medicina.
      (ustedes, yo, nosotros, tú)

   5 Tú lo decidirás.
      (nosotros, usted, yo, ellos)

b Verbos irregulares en el futuro:

caber	(to fit, be contained)	**cabré**
haber	(to have)	**habré**
poder	(to be able)	**podré**
poner	(to put, place)	**pondré**
saber	(to know, know how)	**sabré**
salir	(to go out)	**saldré**
tener	(to have)	**tendré**
valer	(to be worth)	**valdré**
venir	(to come)	**vendré**
decir	(to tell, say)	**diré**
hacer	(to do, make)	**haré**
querer	(to wish, want)	**querré**

[1] If willingness instead of futurity is meant, **querer** must be used:

   ¿**Quiere** usted ir al teatro conmigo?

   Will you (are you willing to, do you wish to) go to the theater with me?

EJERCICIO **B**

Conteste:

1 ¿Por qué no cabrá Juan en el VW?
2 ¿Quiénes dirán la verdad?
3 ¿Por qué no podrás hacer un viaje a Chile?
4 ¿Qué querrás hacer esta noche?
5 ¿Cuántos años tendrá María?
6 ¿Cuánto valdrá el boleto?
7 ¿Cuándo vendrán las señoritas?
8 ¿Qué tiempo hará mañana?
9 ¿En dónde pondrás el libro?
10 ¿De dónde saldrás?

EJERCICIO **C**

Use las palabras indicadas como sujetos del verbo:

1 Nunca sabremos la verdad.
  (usted, yo, ellos, tú)
2 No vendrá hoy.
  (yo, nosotros, ustedes, tú)
3 ¿Quién podrá hacerlo?
  (Renato y Betty, nosotros, tú, yo)
4 No diré eso.
  (Los señores, nosotros, tú, usted)
5 Mi madre pondrá la mesa.
  (las criadas, yo, tú, nosotros)

c **¿Tendrá** hambre?
Can he be hungry?
Sí, **tendrá** mucha hambre.
Yes, he is probably very hungry.

The future may express conjecture or probability in present time.

EJERCICIO **D**

Indique probabilidad, cambiando el tiempo del verbo al futuro:

Modelo ¿Qué hora es?
       ¿Qué hora será?

1 Son las nueve.
2 ¿Cuándo llegan?
3 ¿Dónde está mi libro?
4 ¿Vas al teatro?
5 Tienen hambre.

   6   ¿Cuántos años tiene ella?
   7   ¿Quién llega?
   8   Están en la biblioteca.
   9   ¿Escriben el libro?
  10   ¿Dice ella la verdad?

5   CONDITIONAL (EL CONDICIONAL)

a   Yo sabía que ella lo **estudiaría.**
I knew that she would study it.[1]

The conditional is generally used as in English.

EJERCICIO   **E**

Cambie al condicional:

   1   Ella no lo entenderá.
   2   Ya estudiaremos la lección.
   3   No iré a Bolivia.
   4   Los caballeros estarán aquí.
   5   La señora recibirá el cuadro en enero.

b   Verbos que tienen formas irregulares en el condicional:

¿Sabía usted que él lo **haría?**
Did you know that he would do it?

Verbs that are irregular in the future tense are also irregular in
the conditional. The endings **–ía, –ías, –ía, –íamos, –ían,** are
added to the irregular future stem.

FUTURE	CONDITIONAL
cabré	**cabría**
habré	**habría**
podré	**podría**
pondré	**pondría**
sabré	**sabría**
saldré	**saldría**
tendré	**tendría**
valdré	**valdría**
vendré	**vendría**
diré	**diría**
haré	**haría**
querré	**querría**

[1] "Would" in the sense of "used to" is often equivalent to a Spanish imperfect:
A veces **llegaba** tarde.
At times I would arrive (used to arrive) late.

EJERCICIO **F**

Use las palabras indicadas como sujetos del verbo:

1 Yo no haría tal cosa.
   (nosotras, ustedes, tú, Roberto)
2 ¿Podría usted ir al campo?
   (yo, ellos, nosotros, tú)
3 Nunca tendría tal fortuna.
   (yo, tú, ellos, Carlos)
4 Juan no diría mentiras.
   (los señores, nosotros, tú, usted)
5 La sirvienta pondría la mesa.
   (las criadas, yo, tú, nosotros)

c ¿Qué hora **sería?**
   I wonder what time it was.
   Serían las nueve.
   It was probably nine o'clock.

The conditional may express conjecture or probability in past time.

EJERCICIO **G**

Indique probabilidad cambiando el tiempo del verbo al condicional:

Modelo   ¿Qué hora era?
            ¿Qué hora sería?

1 Eran las diez.
2 ¿Cuándo llegaron?
3 ¿Dónde estaba mi libro?
4 ¿Ibas al teatro?
5 Tenían sed.
6 ¿Cuántos años tenía él?
7 ¿Quiénes llegaban?
8 Estaban en la biblioteca.
9 ¿Escribían la novela?
10 ¿Decía ella la verdad?

6 PRESENT PERFECT (EL PERFECTO)

a he
   has
   ha
   hemos   **hablado (comido, recibido)**
   habéis
   han

The present perfect consists of the present of **haber** plus the past participle.

b **Hemos recibido** la carta.
We have received the letter.
¿Le **ha hablado** usted hoy?
Have you spoken to him today?

The present perfect expresses a past action closely related to the present.

EJERCICIO **H**

Use las palabras indicadas como sujetos del verbo:

1 Ya he comido la naranja.
(nosotros, usted, tú, ellas)
2 ¿Nunca ha visitado usted el museo?
(yo, nosotros, tú, ustedes)
3 No han vivido en Santander.
(usted, nosotros, yo, tú)
4 El alumno no ha entendido bien la lección.
(los alumnos, tú, yo, nosotros)
5 Los estudiantes se han ido a la biblioteca.
(yo, nosotros, tú, ella)

c Formas irregulares del participio pasado:

abrir	(to open)	**abierto**
cubrir	(to cover)	**cubierto**
decir	(to say, tell)	**dicho**
escribir	(to write)	**escrito**
hacer	(to do, make)	**hecho**
morir	(to die)	**muerto**
poner	(to put, place)	**puesto**
romper	(to break)	**roto**
ver	(to see)	**visto**
volver	(to return)	**vuelto**

EJERCICIO **I**

Cambie el verbo al perfecto:

Modelo Yo abro la puerta.
Yo he abierto la puerta.

1 Comemos carne.
2 Ponen el lápiz en la mesa.
3 Cubrimos el libro.

4   Irene rompe el plato.
5   ¿Escribe usted la carta?
6   ¿Dices la verdad?
7   No cierran la ventana.
8   Murieron hoy.
9   Vimos la película.
10 Hice la cama.
11 ¿Te gusta la sopa?
12 ¿Fumas mucho?
13 ¿Vieron el cuadro?
14 ¿Dice usted eso?
15 ¿Rompieron el vaso?

EJERCICIO **J**

Pregúntele a un estudiante:

Modelo   si ha visto a su novio (o novia)
         ¿Has visto a tu novio (o novia)?

1   si ha escrito la carta
2   si ha visto a María
3   por qué no ha dicho la verdad
4   dónde ha puesto las camisas
5   a qué hora ha vuelto a casa
6   por qué no le ha gustado la novela
7   por qué no ha hecho su lección

7   PLUPERFECT (EL PLUSCUAMPERFECTO)

Sabía que **habíamos partido.**
You knew that we had left.

The pluperfect is generally used as in English. It consists of
the imperfect of **haber** plus the past participle.

EJERCICIO **K**

Cambie al pluscuamperfecto:

Modelo   Ya la comí.
         Ya la había comido.

1   escribí
2   leí
3   hice
4   vi
5   abrí
6   cerré

7   tomé
8   puse
9   devolví

EJERCICIO **L**

Conteste:

Modelo   ¿Cuándo iba a verlo?
             Ya lo había visto.

1   escribirlo
2   devolverlo
3   saberlo
4   romperlo
5   tomarlo
6   cubrirlo
7   leerlo
8   recibirlo
9   abrirlo
10 cerrarlo

EJERCICIO **M**

Cambie los verbos al pasado:

Modelo   Dicen que me han visto.
             Decían que me habían visto.

1   El profesor sabe que yo he estudiado.
2   Pienso que ella ha venido.
3   Decimos que ellos no han vuelto.
4   Creen que él ha muerto.
5   Sé que me han roto el vaso.
6   Escriben que lo han sabido.
7   Ven a la mujer que no ha dicho nada.
8   Me doy cuenta de que no lo han hecho.
9   Pensamos que ella ha puesto la mesa.
10 Me dicen que han abierto la puerta.

8   PRETERIT PERFECT (EL PRETÉRITO ANTERIOR)

It consists of the preterit of **haber** plus the past participle.

Luego que **hubo llegado** (llegó), se lo di.
As soon as he had arrived, I gave it to him.

The preterit perfect is used with certain time conjunctions.
In conversation it is ordinarily replaced by the preterit.

9 FUTURE PERFECT (EL FUTURO PERFECTO)

It consists of the future of **haber** plus the past participle.

a Lo **habré hecho** para el domingo.
I will have it done by Sunday.

The future perfect is generally used as in English.

b ¿Lo **habrá escrito** Carlos?
I wonder if Charles has written it?
Lo **habrá escrito.**
He must have written it. He has probably written it.

The future perfect may express conjecture or probability in past time.

10 CONDITIONAL PERFECT (EL CONDICIONAL PERFECTO)

It consists of the conditional of **haber** plus the past participle.

a Sabía que lo **habría hecho.**
I knew that he would have done it.

The conditional perfect is generally used as in English.

b ¿Lo **habría hecho?**
I wondered if he had done it.
Lo **habría hecho.**
He had probably done it.

The conditional perfect may express conjecture or probability in past time.

EJERCICIO **N**

Diga en español:

1 We will have read it by Monday.
2 I wonder if Mary has broken it.
3 She must have seen it.
4 They thought we would have covered it.
5 I wonder if they had said it.
6 As soon as they arrived, we gave it to them.
7 As soon as she knew it, she left.
8 They will have seen it by Friday.
9 I knew that they would not have opened it.
10 She had probably died in the collision.

11 SABER AND CONOCER

a **¿Sabe** usted conducir el coche?
Do you know how to drive the car?
Sabemos que él es inglés.
We know that he is English.
¿Sabe usted español?
Do you know Spanish?

Saber means *to know how, know a fact, know thoroughly* or
by heart.

b **Conozco** al Dr. Mendoza.
I know Dr. Mendoza.
¿Conoce usted bien esta ciudad?
Do you know this city well?

Conocer means *to know, be acquainted with* (persons or things).[1]

c La **conocí** en Madrid.
I met her in Madrid.
¿Cuándo lo **supo** usted?
When did you find out about it?

In the preterit **conocer** means *to meet, make the acquaintance of;*
saber means *to know, learn, find out.*

EJERCICIO O

Diga en español:

1 I don't know the street, but I know where it is.
2 I don't know Miss García, but I know where she works.
3 We don't know the instructor very well, but we know the
  lesson.
4 She doesn't know the store, but she knows where it is.
5 He doesn't know the boys, but he knows where they play.
6 You don't know the town, but you know that she lives
  there.

---

[1] Sometimes the choice between **saber** or **conocer** depends on the meaning the
speaker intends to convey:
Sé que es verdad. *I know it's true.*
Conozco que es verdad. *I know (am aware, recognize) it's true.*
Conozco la lección. *I know the lesson. (I'm acquainted with it).*
Sé la lección. *I know the lesson. (I know it thoroughly).*
Note also the distinction between **saber** and **poder,** both of which may mean *can*
in English. If the verb indicates mental ability, **saber** is used. If the verb expresses
physical ability, **poder** is used:
¿Sabe usted hablar español? *Can you speak Spanish?*
¿Puede usted levantar la silla? *Can you lift the chair?*

7   I don't know the girl's parents, but I know that they are kind.

8   We don't know the president, but we know when he is coming.

9   We met them in Santander last year.

10   I learned it last week.

11   Where did you meet her?

12   We learned about it on returning from Spain.

VI • PRACTICA ESCRITA

1   They are probably reading the novel.

2   I wonder if he is writing a book.

3   Who can it be?

4   John is probably going to the theater.

5   Mary must be seventeen years old.

6   It is probably ten past ten.

7   It is probably one o'clock.

8   They are probably in the library.

9   We probably don't know it.

10   He is probably a student.

11   I wonder if they are hungry?

12   I wonder if he was hungry?

13   He must have known it.

14   They had probably seen it.

15   We knew that they had not yet arrived.

VII • PRACTICA ORAL

A   DIALOGO COMPLEMENTARIO

(Escena: el cuarto de un hotel en Nueva York.)

ENRIQUE   El viaje de Tejas a Nueva York me ha dejado algo cansado.

DIEGO   Creo que debemos ir a la agencia de turismo para recoger nuestros boletos.

ENRIQUE   Vete sin mí. Tengo dolor de cabeza y voy a acostarme.

DIEGO   Descansa bien. Vuelvo muy pronto.

(En la agencia de turismo.)

AGENTE   Buenos días, ¿en qué puedo servirle?

Diego   Soy Diego Morales. He venido a recoger los boletos de nuestro vuelo a España.

Agente   Ah, sí. Ustedes van a estudiar en la Universidad de Madrid por un año. Esta señorita va también. Es Anita Chávez de Pomona, California.

Diego   Mucho gusto en conocerte.

Anita   Igualmente.

Diego   Bueno, gracias por todo, señor. Anita, ¿quieres almorzar conmigo?

Anita   Sí, con mucho gusto.

       (En el restaurante «Sol».)

Diego   Pasa, Anita. Mozo, queremos una mesa cerca de la orquesta. Muchas gracias.

Mozo   ¿Quieren ustedes ver el menú?

Diego   Sí, por favor.

       (Después de un rato.)

Anita   Yo deseo la sopa del día, arroz con pollo, guisantes, papas, ensalada de lechuga y tomate, pan y mantequilla.

Diego   Yo pido lo mismo. Dime, Anita, ¿cuándo llegaste a Nueva York?

Anita   Anteayer. ¿Cuánto tiempo hace que estudias español?

Diego   Hace tres años. A propósito, tengo boletos para una función de «Don Quijote» esta noche. ¿Quieres ir conmigo? Dicen que es una película española muy buena.

Anita   Pensaba hacer las maletas pero puedo dejarlo para después. ¿A qué hora es la función?

Diego   Comienza a las ocho y termina a las diez y media. No es larga y no tardarás mucho en regresar al hotel. Eso te dejará tiempo de sobra para hacer las maletas.

Anita   Ayer recibí una carta de mi madre. Mi padre llega mañana por la mañana en coche para despedirse de mí en el aeropuerto internacional Kennedy. No viene mi madre. Está enferma y tiene que guardar cama.

Diego   Siento mucho que tu mamá esté enferma. Mañana te voy a presentar a mi buen amigo Enrique que también hace el viaje a España con nosotros.

B   EXPRESION ORAL

Diego sale de Nueva York para España. Se encuentra con Anita que también viaja a Europa. Haga el papel de Diego y:

1   preséntela a Enrique
2   pregúntele a dónde va y por qué
3   pregúntele si quiere almorzar
4   pregúntele cuánto tiempo lleva ella en Nueva York
5   pregúntele cuánto tiempo lleva ella en el hotel
6   haga una cita con ella para la noche

C   PLATICA ESPONTANEA

1   ¿Por qué le gustaría a usted hacer un viaje a Europa?
2   ¿De dónde se sale para Europa?
3   ¿Cómo prefiere usted viajar, en vapor o en avión? ¿Por qué?
4   ¿Cuánto tiempo dura el viaje en vapor de Nueva York a Francia?
5   ¿Qué pide usted en el restaurante para el almuerzo?
6   ¿Por qué le gusta (o no le gusta) andar por la Quinta Avenida en Nueva York?
7   ¿Cuándo escribe usted cartas a sus amigos?
8   ¿Por qué le gusta (o no le gusta) Nueva York?
9   ¿Quiénes le han dado a usted el dinero para el viaje?
10   ¿Quiénes van a despedirse de usted?

VIII • COMPOSICION

Sugerencias para un tema: Hablan dos amigos. Uno pregunta al otro:

1   ¿a qué hora va a llegar a Nueva York?
2   ¿cuánto tiempo piensa pasar allí?
3   ¿qué cosas quiere ver?
4   ¿cuándo piensa salir en avión (o vapor) para Europa?
5   ¿qué países va a visitar?
6   ¿qué ciudades?
7   ¿qué ropa lleva?
8   ¿qué quiere comprar?
9   ¿cuándo regresa a los Estados Unidos?

Lección tercera

I · DIALOGO

(Escena: En la terraza del edificio de la Unión Estudiantil. Tres estudiantes, sentados alrededor de una mesa al aire libre, están hablando.)

DIEGO Me han dicho que usted es de la Argentina.

PEPE Sí, hace tres años que estoy aquí. Estudio ciencias políticas y espero volver algún día a mi país como representante al Congreso.

ELENA ¡Qué interesante! ¿Por qué decidió venir a los Estados Unidos?

PEPE Sé que la libertad es preciosa. Quería venir acá para aprender más sobre el concepto de la democracia que tienen ustedes.

DIEGO ¿No sabe Vd. que Elena y yo pensamos casarnos pronto?

PEPE Y ¿quién va a llevar los pantalones en su casa?

DIEGO Yo, desde luego.

ELENA Sí, no quiere perder su libertad.

PEPE Eso me extraña mucho porque, según he observado, en la vida norteamericana las mujeres hacen un papel muy importante en la familia.

DIEGO Tiene usted razón. Nosotros los hombres no podríamos hacer nada sin ellas.

ELENA Gracias, Diego. Me alegro de que te des cuenta de ello. A propósito, Pepe, ¿cuánto tiempo piensa permanecer aquí?

PEPE Un año más. Después iré a Montevideo a pasar unos días con unos amigos míos. Tengo muchas ganas de visitar a los García, a quienes conocí en Buenos Aires hace algún tiempo.
(Se levantan Diego y Elena.)

DIEGO Ya son las cuatro. Siempre damos un paseo por el parque los sábados por la tarde. De modo que vamos a despedirnos de usted ahora.
(Se levanta también Pepe.)

PEPE Me alegro mucho de haberlos conocido. Hasta pronto.

DIEGO Y ELENA Adiós.

Courtesy American Airlines
Edificio Administrativo, Universidad de México

II • MODISMOS Y EXPRESIONES

a propósito	*by the way*
asistir a	*to attend*
depender de	*to depend on*
hacer el papel	*to play the part*
insistir en	*to insist on*
seguir cursos	*to take courses*
tener ganas de	*to feel like*

III • PRACTICA SOBRE MODISMOS Y EXPRESIONES

A   USE CADA MODISMO EN UNA FRASE COMPLETA Y LUEGO TRADÚZ-
CALA AL INGLÉS:

1   a propósito
2   depender de
3   seguir cursos
4   tener ganas de
5   asistir a

B   CONTESTE EN ESPAÑOL:

1   ¿Por qué tiene Vd. tantas ganas de comer?
2   ¿Qué papel hace Carlos en la comedia?
3   ¿Cuántos cursos sigue Vd. este año?
4   ¿De qué depende la paz?
5   ¿A qué clases asistió Vd. ayer?
6   ¿Por qué insiste Juan en ir a la biblioteca esta noche?

IV • REPASO DE VERBOS

A   USE LOS PRONOMBRES INDICADOS COMO SUJETOS DEL VERBO. (REPASE LOS VERBOS **conducir** Y **dar** EN EL APÉNDICE.):

1   ¿Cómo conduce ella?
    (ella y él, ella y yo, yo, nosotros, Vd.)
2   Usted nunca da nada a los pobres.
    (yo, nosotros, ellos)
3   Nosotros no condujimos el coche ayer.
    (yo, ellas, Vd., tú)
4   Quiere que Juan conduzca bien.
    (yo, ellas, nosotros)
5   Se lo dimos ayer.
    (yo, ellos, tú, Vd.)

B   CAMBIE LOS VERBOS A LOS TIEMPOS INDICADOS:

1   ¿Conduce Vd. el otro coche? (imperfecto, pretérito, futuro)
2   No me lo dan. (futuro, perfecto, imperfecto)
3   Quieren que conduzcamos bien. (imperfecto, futuro, condicional)
4   Siento que Vd. no se lo dé. (imperfecto, pretérito, futuro)
5   No doy nada a nadie. (perfecto, pretérito, condicional)

C   DÉ UNA SINOPSIS DEL VERBO:

(Yo) conducir el coche.
(Nosotros) dar limosna a los pobres.

V • GRAMATICA Y EJERCICIOS

12 GENDER OF NOUNS (GENERO DE LOS SUSTANTIVOS)

a el libro   *the book*

Nouns ending in **o** are usually masculine.[1] Common exception:
la mano *the hand.*

b la tinta   *the ink*

Nouns ending in **a** are usually feminine.[2]

c la muchedumbre   *the crowd*
  la lección   *the lesson*
  la libertad   *the liberty*
  la bondad   *the goodness*
  la serie   *the series*

Nouns ending in **umbre, ión, ie, tad, dad** are usually feminine.
Common exception: **el pie**   *the foot.*

d la pared   *the wall*
  el lápiz   *the pencil*

Since the gender of many nouns cannot be determined from
meaning or form, learn the article along with each noun as it
occurs.

EJERCICIO **A**

Complete las oraciones con los sustantivos siguientes:

1   Hablan con el primo.
2   _____ tía.
3   _____ representante.
4   _____ mujer.
5   _____ muchacho.

---

[1] Some nouns are masculine with one meaning and feminine with another. For
example:

el capital	*the capital (money)*	**la capital**	*the capital (of a country)*
el cura	*the priest*	**la cura**	*the cure*
el orden	*the order (of a series)*	**la orden**	*the order (command)*

[2] Common exceptions:

el clima	*the climate*
el día	*the day*
el drama	*the drama*
el mapa	*the map*
el problema	*the problem*
el telegrama	*the telegram*

6 _____ estudiante.
7 _____ señorita.
8 _____ cura.
9 _____ profesor.
10 ¿Tienes un libro?
11 ¿_____ lápiz?
12 ¿_____ pluma?
13 ¿_____ cuaderno?
14 ¿_____ mapa?
15 ¿_____ coche?
16 ¿_____ casa?
17 ¿_____ telegrama?
18 ¿_____ papel?

13 PLURAL OF NOUNS (PLURAL DE LOS SUSTANTIVOS)

a **la mesa**   *the table*
  las mesas   *the tables*

Nouns ending in a vowel usually add **s**.[1]

b **la pared**   *the wall*   **las paredes**   *the walls*
  la lección   *the lesson*   **las lecciones**   *the lessons*
  el rey   *the king*   **los reyes**   *the kings*

Nouns ending in a consonant add **es**.[2]

EJERCICIO **B**

Cambie las frases siguientes al plural, haciendo todos los cambios necesarios:

1 Tengo el lápiz.
2 Hay una botella en la mesa.
3 Es la luz.
4 Debajo del balcón hay un jardín.
5 Tiene el hacha.
6 Ella compra un par de huaraches.
7 El Sr. Ramírez comprende la pregunta.
8 Soy alumno.
9 Escribo la lección.
10 ¿Quién dice que el estudiante estudia el miércoles?
11 No comprende bien el libro.

[1] Nouns ending in an accented vowel often add **es** to form the plural:
  el rubí, *ruby;* **los rubíes** *rubies;* but **el café** *coffee;* **los cafés** *coffees.*
[2] Nouns ending in **z** change **z** to **c** before adding **es:**
  el lápiz *pencil;* **los lápices** *pencils;* **la luz** *light;* **las luces** *lights.*

12 Es médico.
13 Llevaba 'una caja.
14 Voy allí el sábado.
15 Una persona entró en la calle.
16 Será la pared.
17 Me levantaré temprano.
18 Tomo el lápiz.
19 Tengo la flor.
20 Era el general.

14 DEFINITE ARTICLE (ARTICULO DEFINIDO)

	MASCULINE	FEMININE
SINGULAR	el	la[1]
PLURAL	los	las

The definite article occurs more frequently in Spanish than in English.

a **La libertad** es preciosa.
Liberty is precious.
Las bibliotecas son necesarias.
Libraries are necessary.

The definite article is used before a noun in an abstract sense and in a generic sense.

b **El señor García** está presente.
Mr. García is present.
El pobre Carlos se enfermó.
Poor Charles fell ill.
But
Buenos días, Sr. García.
Good morning, Mr. García.
Carlos está aquí.
Charles is here.

The definite article is used before titles, except in direct address, and before a person's name when modified.

The definite article is not used before **don, doña, San, Santo,** and **Santa:**

Es **el día de San Fermín.**
It is St. Fermin's day.

---

[1] The article **la** is replaced by **el** when the noun begins with a stressed **a** or **ha**: **el hacha** *the ax;* **el agua** *the water.* This does not change the gender of the noun. The plurals are **las hachas** and **las aguas.**

c **El español** no es difícil.
Spanish is not difficult.

The definite article is used with names of languages. The article is dropped, however, after the prepositions **en** and **de** and after such common verbs as **hablar, saber, enseñar, aprender,** and **estudiar.**

Mi profesor **de español** es simpático.
My Spanish teacher is nice.
Escribo en español.
I'm writing in Spanish.
Aprendo español.
I'm learning Spanish.

d Voy a **Chile.**
I'm going to Chile.
Vive en **España.**
He lives in Spain.

Names of countries, cities, and other geographical points are generally used without the definite article. Note these important exceptions, however:

la Habana	*Havana*
el Canadá	*Canada*
el Japón	*Japan*
el Perú	*Peru*
la Argentina	*Argentina*
el Brasil	*Brazil*
el Ecuador	*Ecuador*
los Estados Unidos	*the United States*

The definite article is normally used before a geographical name if it is modified:

Vive en **la bella España.**
He lives in beautiful Spain.

e Voy al parque **los sábados.**
I go to the park on Saturdays.
Ya ha llegado **la primavera.**
Spring is here.
Son **las dos.**
It's two o'clock.

The definite article is used before days of the week, seasons, and expressions of time of day.

f **El estudiar** es necesario.
Studying is necessary.

The definite article is used before infinitives functioning as nouns.

g diez centavos **la libra**   *ten cents a pound*
un peso **la docena**   *one dollar a dozen*
dos veces **al día**   *twice a day*

The definite article is used before nouns of weight and measurement, where English uses the indefinite article.

h **Se quitaron el sombrero.**
They took off their hats.

The definite article is used in place of the possessive adjective with articles of clothing or parts of the body, provided the possessor has previously been clearly identified.

EJERCICIO **C**

Use el artículo definido cuando sea necesario y explique la razón de su selección:

1 No vivimos en _____ México.
2 Esta es _____ Sra. Blanco. Buenos días, _____
Sra. Blanco.
3 _____ pintura es un arte.
4 Han aprendido _____ portugués.
5 Venecia está en _____ gloriosa Italia.
6 _____ mujeres llevan faldas.
7 Estas papas cuestan cinco centavos _____ libra.
8 Nos pusimos _____ guantes.
9 Me ha mandado un libro en _____ inglés.
10 _____ pasearse es agradable.
11 _____ Argentina está en Sud América.
12 Hablamos _____ español en la clase.
13 _____ muchachos llevan _____ pantalones.
14 Llegó _____ semana pasada.
15 Se lavaron _____ manos.
16 Es _____ una y cinco.
17 Es un libro de _____ español.
18 _____ estudiar es necesario.
19 _____ capitán está a bordo del vapor.
20 Vivo en _____ Estados Unidos.
21 Voy al cine _____ sábados.
22 Se pone _____ chaqueta.

23 Compro huevos a ocho pesos _____ docena.

24 Ella me llama durante _____ día.

25 _____ señora González no vive aquí.

26 En su libro el autor describe _____ bella España.

27 Nos quitaron _____ sombrero.

28 Venden café a setenta centavos _____ libra.

29 _____ pobre Enrique no pudo venir.

30 Mañana vuelo a _____ Chile.

31 Yo soy _____ protestante; ella es _____ buena católica.

15 CONTRACTIONS OF THE DEFINITE ARTICLE (CONTRACCIONES CON EL ARTICULO DEFINIDO)

de + el = del
a + el = al

Di el libro **al muchacho.**
I gave the book to the boy.
el lápiz **del profesor**
the teacher's pencil

EJERCICIO D

Reemplace las palabras indicadas por los sustantivos siguientes:

1 Es el libro de la *amiga.*
   (maestro, muchachas, señor, señorita)

2 Vamos a la *biblioteca.*
   (cine, playa, Las Vegas, cuarto)

3 Tengo la pluma de la *muchacha.*
   (alumno, estudiantes, médico, enfermera)

4 Veo a la *criada.*
   (tío, los jóvenes, alumno, novia)

16 INDEFINITE ARTICLE (ARTICULO INDEFINIDO)

	MASCULINE	FEMININE	
SINGULAR	**un**	**una**	*a, an*
PLURAL	**unos**	**unas**	*some*

The indefinite article is not used as frequently in Spanish as in English.

a **Soy profesor.**
   I am a teacher.

Es cubana.
She is a Cuban.
Soy protestante.
I am a Protestant.
Es republicano.
He is a Republican.

The indefinite article is omitted before an unmodified predicate noun denoting occupation, nationality, and political or religious affiliation. When modified or stressed, the article is used:

Es un buen abogado.
He's a good lawyer.
¡Es un médico!
He's quite a doctor!

b **mil estudiantes**   *a thousand students*
  otro hombre   *another man*
  ¡Qué mujer!   *What a woman!*
  ¡Tal cuento!   *Such a story!*

The indefinite article is not used before **cien** *one hundred;* **cierto** *certain;* **medio** *half;* **mil** *thousand;* **otro** *another;* and after **qué** *what (a);* **tal** *such (a).*

c Salió **sin sombrero.**
  He left without a hat.
  No tengo libro.
  I don't have a book.

The indefinite article is generally omitted after the preposition **sin** and after a negative.

d **un hombre y una mujer**   *a man and a woman*
  el papel y la tinta   *the paper and ink*

Both the definite and indefinite articles must be repeated before each noun in a series, except when nouns of the same gender are considered as a unit:

el amor y cariño   *love and affection*

EJERCICIO E

Diga en español:

Modelo She is a nurse. Ella es enfermera.
            She is a *nurse.* Ella es una enfermera.

1 He is a doctor. He is a *doctor.*
2 María is a teacher. María is a *teacher.*

3 Juan is a student. Juan is a *student*.
4 Juana is a cook. Juana is a good cook.
5 Don Urbano is a Cuban. Don Urbano is a handsome Cuban.
6 Miss García is a tourist. Miss García is an old tourist.
7 Mr. Moreno is a grandfather. Mr. Moreno is a friendly grandfather.
8 Miss Blanco is a nurse. Miss Blanco is a pretty nurse.
9 Carlos is a businessman. Carlos is a rich businessman.
10 The maid is a Spaniard. The maid is a young Spaniard.
11 Jorge is an athlete. He is a good athlete.
12 Antonio is a lawyer. He is a terrible lawyer!
13 She is a teacher. She is a magnificent teacher!
14 She is an artist. She is a famous artist.
15 He is a dentist. He's quite a dentist!

17 NEUTER ARTICLE LO (EL ARTICULO NEUTRO LO)

Lo peor era que no tenía dinero.
The worst thing was that he had no money.
Lo dicho no es verdad.
What has been said is not true.

The neuter article **lo** is used with adjectives or past participles to form nouns used in an abstract sense.

EJERCICIO **F**

Reemplace las palabras indicadas por los adjetivos entre paréntesis:

1 Esto es lo *peor*.
(bueno, malo, mejor, difícil)
2 Lo *importante* es estudiar.
(primero, práctico, adecuado, único)
3 Hay que hacer lo *posible*.
(necesario, importante, difícil, indicado)

VI • PRACTICA ESCRITA

1 Are you an American?—No, I'm French.
2 Women wear skirts.
3 The Río Grande separates Mexico from the United States.

4 The best thing is to study every day.
5 Lima is the capital of Peru.
6 Mr. White teaches Spanish.
7 Eating is necessary in order to live.
8 The Fernández brothers always prepare the day's lesson.
9 The boys put on their shoes.
10 Last week a certain man left without an umbrella.
11 My aunt and uncle arrived last month.
12 Some think that justice is blind.
13 One needs a hat and a coat when it's cold.
14 A certain woman ate half a grapefruit.
15 What is needed on such an occasion is speed.
16 Send a telegram at once.
17 Please come in, Mr. Pérez.
18 He's a doctor, a good doctor.
19 Do you have any money?
20 What a woman! She told such a story!
21 Do you have a thousand dollars?
22 Can you give me another orange?
23 This book has one hundred pages.
24 He ate up three and a half eggs.
25 She doesn't have any friends.

VII • PRACTICA ORAL

A DIALOGO COMPLEMENTARIO

(En la Universidad de México.)

PABLO   Hola, Luisa, ¿qué cursos sigues este año?

LUISA   Sigo cursos de filosofía, historia, economía, lenguas extranjeras y ciencia política, porque un día quiero representar a mi país en las Naciones Unidas en Nueva York Como tú sabes, mi padre fue embajador.

PABLO   ¡Qué mujer! Y lo malo es que las mujeres siempre insisten en competir con los hombres.

LUISA   Eso depende del punto de vista. A propósito, ¿qué carrera estudias tú?

PABLO   Estudio para ser director de cine. Tengo ganas de ir a Hollywood después de obtener mi doctorado y adquirir allí un conocimiento práctico de la industria cinematográfica. Hay mil cosas que aprender. Luego quisiera regresar y formar una compañía para hacer películas en México. Me parece que en esto hay un futuro estupendo.

LUISA   Claro, podrías producir obras mexicanas como *El periquillo sarniento,* de Fernández de Lizardi y españolas como *A ninguna de las tres,* de Calderón.

PABLO   Y, ¿qué dirías de *Tierra* y *El indio* de Gregorio López y Fuentes o *El águila y la serpiente* de Martín Luis Guzmán? Me encanta esa época de Pancho Villa y la revolución mexicana.

LUISA   Me gusta mucho ese drama de Usigli, ¿cómo se llama, *Corona de sombras?* ¿No hiciste tú el papel de Maximiliano en la función teatral del año pasado?

PABLO   Sí, y fue en aquel entonces que decidí seguir la carrera de director. ¿Tomamos una limonada?

LUISA   Sí, pasemos a la Unión Estudiantil. Ahí está Elena Díaz. Hace mucho tiempo que no la veo.

B   EXPRESION ORAL

1   Pregunte a un amigo (o a una amiga) por qué quiere estudiar en la Universidad de Madrid. ¿Qué piensa estudiar? ¿Cuánto tiempo dura el curso? ¿En qué año de estudio va? ¿Y por qué?

2   Imagínese que usted quiere ser director de películas en Hollywood. ¿Cuáles son los requisitos para tal puesto? ¿Qué novelas o dramas produciría? ¿Y por qué? ¿Qué actores y actrices escogería Vd.?

C   PLATICA ESPONTANEA

1   ¿Cuánto tiempo hace que asiste Vd. a la universidad?
2   ¿Cuánto tiempo le falta para obtener el grado?
3   ¿En qué campo de especialización se interesa usted?
4   ¿Qué cursos sigue Vd. ahora?
5   ¿Por qué insisten las mujeres en competir con los hombres?
6   ¿Para qué estudia Vd.?
7   ¿Por qué estudia Vd.?
8   ¿Qué hay que saber en esa especialización?
9   ¿Qué películas ha visto Vd. recientemente?
10   ¿Quién es su actriz favorita?

VIII • COMPOSICION

Escriba un diálogo entre varios alumnos de la universidad que quieren representar una comedia. Indique quiénes son los alumnos que intervienen en el diálogo y diga algo sobre:

1 cómo se llama la comedia
2 la fecha en que se representará
3 quién es el autor
4 de qué trata la obra
5 por qué es importante o interesante la obra
6 quiénes se encargan de la decoración, del maquillaje y de los trajes

Lección cuarta

I • DIALOGO

(Al mediodía, después de una clase, dos amigas, Carlota
y Juana, entran en un restaurante que está cerca de la
universidad para almorzar. Después de sentarse, piden
la lista al camarero.)

CARLOTA ¿Qué piensas tomar?

JUANA No sé. A ver. (al camarero) El cubierto, por favor.

CARLOTA Para mí también. No vale la pena pedir la carta
porque resulta demasiado caro.

CAMARERO ¿Quieren ustedes la sopa del día o jugo de tomate?

LAS DOS La sopa del día.

(Mientras el camarero pasa a la cocina a traer la sopa,
las dos amigas continúan charlando.)

JUANA ¿Qué te pareció el examen del profesor García?

CARLOTA Dificilísimo. Me parece que no voy a sacar buenas
notas este semestre porque me faltó tiempo para
estudiar.

JUANA Eso es lo que sospechaba yo. Casi todas las noches
tienes una cita con algún muchacho.

CARLOTA Cállate. Ya viene el mozo.

(El camarero les sirve la sopa. Juana nota que hay una
mosca en la sopa.)

JUANA ¡Camarero! ¿Qué es esto? ¿Una mosca?

CAMARERO Creo que sí. Pero no tendrá que pagar más.

CARLOTA Es un bromista. Por este insulto, no le vamos a dejar
propina.

JUANA Vámonos en seguida porque temo que voy a matar al
camarero.

CARLOTA No, cálmate, Juana. (al camarero) Llévese la sopa y
tráiganos un sandwich de jamón con lechuga.

JUANA Pues, si nos quedamos aquí, no voy a comer más que
una ensalada de tomate sin salsa.

CAMARERO La señorita no quiere engordar, ¿verdad?

JUANA Eso es el colmo. Vámonos, Carlota.

Courtesy American Airlines
Corrida de toros en México: el picador

II • MODISMOS Y EXPRESIONES

a pesar de	*in spite of*
asistir a	*to attend*
dar un paseo	*to take a walk*
llegar a (ser)	*to get to be, to become*
muchas veces	*often*
sacar buenas notas	*to get good grades*

III • PRACTICA SOBRE MODISMOS Y EXPRESIONES

A USE LOS MODISMOS SIGUIENTES EN FRASES COMPLETAS Y LUEGO TRADÚZCALAS AL INGLÉS:

1 asistir a
2 a pesar de
3 sacar buenas notas
4 dar un paseo

B DIGA EN ESPAÑOL:

1 I often take a walk in the park.
2 Yesterday I met Mary there.
3 In spite of receiving good grades, John never got to be a lawyer.
4 Next year they will attend the University of Madrid.
5 We became teachers.

IV • REPASO DE VERBOS

A (REPASE LOS VERBOS **ser** Y **estar** EN EL APÉNDICE.) CAMBIE LOS VERBOS

AL SINGULAR:

1 Eramos buenos amigos de los González.
2 Estuvieron en México el año pasado.
3 Fuimos los únicos que llegamos.
4 Estarán en el Japón.
5 Hemos sido malos.

AL PLURAL:

6 He estado en España.
7 El es actor.
8 Había sido médico.
9 Estaré en Chile la semana que viene.
10 Fue actriz.

B CAMBIE LOS VERBOS A LOS TIEMPOS INDICADOS:

1 Eramos cinco en mi familia. (pretérito)
2 Estuvieron en la biblioteca. (condicional)
3 Hemos sido buenos. (presente)

4   Mi tío es abogado. (pretérito)
5   Estoy en Europa. (futuro)
6   Ellos son ricos. (perfecto)
7   Nunca he estado en México. (imperfecto)
8   ¿Sería grande la biblioteca? (imperfecto)
9   Yo estaba en Nogales. (presente)
10 Tú eres estudiante. (pretérito)

C   DÉ UNA SINOPSIS DE LOS VERBOS:

(Tú) ser malo.
(Nosotros) estar en la universidad.

V • GRAMATICA Y EJERCICIOS

SER AND ESTAR

Spanish possesses two verbs meaning *to be,* **ser** and **estar.** These verbs are never used interchangeably. In general, **ser** denotes characteristic or intrinsic qualities, while **estar** is used to describe conditions or indicate location.

18   SER

a **Es mi hermana.**   *She is my sister.*
   Son médicos.   *They are doctors.*
   ¿Quién es ella?   *Who is she?*
   Juan es peruano.   *John is a Peruvian.*

Ser is used with a predicate noun, a pronoun, or an adjective used as a noun.

EJERCICIO A

Sustituya:

1   Yo soy profesor.
    (Carlos, tú, las señoritas, Elena y yo)
2   ¿Quién es él?
    (nosotros, yo, Vd., ella)
3   Ellas son chilenas.
    (yo, nosotros, él, tú)

b La muchacha **es muy bonita.**
   The girl is very pretty.

La biblioteca **es grande.**
The library is big.
Mi máquina de escribir **es portátil.**
My typewriter is portable.
Miguel **es muy amable.**
Miguel is very friendly.

Ser is used with a predicate adjective to express an inherent quality, such as size, shape, color, or personal characteristics.

EJERCICIO **B**

Sustituya:

1 Anita es muy simpática.
(Juan y Anita, nosotros, tú, él)
2 La casa es pequeña.
(el coche, las habitaciones, los aviones, la biblioteca)

c **¿De quién es** este cuaderno de apuntes?
Whose memorandum book is this?
Esta casa **es de mi suegro.**
This house belongs to my father-in-law.
Este vestido **es de seda.**
This dress is made of silk.
El reloj **es de oro.**
The watch is made of gold.
¿De dónde es usted?
Where are you from?
Soy de España.
I'm from Spain.

Ser is used with a prepositional phrase to express ownership, material, or origin.

EJERCICIO **C**

Conteste:

1 ¿De qué es el cuaderno?
2 ¿De quién es el reloj?
3 ¿De qué es el abrigo?
4 ¿De dónde es Vd.?
5 ¿De qué es el pastel?
6 ¿De quién es la casa?
7 ¿De dónde es María?

d **¿Qué hora es?**
What time is it?

Es la una menos uno.
It's one minute to one.
Son las tres y veinte.
It's three-twenty.
Eran las cinco cuando llegaron.
It was five o'clock when they arrived.

Ser is used to express the hour of the day. Note that only the imperfect tense of **ser** can be used to tell past time.

EJERCICIO **D**

Conteste:

1 ¿Qué hora es?
2 ¿A qué hora se desayuna Vd.?
3 ¿A qué hora almuerzan Elena y Pedro?
4 ¿A qué hora comen Vds.?
5 ¿Qué hora era cuando llegó Vd. a la universidad?

e **Es lástima.**   *It's a shame.*
Es evidente.   *It's evident.*

Ser is used in impersonal expressions.

EJERCICIO **E**

Sustituya:

1 Es importante estudiarlo.
   (leerlo, comer bien, vivir aquí, aprenderla)
2 Es necesario hablarle.
   (vender la casa, comprar muchas cosas, verlo aquí, ir mañana)

f **La carta fue escrita por María.**
The letter was written by Mary.

Ser is used in a passive construction.

EJERCICIO **F**

Sustituya:

1 La novela fue escrita por Ramón.
   (el poema, los libros, el documento, la nota)
2 Los cuentos fueron escritos por las muchachas.
   (las direcciones, la carta, el mensaje, el diálogo)

19   ESTAR

a   El Ecuador **está al norte** del Perú.
Ecuador is situated north of Peru.
Estuvimos en el Teatro Nacional anoche.
Last night we were in the National Theater.

Estar is used to express location, whether permanent or temporary.

EJERCICIO   G

Sustituya:

1   El alumno está en la universidad.
   (en el Perú, en casa, en Nueva York, en el teatro)
2   Yo estoy en el parque.
   (en Los Angeles, en el laboratorio, en la biblioteca, en el estudio)

b   El agua **está fría.**
The water is cold.
La ropa **estaba mojada.**
The clothes were wet.
La ventana **está cerrada.**
The window is closed.
Las cartas **están firmadas.**
The letters are signed.

Estar is used with an adjective or past participle to denote a state or condition of long or short duration. The adjective or past participle must agree in gender and number with the subject.

EJERCICIO   H

Sustituya:

1   La puerta está abierta.
   (las ventanas, el libro, la biblioteca, los diccionarios)
2   Los platos están rotos.
   (la taza, las corbatas, el vidrio, los lápices)

c   El pescado **está muy bueno.**
The fish is (tastes) very good.
María no ha cumplido veinticinco años. Pero **está vieja.**
Mary hasn't reached twenty-five. But she is (looks) old.
Los lunes **están muy tristes.**
Mondays are (seem to me) very blue.

Estar is used to denote personal reaction, especially taste, appearance, and opinion.

EJERCICIO I

Sustituya:

1 La carne está muy sabrosa.
(las legumbres, el pescado, la fruta, los duraznos)
2 Las muchachas están bonitas.
(la flor, el coche, la casa, los árboles)

d **Estoy leyendo** el libro.
I am reading the book.

Estar is used to form the progressive tenses.

EJERCICIO J

Un estudiante hace la pregunta y otro contesta:

Modelo (estudiar) ¿Qué está Vd. estudiando?
Estudio español.

1 (leer) _____
2 (escribir) _____
3 (hacer) _____
4 (preparar) _____
5 (olvidar) _____

e The following common adjectives differ in meaning according to the verb used:

	WITH **ser**	WITH **estar**
alegre	*gay (by nature)*	*gay, merry (for a while)*
bueno	*good, kind*	*well (health), good (taste)*
cansado	*tiresome (bore)*	*tired*
enfermo	*invalid*	*sick*
listo	*clever, smart*	*ready*
loco	*silly, a fool*	*crazy*
malo	*bad, wicked*	*ill*
nuevo	*new (newly made)*	*new (unused, as good as new)*
seguro	*sure (safe, reliable)*	*sure (safe, protected)*
triste	*dull*	*sad, gloomy*
vivo	*keen, lively*	*alive*

EJERCICIO **K**

Empleando los adjetivos dados, un estudiante debe de hacer preguntas, primero con **ser** *y después con* **estar,** *y otro estudiante debe contestarle:*

Modelos —¿Es usted bueno?
—Sí, siempre digo la verdad.

—¿Está usted bueno?
—Sí, gozo de buena salud.

1	listo	**4**	enfermo
2	cansado	**5**	triste
3	malo	**6**	vivo

EJERCICIO **L**

Cambie las oraciones para indicar el lugar de origen:

Modelos —Compré el libro en España.
—El libro es de España.

—Yo vivo en Nueva York.
—Yo soy de Nueva York.

1 Se compraron los sombreros en Panamá.
2 Nosotros vivimos en Chicago.
3 El estudiante trajo el auto de Alemania.
4 Vives en Los Angeles.
5 Compramos las flores en el mercado.
6 Viven en Chile.

EJERCICIO **M**

Cambie las oraciones para indicar localidad:

Modelos —Jorge se encuentra en Madrid.
—Jorge está en Madrid.

—Los periódicos se encuentran en la biblioteca.
—Los periódicos están en la biblioteca.

1 La oficina se encuentra en la Quinta Avenida.
2 Evelia y Lolita se encuentran en Puerto Rico.
3 La familia se encuentra en el patio.
4 Los muchachos se encuentran en la biblioteca.
5 La Unión Panamericana se encuentra en Wáshington.
6 El jefe se encuentra en Nueva York.

EJERCICIO **N**

Cambie las oraciones usando el verbo **estar:**

Modelos —Mi padre ya se enfermó.
—Mi padre está enfermo.

—Las muchachas ya se cansaron.

—Las muchachas están cansadas.

1 Felipe y Ana ya se enojaron.

2 Ya nos dormimos.

3 Ya me asusté.

4 La mujer ya se calló.

5 Ya me acosté.

6 Ya se casaron Diego y Gloria.

EJERCICIO **O**

Diga en español:

1 (la ventana) It's small, but it's open.

2 (el médico) He's good, but he's ill.

3 (el coche) It's new, but it's not here.

4 (los lápices) They are mine, and they are on the table.

5 (Anita) She's pretty, but she's not here today.

6 (el libro) It's of paper, but it's not torn (roto).

7 (Teodoro) He's Cuban, but he's not in Cuba.

8 (sus padres) They are from Los Angeles, but now they are
   in Texas.

9 (mis amigos) They are American, but they are not in the
   United States.

10 (las puertas) They are heavy, but they are open.

11 (las novelas) They are new, but they are not in the library.

12 (la casa) It's new and it's cold.

13 (la cartera) It's Mary's, but she's not here.

14 (el avión) It's big, but it's far away from here.

15 (los pasajeros) They are Portuguese, but they are in California.

EJERCICIO **P**

Diga en español:

1 (the window) It's large, but it's open.

2 (my niece) She's tall, but she's not here.

3 (the fish) It's small, but it's good.

4 (the letters) They are mine, and they are on the table.

5 (the book) It's interesting, but it's not here.

6 (his sister) She's blonde, and she's in the library.

7 (the doctor) He's friendly, but he's in Nicaragua.

8 (Miguel) He's an American, but he's in Chile.

9 (María) She's brunette, but she's not present.

10 (the family) It's numerous, but it's in New York.

11 (the bus) It's new but it's broken down.

12 (the door) It's small, but it's not open.
13 (the dentists) They are from Mexico, but they are not here.
14 (the boy) He's bad, but he's not sick.
15 (the roses) They are red, but they are not fresh.

EJERCICIO **Q**

Conteste:

1 ¿De qué es la silla?
2 ¿Por qué estás triste los lunes?
3 ¿Qué está Vd. leyendo?
4 ¿Cómo están sus padres?
5 ¿Por qué estaba ausente su hermana?
6 ¿De quién es este sombrero?
7 ¿De qué colores son las rosas?
8 ¿Cuándo estuvo Vd. en Europa?
9 ¿Dónde estarán Vds. el verano que viene?
10 ¿Qué hora es?
11 ¿De dónde es Vd? ¿Dónde está Vd. ahora?
12 ¿Dónde estaba la oficina?
13 ¿Por qué está mojada la ropa?
14 ¿Cómo es la alumna?
15 ¿Qué hora era cuando llegó Vd. esta mañana?
16 ¿Qué estaba Vd. estudiando?
17 ¿Por quién fue escrita la novela?
18 ¿Dónde está México?
19 ¿De qué es el reloj?
20 ¿Por qué estaba cerrada la ventana?

VI • PRACTICA ESCRITA

1 He is studying the lesson. (use progressive construction)
2 My two brothers are lawyers.
3 Spain is in Europe.
4 The milk is warm.
5 The soup is good.
6 The novel was written by Cervantes.
7 The boy is tall.
8 She is old and poor.
9 Are you from Mexico?
10 Whose watch is that?
11 The window is large, but it's broken.

12 My niece is pretty, but she's not here.
13 The door is small, but it's open.
14 I'm a Cuban, but I'm not happy.
15 They're Mexican, but they're not present.

VII • PRACTICA ORAL

A DIALOGO COMPLEMENTARIO

(En una pensión de Madrid.)

LA PATRONA Oye, Eduardo, ¿dónde has estado? Hacía tiempo que te buscaba y no te encontré por ninguna parte.

EDUARDO Después de tanto estudiar para ese curso del Dr. Lapesa, estaba un poco cansado y por eso decidí dar un paseo. ¿Por qué me lo pregunta?

LA PATRONA Porque está aquí uno de tus amigos norteamericanos.

RICARDO Hola, Eduardo.

EDUARDO ¡Qué tal, Ricardo, tú por aquí! ¿Por qué has tardado tanto en venir a verme?

RICARDO Pues, hombre, no quisiera mentirte. No hay excusas. He estado ocupado hasta los codos. ¿Qué tal la vida aquí en casa de la viuda de Torres?

EDUARDO Muy buena. Estoy contento. La viuda es simpática y amable. Si has estado tan ocupado, sin duda eso indica que sacas buenas notas este año.

RICARDO Un poquito mejor que el año pasado a pesar de todas las actividades.

EDUARDO ¿A qué actividades te refieres?

RICARDO Pues, ¿no sabías que soy muy aficionado a los deportes: fútbol, toreo, jai-alai, etc. y que siempre asisto a los partidos? Me gustan sobremanera las corridas de toros. Por fin conocí a un famoso matador y me enseñó el arte de la tauromaquia. Es muy listo y trabajador. Pasamos horas juntos.

EDUARDO Si continúas así, uno de estos días llegarás a ser torero también.

RICARDO El matador vive en las afueras de Madrid. Allá tiene una hacienda. Su mujer es de Barcelona donde está ahora visitando a sus padres. Tienen dos hijos preciosos, un niño de siete años y una niña de cinco.

EDUARDO   Basta, por Dios. Eres muy conversador. Esta noche vienen mis amigos Lupe, Carlos y otros, y vamos a comer en un restaurante que lleva el pintoresco nombre de «Las cuevas de Luis Candelas». ¿Quieres ir con nosotros?

RICARDO   ¡Qué bueno! Creo que mi amigo el matador tendrá mucho gusto en acompañarnos.

B EXPRESION ORAL

Hace mucho tiempo que dos amigos no se han visto. El uno pregunta al otro:

1 ¿Dónde estudia, qué estudia, y por qué?
2 ¿Por qué volvió a casa?
3 ¿Con quién se casó?
4 ¿De dónde es la esposa?
5 ¿Cuántos hijos tienen?
6 Lo invita a un restaurante, ¿qué pide?
7 ¿Por qué no quiere visitar este restaurante otra vez?

C PLATICA ESPONTANEA

1 ¿Qué hace usted cuando está cansado de tanto estudiar?
2 ¿Cuándo da Vd. un paseo por el parque? ¿Con quién?
3 ¿Por qué le gustaría (o no le gustaría) estudiar en una universidad lejos de su casa?
4 ¿Por qué no quiere Vd. trabajar después de las horas de estudio?
5 ¿Qué le regalan sus padres cuando saca Vd. buenas notas?
6 ¿A quiénes escribe Vd. cartas? ¿Se las escribe a menudo?
7 ¿Cuánto tiempo hace que no ha escrito Vd. a sus padres?
8 ¿Qué hace Vd. cuando está triste?

VIII • COMPOSICION

Escriba un diálogo entre dos alumnos que dan un paseo por el parque:

1 ¿Con quiénes se encuentran?
2 ¿Qué desean ver?

3   ¿Qué animales hay en el parque zoológico?
4   ¿En dónde van a tener el «picnic»?
5   ¿Por qué les gusta pasearse por el parque?
6   ¿A qué hora piensan volver a casa?

Lección quinta

I • DIALOGO

MARTÍN   Marta, vamos a pasearnos por el sendero rumbo a las residencias.

MARTA   Ya que acabo de salir de la última clase, me da lo mismo. Quiero llegar a mi residencia a la hora del almuerzo. Vamos ahora mismo.

MARTÍN   El paseo nos abrirá el apetito. Una cosa se me ocurre. Carlos me dio dos billetes para la función de teatro esta noche. ¿Quieres ir conmigo?

MARTA   ¡Cómo no! ¿Por qué te los dio a ti?

MARTÍN   Porque es un buen amigo mío. Somos del mismo pueblecito.

MARTA   Te lo pregunto porque el otro día lo vi pasearse hablando consigo mismo.

MARTÍN   No me sorprende nada. El pobrecito está enamorado de una muchacha que ha conocido a otro que le gusta más. Por eso siempre tiene el aspecto muy triste.

MARTA   No·dejes de llamarme esta tarde a eso de las cinco para decirme a qué hora piensas llegar.

MARTÍN   Está bien. Esta noche voy a traerte un ramillete de flores.

MARTA   ¿Cuál es la comedia para hoy?

MARTÍN   *Fuenteovejuna* de Lope de Vega.

MARTA   Pues, he aquí mi residencia. Hasta luego, Martín.

MARTÍN   Hasta la vista, Marta.

II • MODISMOS Y EXPRESIONES

abrirse el apetito	*to whet one's appetite*
ahora mismo	*right now*
dar con	*to run across*
dar de comer a	*to feed*
decirse a sí mismo	*to say to oneself*
entrar en	*to enter*
figurarse (imaginarse)	*to imagine*
helo aquí	*here it is*
impacientarse (por)	*to become impatient (to)*
me da lo mismo	*it's all the same to me*
no dejar de	*not to fail to*

pasearse por   *to stroll along*
rumbo a   *in the direction of*
ya que   *since*

By Jim Cron from Monkmeyer
En el supermercado, Ciudad de México

III • PRACTICA SOBRE MODISMOS Y EXPRESIONES

A USE CADA MODISMO EN UNA FRASE COMPLETA Y LUEGO TRADÚZCALA AL INGLÉS:

1 ahora mismo
2 helo aquí
3 entrar en
4 ya que
5 me da lo mismo

B HAGA PREGUNTAS:

1 Mañana daremos algo de comer a los niños del hospital.
2 Juan se dice a sí mismo, andando por el sendero, que nunca podrá salir bien en el examen de química.
3 Ella da con sus amigos al volver a la residencia.
4 Olga no dejó de escribirme todas las semanas.
5 Ellas se impacientan por saber la verdad.
6 Figúrese mi sorpresa cuando mi novia no quiso ir al concierto conmigo.
7 Me abre el apetito la cocina mexicana porque es muy sabrosa.
8 Queríamos pasearnos por la Quinta Avenida para mirar los escaparates.
9 El vapor iba rumbo a Cádiz cuando ocurrió un incendio.
10 Me imaginaba que mi padre había sufrido un ataque de úlceras.

IV • REPASO DE VERBOS

A USE LOS PRONOMBRES INDICADOS COMO SUJETOS DEL VERBO. (REPASE LOS VERBOS **decir** Y **haber** EN EL APÉNDICE.):

1 Tú no lo dices.
(yo, nosotros, Vd., ellas)
2 Ellos se lo dirán mañana.
(nosotros, tú, yo, ella)
3 El se lo dijo ayer.
(nosotros, yo, tú, Vds.)
4 Yo se lo he dicho.
(Vd., tú, nosotros, ellos)

B CAMBIE EL VERBO AL TIEMPO INDICADO:

1   Yo siempre decía la verdad. (presente)
2   Hay un libro en la mesa. (imperfecto)
3   Ellos me lo dicen. (perfecto)
4   ¿Qué hay de nuevo? (perfecto)
5   Nosotros nunca decíamos eso. (futuro)
6   Mañana hay una película. (futuro)
7   ¿Dirán Vds. eso? (condicional)
8   Había un lápiz en la caja. (presente)
9   Yo siempre digo eso. (imperfecto)
10 Había un ladrón en la casa. (pretérito)

C DÉ UNA SINOPSIS DE LOS VERBOS:

1   (Yo) decir la verdad.
2   Hoy no hay café.

V • GRAMATICA Y EJERCICIOS ORALES

20 PERSONAL A (LA PREPOSICION PERSONAL A)

Veo **a María.**
I see Mary.
Saludamos **a la bandera** americana.
We salute the American flag.

When the direct object of the verb is a person or a personified
object, it is preceded by **a.**

EJERCICIO **A**

Forme oraciones:

Modelo el coche / Juan
            Veo el coche, pero no veo a Juan.

1   el tranvía / Marta
2   la casa / Luis y Concha
3   la universidad / los alumnos
4   el jardín / las señoritas
5   los aviones / mis parientes

EJERCICIO **B**

Use los sustantivos siguientes como complementos del verbo:

1   Miramos el cuadro.

(la profesora, la televisión, el comerciante, los carteros, la policía, el libro)
2 Saludan a Juan.
(la bandera, los soldados, el capitán, el general)

21 PERSONAL PRONOUNS (PRONOMBRES PERSONALES)

Subject	*Indirect Object*	*Direct Object*	*Prepositional*
yo	me	me	mí
tú	te	te	ti
usted	le (se)	le, la	usted, sí
él	le (se)	le, lo[1]	él, sí
ella	le (se)	la	ella, sí
	le (se)	lo (neut.)	
nosotros, −as	nos	nos	nosotros, −as
vosotros, −as	os	os	vosotros, −as
ustedes	les (se)	les	ustedes, sí
ellos	les (se)	les, los	ellos, sí
ellas	les (se)	las	ellas, sí

With the preposition **con,** the pronouns **mí, ti** and **sí** become **conmigo, contigo,** and **consigo.**

Usted (ustedes) is the conventional form of address in Spanish. **Tú** and **vosotros** are familiar forms, used to address members of one's family, intimate friends and children. The plural of **tú** is **ustedes** in Latin America and **vosotros** in Spain.

22 SUBJECT PRONOUNS (PRONOMBRES PERSONALES USADOS COMO SUJETOS)

a **Yo** puedo hacerlo, pero **él,** no.
   I can do it, but he can't.

Since the Spanish verb usually indicates both person and number, the subject forms of personal pronouns are used only for emphasis or contrast. The subject pronoun **usted (ustedes),** however, is used regularly, and **yo** is used with the imperfect tense to distinguish the first person from the third:

---

[1] The direct objects **lo, los** are used more frequently in Latin America than in Spain when referring to persons.

Yo iba al parque todos los domingos.
I used to go to the park every Sunday.
Ella iba al parque todos los domingos.
She used to go to the park every Sunday.

EJERCICIO C

Use los pronombres siguientes como sujetos del verbo:

Modelo   Yo puedo cantarla, pero ella no. (usted)
Yo puedo cantarla, pero usted no.

1   Luis sabe hacerlo, pero yo no.
(nosotros, tú, usted)
2   La muchacha quiere oírlo, pero él no.
(ustedes, yo, ellas)
3   Los niños vienen a jugar, pero tú no.
(ella, yo, usted)

23   DIRECT OBJECT PRONOUNS (PRONOMBRES COMO COMPLEMENTOS DIRECTOS DEL VERBO)

Tengo **el libro.**   **Lo** tengo.
I have the book.   *I have it.*
No he visto **los libros.**   No **los** he visto.
I haven't seen the books.   *I haven't seen them.*

The direct object pronoun replaces a noun used as a direct object and agrees in gender and number with the noun it replaces. The direct object pronoun precedes the verb or the auxiliary in a compound tense.

EJERCICIO D

Conteste las preguntas:

Modelos   ¿Tienes la pluma?   Sí, la tengo.
¿Tienes los libros?   No, no los tengo.
¿Tienes las plumas?   No, no las tengo.

1   ¿Tienes el papel?   Sí, _____.
2   ¿Traes los lápices?   Sí, _____.
3   ¿Necesitas la carta?   No, no _____.
4   ¿Buscas las invitaciones?   Sí, _____.
5   ¿Quieres la caja?   Sí, _____.
6   ¿Compras los cuadernos?   Sí, _____.
7   ¿Vendes los zapatos?   Sí, _____.
8   ¿Traes el paraguas?   No, no _____.
9   ¿Recibes las flores?   No, no _____.
10   ¿Necesitas el abrigo?   No, no _____.

EJERCICIO **E**

Conteste:

Modelos   ¿Estudia usted la lección?
Sí, la estudio.

¿Estudian ustedes la lección?
Sí, la estudiamos.

1   ¿Aprende usted la canción?
2   ¿Aprenden ustedes la canción?
3   ¿Aprenden ellos la canción?
4   ¿Estudia usted el libro?
5   ¿Estudian ustedes el libro?

Modelo   ¿Ella come carne?
Sí, y yo la como también.

6   ¿El vende su casa?
7   ¿Ella compra el coche?
8   ¿Ellos traen los libros?
9   ¿El lee la carta?
10   ¿Ella vende los boletos?

Modelo   ¿Vio usted el árbol?
No, no lo vi.

11   ¿Recibiste la carta?
12   ¿Terminaste el cuento?
13   ¿Leyeron ustedes las novelas?
14   ¿Entendió ella la lección?

Modelo   ¿Escribes la tarea?
Sí, la escribo.

15   ¿Tiene ella el vestido?
16   ¿Aprenden ustedes las lecciones?
17   ¿Toma usted la manzana?
18   ¿Reciben ustedes los periódicos?

b   Voy a estudiar**lo**   (or)   **Lo** voy a estudiar.
I am going to study it.
Voy (estoy) estudiándo**lo.**   (or)   **Lo** voy (estoy) estudiando.
I am studying it.

The direct pronoun object may follow an infinitive or present participle, in which case it is attached to it.

EJERCICIO   **F**

Sustituya. Primero use el pronombre después del verbo, y luego póngalo delante:

Modelo   Voy a ver la película.
Voy a verla.
La voy a ver.

1   Quiero comer pan.
(frutas, dulces, postre, papas)
2   Queremos beber leche.
(café, té, cerveza, vino)
3   No quieren ver la obra.
(los cuadros, las cintas, el libro, las películas)
4   No puedo comprar el regalo.
(los regalos, la caja, las rosas, el lápiz)
5   ¿Piensas traer flores?
(vasos, papel, uvas, dulces)
6   Están tomando café.
(leche, vino, chocolate, limonada)
7. Elena está aprendiendo francés.
(sus lecciones, lenguas extranjeras, el drama)
8   Estamos cerrando la puerta.
(la ventana, el libro, los cuadernos, la caja)
9   Sigo trayendo lápices.
(flores, café, cajas, fruta)
10 Estoy mirando la televisión.
(las fotos, el cuadro, los edificios, a las señoritas)

c   Tó**melo,** señor.   *Take it, sir.*
Tó**malo,** Luis.   *Take it, Louis.*

In an affirmative command or imperative, the pronoun object
is attached.

d   No **lo** tome usted.   *Don't take it.*
Que **lo** tome su padre.   *Let your father take it.*

In negative imperatives and in indirect affirmative commands,
pronoun objects stand before the verb.

EJERCICIO G

Cambie al negativo:

1   ¡Escríbame la lección!
2   ¡Póngase el abrigo!
3   ¡Préstemelo hoy!
4   ¡Déselo usted a él!
5   ¡Explíquenselos ustedes!
6   ¡Mándenmelas en seguida!
7   ¡Muéstrenoslos ahora!

8   ¡Cásate con ella!
9   ¡Devuélvanselo a ella mañana!
10 ¡Déselo a él!

EJERCICIO H

Cambie al afirmativo:

1   ¡No se los preste Vd. a él!
2   ¡No me las den Vds.!
3   ¡No nos la escriban!
4   ¡No se lo ponga Vd.!
5   ¡No se la expliquen Vds.!
6   ¡No se lo quite Vd.!
7   ¡No me los devuelva Vd.!
8   ¡No nos las lean Vds.!
9   ¡No se los traiga Vd.!
10 ¡No me la manden Vds.!

EJERCICIO I

Sustituya los sustantivos por pronombres:

Modelo   Yo leo la lección.
             Yo la leo.

1   Yo voy comiendo fruta.
2   Yo no bebo café.
3   Jorge y Matilde no han podido abrir la caja.
4   No pueden cerrar las ventanas.
5   Veo a María.
6   Abrimos el libro.
7   El profesor va explicando la lección.
8   Señor Contreras, no tome los libros.
9   Seguimos estudiando portugués.
10 ¿Tiene usted manzanas?
11 No hay dinero.
12 Ella va a comprar lápices.
13 El hombre no vende máquinas de escribir.
14 No hemos visto el sombrero.
15 ¡No miren a las muchachas!

e   **¿Son españoles?**   *Are they Spaniards?*
    Sí, **lo** son.   *Yes, they are (it).*
    ¿Está usted cansado?   *Are you tired?*
    Sí, **lo** estoy.   *Yes, I am (it).*

The neuter pronoun **lo** is used with **ser** and **estar** to refer to a preceding statement or idea without repeating it.[1]

EJERCICIO **J**

Sustituya y conteste afirmativamente:

Modelo ¿Son norteamericanos?
　　　　　Sí, lo son.

1 estudiantes
2 muchachos
3 franceses
4 médicos
5 señoras

Modelo ¿Están ustedes enfermos?
　　　　　Sí, lo estamos.

6 malos
7 contentos
8 satisfechos
9 tristes

f Los libros **los** tenemos aquí.
　We have the books here.

When a direct noun object precedes the verb, a corresponding pronoun object is required directly before the verb.

EJERCICIO **K**

Use los sustantivos como complementos del verbo:

Modelo Los libros los tengo aquí.

1 las cartas
2 el dinero
3 la caja
4 las plumas
5 los lápices

24 INDIRECT OBJECT PRONOUNS (PRONOMBRES USADOS COMO COMPLEMENTOS INDIRECTOS DEL VERBO)

a **Le** explico la lección.
　I explain the lesson to him.
　Le he explicado la lección.
　I have explained the lesson to him.

---

[1] When **todo** is used as object of the verb, the neuter pronoun **lo** precedes the verb:
Lo sabe **todo.** *He knows everything.*

In Spanish the indirect object pronoun is placed before the verb and before the auxiliary in a compound tense.

b **Le** quiero explicar la lección. Quiero explicar**le** la lección.
I wish to explain the lesson to him.
Le voy (estoy) explicando la lección. Voy (estoy) explicándo**le** la lección.
I am explaining the lesson to him.

The pronoun may follow an infinitive or present participle, in which case it is attached to it.

c **Le** dieron el libro **a María.**
They gave the book to Mary.

When an indirect noun object follows the verb, a corresponding pronoun object is frequently used to anticipate the indirect noun object.

EJERCICIO **L**

Use los sustantivos que siguen como complementos indirectos del verbo, cambiando el pronombre si es necesario:

Modelo   El estudiante le da los dulces a Concha. (a las señoritas)
          El estudiante les da los dulces.

1 El profesor le explica la lección al muchacho.
   (a las señoritas, a Elena, a Elena y Hugo, a los estudiantes)
2 La señora le dio el libro a Jorge.
   (a María y Alberto, a Juan, a las alumnas)
3 Jorge no les escribe a las muchachas.
   (a sus hijos, al chico, a los jugadores)
4 La muchacha no le quería mandar una carta a Roberto.
   (a Ernesto, al muchacho, a Octavio y María)
5 Los estudiantes no pueden mandarles la postal a las profesoras.
   (a sus tíos, a los criados, a Roberta)
6 Las muchachas no le quieren hablar al policía.
   (al comerciante, a las meseras, a Julia)
7 El profesor les va enseñando la lección a los alumnos.
   (a Juan y Concha, a la señorita, a los estudiantes)
8 ¿Quiere usted entregarle las cartas a la criada?
   (al médico, a Doña Luz, a las muchachas)
9 ¿Puede usted decirles la verdad a Roberto y Luisa?
   (a Juan, a los jefes, a las señoras)
10 Vamos a mandarle dulces a la profesora.
    (a nuestro padre, a las criadas, a Margarita)

25 INDIRECT OBJECT WITH INTRANSITIVE VERBS (COMPLEMENTO INDIRECTO CON VERBOS INTRANSITIVOS)

Me gusta el libro.
I like the book. (literally, *The book pleases me.*)
Les faltan lápices.
They need pencils. (literally, *Pencils are lacking to them.*)
Nos parece caro.
It seems expensive to us.

Some concepts are expressed in Spanish by intransitive verbs with indirect objects. The most common of these verbs are:

gustar	*to like, be pleasing to*
faltar	*to lack, need*
parecer	*to seem, appear, think*

Note that **gustar** and **faltar** reverse the order of subject and object as compared to English. The Spanish subject becomes the English object and vice versa.

EJERCICIO **M**

Use los pronombres siguientes para completar la oración:

Modelo A mí me falta el coche.

1 A él _____.
2 A ella _____.
3 A nosotros _____.
4 A ellos _____.
5 A ellas _____.

EJERCICIO **N**

Conteste:

1 ¿Le gusta a usted la novela?
2 ¿Le gusta a ella el libro?
3 ¿Les gusta a ellos el drama?
4 ¿Les gusta a Vds. el cuento?
5 ¿Le gusta al Sr. Martínez la película?

EJERCICIO **O**

Sustituya y haga los cambios necesarios:

Modelo a usted / nadar
¿Le gusta a usted nadar?
Sí, a mí me gusta nadar.

1 a ella / coser

2 a él / correr
3 a nosotros / charlar
5 a ustedes / aprender
6 a ti / las novelas
7 a ustedes / las películas
8 a ella / las revistas

EJERCICIO **P**

Sustituya haciendo los cambios necesarios:

Modelo   a ellos / los deportes
¿A ellos les gustaron los deportes?
Sí, a ellos les gustaron los deportes.

1 a él / la corrida de toros
2 a usted / la carta
3 a ti / el baile
4 a ustedes / el partido de fútbol
5 a ella / el programa

EJERCICIO **Q**

Sustituya haciendo los cambios necesarios:

Modelo   a ti / el libro
¿A ti te pareció interesante el libro?
Sí, a mí me pareció interesante el libro.

1 a usted / la novela
2 a él / la comedia
3 a ellos / el drama
4 a nosotros / el poema
5 a ustedes / el cuento
6 a ella / la historia

26 INDIRECT OBJECT AFTER SPECIAL VERBS (USO ESPECIAL DEL COMPLEMENTO INDIRECTO)

Le compré un libro **a Juan.**
I bought a book from John.
Nos han robado el dinero.
They have stolen the money from us.
El miedo **me ha quitado** el apetito.
Fear has taken away my appetite.
Le pidió un peso a su padre.
He asked his father for a dollar.
No **me pierdas** los sombreros.
Don't lose the hats.

Verbs like **comprar, pedir, perder, robar, quitar** (generally denoting loss, gain, or changing hands), require the indirect object of the person and the direct object of the thing. The construction is peculiarly idiomatic (note the English equivalents).

27 PREPOSITIONAL PRONOUNS (LOS PRONOMBRES PERSONALES CON PREPOSICIONES)

a Lo compré **para mí.**
I bought it for myself.
Aquí está la caja, pero no hay nada **en ella.**
Here is the box, but there is nothing in it.

Prepositional pronoun forms are used with any preposition. These forms are identical with the subject pronouns except for **mí, ti** and **sí** which use the special forms **conmigo, contigo,** and **consigo:**

María va **conmigo.**
Mary is going with me.
Juan se llevó el libro **consigo.**
John took the book with him.

b Voy a **dárselo a él.**
I'm going to give it to him.
El **me lo dio a mí** y no a mi hermano.
He gave it to me, and not to my brother.

Prepositional forms may be used in conjunction with indirect or direct objects for clearness or emphasis.

EJERCICIO **R**

Conteste las preguntas siguientes:

Modelo ¿Fue para usted?
No, para mí, no.

1 ¿Fue para ellos?
2 ¿Fue para mí?
3 ¿Fue para ella?

Modelo ¿Van los hermanos Morelos conmigo?
No, no van contigo.

4 ¿Van los hermanos Morelos hacia mí?
5 ¿Van los hermanos Morelos en vez de mí?
6 ¿Van los hermanos sin mí?

Modelo ¿Estudia María con usted?
¿Conmigo? No, nunca.

7 ¿Estudia María con Juan?
8 ¿Estudia María con Juan y Alberto?
9 ¿Estudia María con nosotros?

Modelo ¿Es la flor para mí?
Para usted no, para ella.

10 ¿Es el regalo para mí?
11 ¿Es la caja para él?
12 ¿Es el paquete para mí?

c **Juan** sólo piensa **en sí.**
John only thinks of himself.
Las muchachas siempre hablan **de sí mismas.**
The girls always talk about themselves.

Following a preposition, the pronoun **sí** is used to refer to a third-person subject, masculine or feminine, singular or plural.

Note: The following words are not considered prepositions in Spanish and take subject rather than object pronouns:

como   *as*
entre   *between, among*
excepto   *except*
incluso   *including*
según   *according to*

Haga **como yo.**
Do as I do.
Entre tú y yo, creo que la novela no es buena.
Between you and me, I don't think the novel is good.
Todos fueron **incluso yo.**
All went, including me.
Según él, ellos no vienen hoy.
According to him, they are not coming today.

EJERCICIO **S**

Sustituya:

Modelo Mi hermano *me* perdió el reloj.
(a él)
Mi hermano le perdió el reloj.

1 Le vendí un anillo *a Ricardo.*
(a María, a María y Tomás, a los muchachos)
2 *Me* han robado la plata.
(a nosotros, a él, a ellos, a ti)

3 La emoción *nos* ha quitado el apetito.
(a mí, a ellas, a ti, a usted)
4 Les pedí un favor *a las señoritas.*
(a los jóvenes, a Juan, a Elba, a su padre)
5 Alberto *me* perdió el sombrero.
(a nosotros, a ti, a ellos, a Irene)

28 TWO PRONOUNS AS OBJECTS OF THE VERB (DOS PRONOMBRES COMO COMPLEMENTOS DEL VERBO)

a **Me lo** dio ayer.
He gave it to me yesterday.

An indirect object pronoun precedes another object pronoun.
By exception, **se** always precedes another object pronoun:
Se me olvidó el libro.
I forgot the book.

b Voy a dár**selo** a usted mañana.
I'm going to give it to you tomorrow.

When two third-person pronouns are used together, the indirect pronoun is always **se** (not **le** or **les**).

EJERCICIO **T**

Repita las frases, cambiando los sustantivos a pronombres:

Modelo Juanita me da la rosa.
Juanita me la da.

Yo le doy la rosa a Juanita.
Yo se la doy.

1 ¿Me quiere dar el libro?
2 Mamá nos deja la comida.
3 ¿Me puede planchar esta camisa?
4 El dependiente me ha vendido una corbata.
5 Doña Ana no nos ha enseñado las lecciones.
6 ¿Quién te quitó el gabán?
7 ¿Quiénes te explicaron la lección?
8 Queremos entregarte el caballo.
9 ¿Antonio te mostró la universidad?
10 ¿La dependienta te vendió la chaqueta?
11 La profesora nos dejó el recado.
12 Los empleados nos trajeron los papeles.
13 ¿Quién nos dio las noticias?
14 ¿Quiere explicarnos la palabra?

15 ¿Nos pueden tener la ropa interior para mañana?
16 Le mostraré el coche la semana que viene.
17 Ahora les sigo vendiendo los libros.
18 Le voy a prometer las sillas.
19 Yo les daré limosna a los pobres.
20 Présteme la peinilla, por favor.

VI • PRACTICA ESCRITA

1 Why are you returning the book to me?
  They are sending it to me.
2 Why is he writing the letters to them?
  We are writing them to them.
3 They are not asking him for the invitation.
  I am asking him for it.
4 Why are they bringing me the news?
  She is bringing it to me.
5 We can't sell her the house. Will you sell it to him?
6 Explain the rule to me. Explain it to me.
7 Give him the books. Give them to him.
8 Write her a letter. Write it to her.
9 Tell us the truth. Tell it to us.
10 Don't give them the message. Don't give it to them.
11 Don't bring us the fried potatoes. Don't bring them to us.
12 Don't send him the card. Don't send it to him.
13 Don't lose the books. Don't lose them.

VII • PRACTICA ORAL

A DIALOGO COMPLEMENTARIO

(En la lavandería.)

DEPENDIENTE ¿En qué puedo servirle?

TOMÁS Aquí traigo un paquete con ropa sucia: cuatro pares de calcetines, cinco camisas, siete pañuelos, seis camisetas y seis calzoncillos, tres sábanas y tres fundas. Esta ropa es mía. En el otro paquete más grande hay ropa de mi compañero de cuarto.

DEPENDIENTE   ¿Para cuándo la quiere?

TOMÁS   Para el viernes, si es posible.

DEPENDIENTE   ¿Va a pasar por aquí o quiere que se la enviemos? Hay un descuento del diez por ciento si la recoge usted.

TOMÁS   Bueno, yo paso por aquí el viernes por la tarde. *(En la tintorería.)*

DEPENDIENTA   Buenos días, señor, ¿qué tal?

TOMÁS   Bien, gracias. Le traigo un traje, chaqueta y pantalones. Los quiero lavados en seco.

DEPENDIENTA   ¿Para cuándo los necesita usted?

TOMÁS   Para pasado mañana si es posible.

DEPENDIENTA   Está bien. He aquí el recibo. *(En la droguería.)*

TOMÁS   Se me olvidó lo que tengo que comprar aquí.

BEATRIZ   ¿No era algo para el pelo?

TOMÁS   Ah, sí, brillantina. Señorita, una botellita de brillantina, por favor. También quiero una caja de toallitas de papel, dos pastillas de jabón, un peine y un despertador.

BEATRIZ   ¿Para qué quieres el despertador?

TOMÁS   ¿Para qué? Para despertarme por la mañana. Tengo tanto que estudiar que no puedo acabar mis tareas hasta altas horas de la noche; eso me cansa tanto que es difícil despertarme.

DEPENDIENTA   Siete cincuenta, por favor.

BEATRIZ   Vamos ahora al supermercado. Tengo que comprar algunas cosas para mis amigas. *(En el supermercado.)*

TOMÁS   *(Empujando el carrito)* ¿Qué quieres aquí?

BEATRIZ   A ver, una caja de jabón en polvo. Voy a lavar unas cosas.

TOMÁS   Está en la próxima sección. Y, ¿qué más?

BEATRIZ   Vamos a la carnicería. Necesito carne para preparar hamburguesas. Mañana tenemos un «picnic» en el patio de la casa de los señores Brown.

TOMÁS   Ah, sí. He oído decir que ese profesor y su esposa tienen tertulias muy interesantes en el patio de su casa una vez al mes. Allá repasan y discuten la literatura española que él ha enseñado en las cuatro últimas semanas. Tengo ganas de matricularme en ese curso.

Beatriz ¡Figúrate qué informalidad! Y todos estamos muy entusiasmados porque aprendemos mucho con poco esfuerzo.

B EXPRESION ORAL

Cuente a un amigo el paseo que dio usted por el parque zoológico.

1 Mencione unos animales; lo que les dio de comer.
2 ¿Con quiénes se encontró usted?
3 ¿A dónde fue a comprar refrescos?
4 ¿Qué comió y bebió?
5 ¿A dónde va uno de sus amigos pronto?
6 ¿Para qué?

C PLATICA ESPONTANEA

1 ¿Dónde pasa usted el verano?
2 ¿Qué hace usted en el verano?
3 ¿Piensa usted hacer un viaje a Europa el verano que viene?
4 ¿Por qué no fue usted al campo el verano pasado?
5 ¿Cuánto tiempo hace que no pasa usted el verano en las montañas?
6 ¿Por dónde se pasea usted usualmente?
7 ¿Con quién dio usted en el parque el otro día?
8 ¿Qué hacía usted en el parque?
9 ¿Por qué no se permite dar de comer a los animales en el parque?
10 ¿Qué hace usted para abrirse el apetito?

VIII · COMPOSICION

Escriba un diálogo entre varios alumnos sobre el tema de los regalos de Navidad. Indique:

1 por qué recibió un alumno un paquete de su tía.
2 cuándo llegó el paquete.
3 qué contenía.
4 qué piensa hacer el alumno para expresarle el agradecimiento a su tía.
5 qué regalo piensa darle a su novia para la Navidad.

Lección sexta

I • DIALOGO

(Anita y Miguel están sentados en un coche frente a un kiosco de refrescos.)

MIGUEL   De todas las estaciones del año, me gusta más el verano porque puedo descansar, tomar el fresco y nadar en el río.

ANITA   Me gusta más el invierno. Soy muy aficionada a patinar y esquiar.

MIGUEL   No me gusta el frío. Además, siempre hace mal tiempo en el invierno. A propósito, ¿no te gustaría hacer una excursión al Lago del Diablo hoy?

ANITA   ¿No te das cuenta de que nos falta tiempo para hacer los preparativos? ¿Qué te parece mañana, domingo?

MIGUEL   Es que no puedo ir este domingo sino el próximo. Te agradecería mucho si prepararas lo necesario. Con mucho gusto pago yo los gastos de la excursión.

ANITA   Bajemos del coche un rato. Quiero tomar una limonada. ¿Qué tomas tú?

MIGUEL   Limonada también. Parece que la que atiende no se acerca a mi coche.

ANITA   ¿Cuánto dista el lago de aquí?

MIGUEL   Sólo unas sesenta millas.

(En el Lago del Diablo.)

ANITA   ¡Uf! Hace mucho calor y además estoy rendida. ¿No quieres remar un poco?

MIGUEL   ¿Yo? ¡No! Prefiero quedarme sentado aquí para tomar el sol.

ANITA   En ese caso, voy a nadar un rato.

(Ella se mete al lago.)

MIGUEL   Se acerca una lancha. Oye, Anita, sube en seguida porque viene gente.

ANITA   A los pocos minutos subo. ¿No ves que gozo del agua fresca?

MIGUEL   Pero Anita, ya vas fuera de los límites donde se permite nadar. Acércate inmediatamente.

ANITA   Está bien. Subo de buena gana porque veo que es la lancha de la policía.

Courtesy Pan American Airways
Lago Atitlán en Guatemala

II • MODISMOS Y EXPRESIONES

a los pocos minutos	*in a few minutes*
acercarse a	*to approach*
agradecerle a uno	*to be grateful to someone for*
bajar de	*to get off, to get out of; to take down*
darse cuenta de	*to realize*
es que	*the fact is that*
faltar	*to be lacking, need*
fijarse en	*to notice*
fuera de	*outside of*
hacer calor	*to be warm (weather)*
subir	*to get on, bring up, come up (out)*

III • PRACTICA SOBRE MODISMOS Y EXPRESIONES

A USE CADA MODISMO EN UNA FRASE COMPLETA, Y LUEGO TRADÚZ-CALA AL INGLÉS:

1 agradecerle a uno
2 darse cuenta de
3 fuera de
4 hacer calor
5 a los pocos minutos

B CONTESTE EN ESPAÑOL:

1 Ayer hizo frío. ¿Qué tiempo hará mañana?
2 Elena se acercó a la colina para ver mejor el incendio. ¿Por qué se acercó usted a la ventana?
3 Me faltan dos libros. ¿Qué le falta a usted?
4 Le agradecieron los alumnos el favor a Juana. ¿A quién le agradece usted el favor?
5 No nos dimos cuenta de que habían hecho el trabajo. ¿De qué no se dio cuenta usted?

IV • REPASO DE VERBOS

A (REPASE LOS VERBOS **hacer** E **ir** EN EL APÉNDICE.) CAMBIE LOS VERBOS

AL SINGULAR:

1 Hacemos la lección ahora.
2 Dudábamos que fueran a Madrid.
3 Hemos hecho el baúl.
4 Van a Galicia.
5 Me hicieron varias preguntas sobre Velázquez.

AL PLURAL:

6 Fui al baile anoche.
7 Ella prohibió que él hiciese el viaje a Vigo.
8 Iré a California pronto.
9 ¿Me haría usted el favor de hablar más despacio?
10 Voy al cine con Ana.

B USE LOS PRONOMBRES INDICADOS COMO SUJETOS DEL VERBO:

(PRESENTE)

1 Yo no voy al cine.
(nosotros, tú, él, ustedes)
2 Tú no lo haces bien.
(ellos, nosotros, yo, Ud.)

(IMPERFECTO)

3 Yo no iba al cine.
(Uds., él, tú, nosotros)
4 Tú no lo hacías bien.
(Ud., ellos, nosotros, yo)

(FUTURO)

5 Yo no iré al cine.
(él, tú, nosotros, Uds.)
6 Tú no lo harás bien.
(ellos, nosotros, yo, Ud.)

(PERFECTO)

7 Yo no he ido al cine.
(tú, nosotros, él, Uds.)
8 Tú no lo has hecho bien.
(yo, Ud., ellos, nosotros)

C CONTESTE LAS PREGUNTAS SIGUIENTES:

1 ¿Por qué no fue usted a la biblioteca?
2 ¿Por qué irán a Europa el año que viene?
3 ¿Qué hizo Ud. anoche?
4 ¿Qué tiempo hacía cuando llegó a su casa anoche?

D DÉ UNA SINOPSIS DE LOS VERBOS:

(Yo) hacer el viaje.
(Nosotros) ir a Chile.

V • GRAMATICA Y EJERCICIOS ORALES

29 AFFIRMATIVE AND NEGATIVE WORDS (INDEFINIDOS:
PRONOMBRES, ADJETIVOS Y ADVERBIOS)

AFFIRMATIVE		NEGATIVE	
algo	*something, somewhat (rather)*	**nada**	*nothing, not anything*
alguien	*someone, somebody*	**nadie**	*no one, nobody not any one*
algún(o) } **alguna**	*some, either (one)*	**ningún(o)** } **ninguna**	*no, none, not any, neither*
algunos } **algunas**	*some*	**ningunos** } **ningunas**	*no, none, not any*

		nunca,	
		jamás	*never, not ever*
también	*also*	**tampoco**	*neither, not either*
o . . . o	*either . . . or*	**ni . . . ni**	*neither . . . nor*

30 USES OF AFFIRMATIVE AND NEGATIVE WORDS (USOS DE LOS INDEFINIDOS)

a **Alguien** viene.
Somebody is coming
Tengo **algo** para Vd.
I have something for you.

Affirmative words are generally used as their English equivalents.

b **No** viene **nadie.**
Nadie viene.
Nobody is coming.

When a negative word follows the verb, **no** must precede the verb.

EJERCICIO **A**

Escriba oraciones nuevas sin usar la palabra **no,** *manteniendo el mismo significado:*

Modelo No viene nadie.
Nadie viene.

1 No tengo nada.
2 No me gusta ninguna de las tres.
3 No iré tampoco.
4 No estudian nunca.
5 No van a cantar jamás.
6 No me gusta nada estudiar.

c Me habló **alguno** de los niños.
One of the children spoke to me.
No me habló **ninguno** de los niños.
None of the children spoke to me.
Alguien está en casa.
Somebody is at home.
Nadie está en casa.
Nobody is at home.

Alguno and **ninguno** refer to a person previously mentioned; **alguien** and **nadie** refer to no definite person.

Lección sexta

d Tiene **(algún)** objeto en hacerlo.
He has some reason for doing it.
No tiene **(ningún)** objeto en hacerlo.
He has no reason for doing it.

Alguno and **ninguno** lose final **o** and become **algún, ningún** before a masculine singular noun. Ordinarily **algún** and **ningún** are not expressed in Spanish, except for emphasis.

e **No** tengo **nada.**
I haven't anything.
No veo a **nadie.**
I don't see anybody.

Algo and **alguien** may never be used in a negative sentence. They are replaced by **nada** and **nadie,** respectively.

f **No** tiene **importancia alguna.**
It doesn't matter at all.
El lo hizo **sin duda alguna.**
He did it without any doubt at all.
No tengo **libro alguno.**
I don't have any book at all.

In a negative sentence (**sin** has negative force), **alguno** stands after a noun.

g Veo a **alguien.**
I see someone.
No veo a **nadie.**
I don't see anyone.

Personal **a** always precedes **alguien, nadie, alguno, ninguno** used as pronoun objects of a verb.

h Es la montaña más alta que yo **jamás** haya visto.
It is the tallest mountain I have ever seen.
¿Le ha hablado **jamás?**
Have you ever spoken to her?

Jamás in the sense of "ever" is used after a superlative or in a question.

i Es un libro **algo** interesante.
It's a rather interesting book.
No es **nada** inteligente.
She's not at all intelligent.

No me gusta **nada.**
I don't like it at all.

Algo and **nada** are sometimes used as adverbs.

j **(O)** démelo **o** préstemelo.
Either give it to me or lend it to me.
No tengo **(ni)** papel **ni** lápiz.
I have neither paper nor pencil.

In correlation, **(o) . . . o** means *(either) . . . or;* **(ni) . . . ni,** *(neither) . . . nor.*

k **Tampoco** iré.
Neither will I go.
No iré **tampoco.**
I will not go either.
(Ni) yo **tampoco.**
Nor I either.

(Ni) . . . tampoco means *neither, not . . . either, nor . . . either.*

l **No** pido **nunca nada** a **nadie.**
I never ask anything of anyone.

Two or more negatives in the Spanish sentence do not make it affirmative.

Nunca pido **nada** a **nadie.**
I never ask anything of anyone.

If one of the negative words is placed before the verb, **no** is omitted.

EJERCICIO **B**

Cambie a la forma negativa:

1 Alguien canta.
2 Tengo algo para ella.
3 Algún amigo mío me lo escribió.
4 Juan es algo estúpido.
5 Me lo dijo alguna de las muchachas.
6 ¡O entre o salga!
7 ¡Cante Vd. alguna canción mexicana!
8 Alguien quiere verme.
9 El libro es algo interesante.
10 Me dio algún dinero.
11 ¿Vamos a Patagonia algún día?
12 El resultado fue algo serio.

13 Yo tengo una revista también.
14 Aquí se puede hacer algo.
15 Alguien entra en la casa.

EJERCICIO C

Exprese en la forma afirmativa:

1 Nadie tiene la revista.
2 ¿Ninguno de ustedes quiere una limonada?
3 Nunca tomamos el colectivo.
4 No recibí una carta tampoco.
5 La alumna no es ni inteligente ni bonita.
6 Miguel no tiene nada en la mano.
7 No viene nadie a ver la película.
8 Ninguna de las alumnas faltaba a la clase.
9 Nunca pongo azúcar en el café.
10 Tampoco pueden asistir a la reunión.

EJERCICIO D

Diga en español usando las dos formas posibles en el negativo:

Modelo Nobody studies.
　　　　　Nadie estudia. No estudia nadie.

1 Nobody loves me.
2 None of you wants to attend the meeting.
3 Never do I look at television in the morning.
4 Neither did she leave.
5 Neither John nor Lucia is coming tonight.
6 Nobody likes the cold weather.

31 NUMERALS (NUMERALES)

a Cardinal Numbers

0	**cero**	18	**diez y ocho**	
1	**uno, –a**		**(dieciocho)**	
2	**dos**	19	**diez y nueve**	
3	**tres**		**(diecinueve)**	
4	**cuatro**	20	**veinte**	
5	**cinco**	21	**veinte y uno**	
6	**seis**		**(veintiuno)**	
7	**siete**	22	**veinte y dos**	
8	**ocho**		**(veintidós)**	
9	**nueve**	30	**treinta**	

10	**diez**	31	**treinta y uno**[1]
11	**once**	40	**cuarenta**
12	**doce**	50	**cincuenta**
13	**trece**	60	**sesenta**
14	**catorce**	70	**setenta**
15	**quince**	80	**ochenta**
16	**diez y seis**	90	**noventa**
	(dieciséis)	100	**cien, ciento**[2]
17	**diez y siete**	101	**ciento uno**
	(diecisiete)	102	**ciento dos**

200	**doscientos**	800	**ochocientos**
300	**trescientos**	900	**novecientos**
400	**cuatrocientos**	1,000	**mil**[3]
500	**quinientos**	2,000	**dos mil**
600	**seiscientos**	1,000,000	**un millón**[4]
700	**setecientos**	2,000,000	**dos millones**

b Ordinal Numbers

primero	*first*
segundo	*second*
tercero	*third*
cuarto	*fourth*
quinto	*fifth*
sexto	*sixth*
séptimo	*seventh*
octavo	*eighth*
noveno (nono)	*ninth*
décimo	*tenth*

32 USE OF ORDINALS (USO DE LOS ORDINALES)

a **el primero de junio**   *the first of June*
   el cuatro de julio   *the fourth of July*

Only **primero** is used in dates. Beyond the first of the month, cardinal numbers are used.

[1] Numbers beyond 29 may not be written as one word.

[2] **Ciento** becomes **cien** before a noun and before **mil** and **millones: cien plumas** *100 pens;* **cien mil hombres** *100,000 men;* but **ciento diez libros** *110 books.*

[3] **Mil** is also used in dates: 1942 **mil novecientos cuarenta y dos.**

[4] **De** must follow **millón** before a noun: **dos millones de mujeres** *two million women.*

b	**Carlos Quinto**	*Charles V*
	Pablo Sexto	*Paul VI*
	Alfonso Doce	*Alfonse XII*
	Juan Veintitrés	*John XXIII*

Titles of rulers and popes require ordinal numbers through **décimo** and cardinal numbers beyond.

c	**la sexta página**	*the sixth page*
	la página seis	*page six*
	capítulo quince	*chapter fifteen*

Pages, chapters, and volumes may be designated by either cardinal or ordinal numbers. Beyond **décimo,** only cardinal numbers are used.

EJERCICIO **E**

Diga los números siguientes en español:

1	1066	**8**	ninth
2	1492	**9**	537
3	seventh	**10**	1,000
4	100,000[1]	**11**	759
5	3,000,000	**12**	fourth
6	150	**13**	1776
7	945	**14**	sixth

33 TIME OF DAY (LA HORA)

¿Qué hora es?	*What time is it?*
¿A qué hora?	*At what time?*
A la una.	*At one o'clock.*
Es la una.	*It's one o'clock.*
Es la una y cuarto.	*It's a quarter past one.*
Es la una y quince.	*It's 1:15.*
Son las dos.	*It's two o'clock.*
Son las tres.	*It's three o'clock.*
Son las cinco menos diez.	*It's 4:50.*
Son las dos menos cuarto.	*It's a quarter to two.*
Es mediodía.	*It's noon.*
a las tres de la madrugada	*at three in the morning*

[1] In Spanish-speaking countries, the use of the decimal point and comma is reversed. In Spanish usage, *100,000* becomes **100.000** and *4.8* becomes **4,8.**

a las siete de la mañana   *at seven A.M.*
a las dos de la tarde   *at 2 P.M.*
a las diez de la noche   *at 10 P.M.*

When definite time is given, **de** is equivalent to English *in.*
When no definite time is expressed, **por** is equivalent to *in:*

Estudio **por la noche.**
I study at night (in the evening).

EJERCICIO **F**

Diga la hora en español:

 1 1:25
 2 12:45
 3 5:15
 4 6:12
 5 7:05 A.M.
 6 11:40 P.M.
 7 8:50 A.M.
 8 3:30
 9 4:55
10 9:28
11 10:20
12 2:14 A.M.

34 SEASONS (LAS ESTACIONES)

la primavera   *spring*
el verano   *summer*
el otoño   *fall*
el invierno   *winter*

35 DAYS OF THE WEEK (LOS DIAS DE LA SEMANA)

el domingo   *Sunday*
el lunes   *Monday*
el martes   *Tuesday*
el miércoles   *Wednesday*
el jueves   *Thursday*
el viernes   *Friday*
el sábado   *Saturday*

36 MONTHS OF THE YEAR (LOS MESES DEL AÑO)

enero	*January*
febrero	*February*
marzo	*March*
abril	*April*
mayo	*May*
junio	*June*
julio	*July*
agosto	*August*
septiembre	*September*
octubre	*October*
noviembre	*November*
diciembre	*December*

EJERCICIO G

Complete las frases:

1 Los días de la semana son _____.
2 Los meses del año son _____.
3 Las estaciones del año son _____.

VI • PRACTICA ESCRITA

1 Is anyone here?—No, nobody is here.
2 Did he tell you (that) he was looking for somebody?—No, he told me nothing. I suppose (that) he wasn't looking for anybody.
3 Is something happening to this stranger?—No, nothing is happening to him.
4 Have you ever received a letter from her?—No, she never writes to me now.
5 Will (present of *querer*) either you or Pepe open the window? Neither Pablo nor Juan can open that window.
6 Some day you will know the truth. They will never know the truth.
7 Did any of you bring money? None of the girls brought a purse.
8 Will you buy bread?—No, I won't buy it either.
9 Does anyone deserve it?—Nobody deserves it.
10 Do you ever look at television?—I never look at it.
11 This lesson is somewhat difficult, don't you think?—No, I don't find it difficult at all.

VII • PRACTICA ORAL

A DIALOGO COMPLEMENTARIO

(En el aeropuerto de Bogotá.)

RITA Hermano, Esteban, ¡qué gusto verte aquí! Desde la muerte de mamá, mi esposo y yo seguimos viviendo en la misma casa. Allá nos espera Miguel.

ESTEBAN ¡Ay! Rita. ¡Qué bueno regresar a mi país!

RITA ¿Qué tal el viaje en avión?

ESTEBAN ¡Magnífico! No hubo vaivén, ni vibración ni nada de eso.

RITA ¿Cómo van tus estudios en California?

ESTEBAN ¡Muy bien! Gané una beca para pasar el año en la Argentina estudiando la novela moderna. Vamos a subir a este taxi.

CHÓFER ¿A dónde?

RITA A la Avenida Caracas, número 59–21, en el barrio de Chapinero. Vaya derecho por la carrera séptima y doble a la izquierda al llegar a la calle 57. Siga por esta calle hasta encontrar la Avenida Caracas, luego doble a la derecha y siga por dos cuadras.

CHÓFER Muy bien. Ya he metido las maletas en el baúl.

ESTEBAN Nunca le pido nada a nadie, pero, Rita, necesito cigarrillos. ¿Tienes uno?

RITA Es que no fumo nunca.

CHÓFER Ni yo tampoco, pero le ofrezco esto. *(Le da a Esteban un paquete.)* Tómelo, señor.

ESTEBAN Mil gracias. Rita, ¿y si tu esposo no me recibe con cordialidad? ¿No les molestará a Vds. mi presencia en la casa?

RITA ¡Qué va! No te preocupes. Miguel es muy buena persona.

CHÓFER Ya hemos llegado. Siete cincuenta, por favor. ¿Les subo las maletas?

ESTEBAN No, gracias. Tome esta propina.

MIGUEL Rita, te vi llegar desde la ventana. Esteban, bienvenido. Aquí tienes tu casa. Pasa. Déjame ayudarte con las maletas.

ESTEBAN Mucho gusto, Miguel. Vds. son muy amables conmigo.

B EXPRESION ORAL

Invite a un amigo (o amiga) a hacer una excursión al campo en su coche.

1 Decida quién ha de hacer los preparativos.
2 Si es muchacha, pregúntele lo que piensa preparar.
3 ¿A dónde van ustedes?
4 ¿A cuántas millas de la universidad?
5 ¿Cuánto tiempo se necesita para llegar allí?
6 ¿A qué hora la recoge usted?
7 ¿Qué piensan hacer después de llegar?
8 ¿Quiénes los acompañan?
9 ¿Cuándo regresan?

C PLATICA ESPONTANEA

1 Cuando hace mucho calor, ¿qué hace usted?
2 ¿Por qué no le gusta el calor?
3 ¿Cuándo piensa usted hacer un viaje a México?
4 ¿Quién está fuera de la clase?
5 A los pocos minutos de llegar a la universidad, ¿a dónde va usted?
6 ¿Por qué no baja usted del coche cuando se pone en marcha?
7 ¿Cuántos hombres se necesitan para subir un piano?
8 ¿Dónde busca usted taxi?
9 ¿Con quién se encontró usted anoche?
10 ¿De qué se dio cuenta usted al salir mal en el examen?

VIII • COMPOSICION

Supóngase que usted tiene que coger un taxi para llegar al aeropuerto. Escriba una conversación entre usted y el chófer con comentarios sobre:

1 el precio del viaje de su casa al aeropuerto
2 las condiciones del aeropuerto
3 cuánto tiempo se tarda en llegar
4 cuánto equipaje tiene usted
5 a qué hora sale el avión
6 quién le acompaña en el viaje; a dónde va
7 por qué no fuma el chófer

Lección séptima

I • DIALOGO

JORGE Hola, Elena. Hoy tenemos que empezar a hacer planes para conmemorar el día de la raza, el doce de octubre.

ELENA ¿Por qué? Estoy de vacaciones y no quiero molestarme con esa tarea en el verano.

JORGE No olvides que el célebre día llega en dos meses, y si queremos tener un programa interesante, debemos hacer los preparativos ahora y no dejarlo todo para el último momento.

ELENA Está bien. Tú tienes razón, como de costumbre. ¿Qué piensas hacer?

JORGE En primer lugar, vamos a decidir si habrá banquete o no.

ELENA ¡Claro que sí! Y además creo que debe haber música, baile y canciones de Hispanoamérica.

JORGE Estoy de acuerdo con eso. ¿Quieres encargarte de la comida? Tú eres una buena cocinera y te gusta cocinar. Ana y unas muchachas podrían ayudarte.

ELENA Y María podría encargarse de las decoraciones. Vamos a colgar las banderas de las naciones panamericanas en las paredes.

JORGE ¡Magnífica idea! Y yo me encargo del programa de música y bailes. Conozco a una pareja venezolana que sabe bailar el joropo muy bien. Voy a pedirles que lo bailen.

ELENA Y yo voy a preguntarle a Marta si le interesa dirigir un coro latinoamericano. Está en la Escuela de Música y estudia canto. Me gustan tus planes.

JORGE Y a mí me gustan los tuyos también. A propósito, ¿qué piensas cocinar?

ELENA Estaba pensando en preparar paella a la valenciana, por ejemplo, ¿qué te parece?

JORGE ¡Sabrosísima! A mí me gusta mucho. ¿Sabes que después de tanto hablar de cosas de comer se me ha abierto el apetito?

ELENA Pues, entonces, hasta luego.

JORGE Hasta luego.

By Dieter Grabitzky from Monkmeyer
Gira por Lima, Perú: Pila de la Plaza de Armas

II • MODISMOS Y EXPRESIONES

(a) la hora de la comida	*(at) dinner time*
a propósito	*by the way*
claro que sí	*of course*
como de costumbre	*as usual*
en primer lugar	*in the first place*
encargarse de	*to take charge of*
estar de acuerdo (con)	*to agree (with)*

estar de vacaciones   *to be on vacation*
por ejemplo   *for example*

III • PRACTICA SOBRE MODISMOS Y EXPRESIONES

A   USE CADA MODISMO EN UNA FRASE COMPLETA, Y LUEGO TRADUZCA AL INGLÉS:

1   a propósito
2   como de costumbre
3   estar de vacaciones
4   estar de acuerdo

B   DIGA EN ESPAÑOL:

1   They arrived late as usual.
2   In the first place, we must decide whether to bring a car or to rent one.
3   My friend always arrives at dinner time.
4   Of course we are not going without them.
5   Has Robert ever taken charge of a play?
6   For example, there are many ways of reading a book.

IV • REPASO DE VERBOS

A   (REPASE LOS VERBOS **jugar** Y **oír** EN EL APÉNDICE.)
CAMBIE LOS VERBOS

AL PLURAL:

1   No juega bien.
2   He jugado al fútbol.
3   Yo jugaba todos los días al golf.
4   Oigo la radio todas las noches.
5   ¿Me oyó Ud.?
6   Ud. oía la verdad.

AL SINGULAR:

7   No jugábamos bien.
8   ¡Jueguen Vds. bien!
9   Jugaremos al tenis la semana que viene.
10   Dijeron que no oirían la verdad.
11   Oíamos al profesor.
12   ¡Oigan a la muchacha!

B USE LOS SUSTANTIVOS Y PRONOMBRES INDICADOS COMO SUJETOS
DEL VERBO:

(PRESENTE)

1 Ud. no oye bien.
(ellos, nosotros, tú, yo)

2 Nosotros no jugamos al béisbol.
(tú, Ana y María, yo, él)

(PRETÉRITO)

3 Ud. no oyó bien.
(nosotros, tú, él y yo, yo)

4 Nosotros no jugamos al béisbol.
(Ud., yo, tú, ellos)

(FUTURO)

5 Ud. no oirá al presidente desde allá.
(nosotros, Uds., tú, yo)

6 No jugaremos nunca al béisbol.
(Yo, ellas, ella, tú)

C DÉ UNA SINOPSIS DEL VERBO:

(yo) jugar al golf.
(Uds.) oír la conferencia.

V • GRAMATICA Y EJERCICIOS ORALES

37 POSSESSIVE ADJECTIVES (ADJETIVOS POSESIVOS)

Possessive adjectives are divided into two groups: those that
precede the noun and those that follow the noun.

a Possessive adjectives preceding the noun

SINGULAR	PLURAL	
mi	mis	*my*
tu	tus	*your* (fam.)
su	sus	*his, her, its, your*
nuestro, –a	nuestros, –as	*our*
vuestro, –a	vuestros, –as	*your* (fam.)
su	sus	*their, your*

b **Mi ropa** está en el armario.
My clothes are in the closet.

Su casa está en Madrid.
Their house is in Madrid.
Nosotros vamos en **nuestro coche.**
We are going in our car.
Mi esposa y **mi hijo** están aquí.
My wife and son are here.

Possessive adjectives, like other adjectives, agree in gender and number, not with the possessor (as in English), but with the thing possessed. **Mi, tu, su** have the same forms for both genders. Possessive adjectives must be repeated before each noun in a series.

Since **su** may mean *your* (singular or plural), *his, her, their,* or *its,* the meaning may be clarified by placing the definite article before the noun and the phrases **de él, de ella, de usted,** and so forth, after the noun:

Es **su libro.**
It's his (her, their, your) book.
But
Es **el libro de ella.**
It's her book.

EJERCICIO **A**

Use los sustantivos indicados, haciendo todos los cambios necesarios:

Modelo Mi libro es grande. (libros)
Mis libros son grandes.

1 Mi cuaderno es pequeño.
(casa, coches, flores)
2 Nuestro tocadiscos no es bueno.
(biblioteca, lápices, tarjetas)
3 ¿Dónde está tu mamá?
(papá, sobrino, hermanas)
4 Juan tiene su cortaplumas.
(invitaciones, cartas, plumas)
5 Esa toalla es limpia.
(traje, calcetines, corbata.)
6 Tu chaqueta está rota.
(blusas, vestido, falda)
7 Sí, mi coche es bonito.
(barcos, toalla, flores)
8 Nuestra biblioteca es grande.
(dormitorio, escuelas, cuartos)
9 No, nuestra sala no es grande.
(coche, alcoba, aviones)

10 Su padre es rico.
(tías, abuelas, hermanas)

c Possessive adjectives following noun

SINGULAR	PLURAL	
mío, −a	**míos, −as**	*my*
tuyo, −a	**tuyos, −as**	*your* (fam.)
suyo, −a	**suyos, −as**	*his, her, its, your*
nuestro, −a	**nuestros, −as**	*our*
vuestro, −a	**vuestros, −as**	*your* (fam.)
suyo, −a	**suyos, −as**	*their, your*

d Ven acá, **niña mía.**
Come here, my child.
¡Dios mío!
My God!
Es **amiga suya.**
She is a friend of his.

Possessive adjectives that follow the noun have three main uses: in direct address, in exclamations, and as the equivalent of English *of mine, of yours, of his, of hers,* and so on.

EJERCICIO **B**

Reemplace los sustantivos y haga los cambios necesarios:

1 Es amigo mío.
(amigos, hermanas, tía)
2 Son parientes nuestros.
(abuelas, primo, hermano)
3 Ven acá, niña mía.
(hija, amigo, abuela)

38 POSSESSIVE PRONOUNS (PRONOMBRES POSESIVOS)

SINGULAR

el mío	**la mía**	*mine*
el tuyo	**la tuya**	*yours* (fam.)
el suyo	**la suya**	*his, hers, its, yours*
el nuestro	**la nuestra**	*ours*
el vuestro	**la vuestra**	*yours* (fam.)
el suyo	**la suya**	*theirs, yours*

PLURAL

los míos	las mías	*mine*
los tuyos	las tuyas	*yours* (fam.)
los suyos	las suyas	*his, hers, its, yours*
los nuestros	las nuestras	*ours*
los vuestros	las vuestras	*yours* (fam.)
los suyos	las suyas	*theirs, yours*

a Esta **alcoba** es más pequeña que **la mía.**
This bedroom is smaller than mine.
Este **coche** cuesta más que **el nuestro.**
This car costs more than ours.

Possessive pronouns differ from possessive adjectives in that the pronouns are ordinarily used with the definite article.

b Tengo mi **libro** y **el suyo** (or **el de ella**).
I have my book and hers.

El suyo, etc. may be replaced by **el de él, el de ella, el de usted,** etc. for clearness.

c ¿De quién es esta **pluma? Es mía.**
Whose pen is this? It's mine.
But
¿Cuál de los libros desea usted?
Which book do you want?
El que deseo es **el suyo.**
I want his.

In answering the question "whose?" the definite article **el** (and the like) is omitted immediately after the verb **ser,** but in answering the question "which one?" the definite article is not omitted.

EJERCICIO C

Sustituya los sustantivos por pronombres:

Modelo   Mi lápiz es amarillo.
                    El mío es amarillo.

1 Mi libro es grande.
2 No tengo los animales de él.
3 Ud. tiene el paraguas.
4 Nuestro coche está en el garaje.
5 Sus carteles están en la mesa.

6   No quiero su plato.
7   Deme sus cartas.
8   Mi casa es pequeña.
9   Nuestras cartas están bien escritas.
10   Mis plumas son bien baratas.

EJERCICIO   **D**

Conteste las preguntas siguientes:

1   ¿De quién es esta casa?
2   ¿De quién es este coche?
3   ¿De quién es aquella caja?
4   ¿De quiénes son esos libros?
5   ¿De quiénes son estas maletas?
6   ¿De quién son estos guantes?
7   ¿De quién es esta flor?
8   ¿De quién es esa corbata?
9   ¿De quién es aquel documento?
10   ¿De quiénes son aquellas chaquetas?

39   DEMONSTRATIVE ADJECTIVES (ADJETIVOS DEMOSTRATIVOS)

SINGULAR

M.	F.	
este	esta	*this*
ese	esa	*that*
aquel	aquella	*that*

PLURAL

M.	F.	
estos	estas	*these* (aquí *here*)
esos	esas	*those* (ahí *there*)
aquellos	aquellas	*those* (allí *there*)

Demonstrative adjectives modify nouns. **Este (esta, estos, estas)** corresponds to the adverb **aquí** *(here, near the speaker)*, **ese (esa, esos, esas)** to **ahí** *(there, near the person spoken to)*, and **aquel (aquella, aquellos, aquellas)** to **allí** *(there, far away from both people involved)*.

Esta mujer es mi esposa.
This is my wife.
Aquellos hombres son soldados.
Those men are soldiers.

Esta pluma y este lapíz son míos.
This pen and pencil are mine.

Demonstrative adjectives, like other adjectives, agree in gender and number with the noun they modify and must be repeated before each noun.

EJERCICIO E

Use los sujetos indicados, haciendo todos los cambios necesarios:

Modelo   Este lápiz es mío. (esta pluma)
Esta pluma es mía.

1   Ese zapato es mío.
(esta flor, estos libros, esas corbatas)
2   Esa torre es alta.
(este hombre, esas montañas, aquellos árboles)
3   Esta alcoba es muy pequeña.
(este coche, esas maletas, esos platos)
4   Este guante es más bonito.
(esta calle, estos guantes, esas cajas)
5   Aquellas casas son blancas.
(aquel billete, esa lancha, aquellos calcetines)
6   Ese chaleco es tuyo.
(aquella camisa, estos zapatos, ese traje)
7   Aquel hombre es rico.
(aquella mujer, esas muchachas, esta señorita)

40 DEMONSTRATIVE PRONOUNS (PRONOMBRES DEMOSTRATIVOS)

SINGULAR

M.	F.	
éste	**ésta**	*this one*
ése	**ésa**	*that one*
aquél	**aquélla**	*that one*

PLURAL

M.	F.	
éstos	**éstas**	*these*
ésos	**ésas**	*those*
aquéllos	**aquéllas**	*those*

a   No quiero **estos** zapatos sino **aquéllos.**
I don't want these shoes but those.

Demonstrative pronouns differ from demonstrative adjectives in that they bear written accents.

b Juan y José son hermanos. **Este** toca el piano y **aquél** el violín.
John and Joseph are brothers. The former plays the violin and the latter the piano.

The pronouns **éste, ésta, éstos, éstas** are sometimes used to mean *the latter* and **aquél, aquélla, aquéllos, aquéllas,** *the former.* Note that in Spanish, contrary to English, **éste** *(the latter)* usually comes before **aquél** *(the former).*

EJERCICIO **F**

Imite el modelo haciendo todos los cambios necesarios:

Modelo   Esta flor es mía. Esta es mía.
  Este billete es mío. Este es mío.

1   Ese lápiz es tuyo.
  (esas corbatas, estos libros, esta caja)
2   Aquellas lanchas son pequeñas.
  (aquellos calcetines, aquella maleta, ese billete)
3   Este guante es muy bonito.
  (esas cajas, esta flor, esos libros)
4   Esta alcoba es amarilla.
  (esos platos, ese coche, aquellas plumas)
5   Ese traje es mío.
  (estos chalecos, esa camisa, aquellos zapatos)
6   Aquel caballero es mexicano.
  (esa mujer, estas señoritas, ese muchacho)
7   Esa familia es muy rica.
  (esta leche, aquel profesor, aquellas chicas)

41 FOURTH DEMONSTRATIVE (USOS ESPECIALES DE LOS PRONOMBRES DEMOSTRATIVOS EL, LA, LOS, LAS)

el (la, los, las) de   *that (or those) of; the one (or ones) with (in, on)*

el (la, los, las) que   *that (those) which (who); the one (ones) which, who.*

El que está aquí es mi padre.
The one who is here is my father.
Se venden libros en **esta librería** y también en **la de la esquina.**
Books are sold in this bookstore and also in the one on the corner.

Before a clause introduced by **que** and before a phrase introduced by **de,** the demonstrative **el (la, los, las)** is generally used in place of the regular demonstrative.

EJERCICIO G

Use los sujetos indicados, haciendo todos los cambios necesarios:

Modelo   Estas flores y las del jardín son bonitas. (este árbol)
Este árbol y el del jardín son bonitos.

1   Estas flores y las del jardín son bonitas.
(esos árboles, aquellas plantas, estos pájaros)
2   Este lápiz y el de Juan son baratos.
(esta corbata, esos trajes, esas camisas)
3   Esa lancha y la de María son pequeñas.
(aquellas cajas, este vestido, esos pañuelos)
4   Aquellas alcobas y las del palacio son grandes.
(esos cuartos, estas cocinas, estos coches)
5   Estos trajes y los de Alberto son caros.
(aquella maleta, ese coche, esas camisas)
6   Estas cartas y las del Sr. Gómez son importantes.
(aquel documento, esas maletas, estos libros)
7   Ese sitio y el de allá son bonitos.
(estos lugares, esa montaña, aquellas nubes)

42   NEUTER DEMONSTRATIVE PRONOUNS (PRONOMBRES DEMOSTRATIVOS NEUTROS)

esto	*this*	**aquello**	*that (remote in time)*
eso	*that*	**lo (que)**	*what*

a   **Esto** no vale la pena.
This isn't worth bothering about.
Eso es magnífico.
That (situation) is magnificent.
Aquello pasó en 1492
That happened in 1492.

Neuter demonstrative pronouns, which have no corresponding adjective forms, have no written accent. They refer to a statement, general idea, or an object whose gender is unknown.

b   **Lo que** me dice usted me asombra mucho.
What (that which) you tell me surprises me very much.

Lo que is equivalent to English *what* in the sense of "that which."

VI • PRACTICA ESCRITA

1 My house is on Fifth Avenue. Where's yours?
2 His tie is on the table. Where's John's?
3 She has her book. Where's mine?
4 They don't have their records. Where are hers and Mary's?
5 Our dictionary is large. My father's is small.
6 This house and that one are large.
7 This boy and the one who is coming are friends of mine.
8 That mountain is very high; this one is rather small.
9 These watches and those run well.
10 Those hats and these are expensive.
11 What they told us was not the truth.
12 You know what I mean, don't argue with me.
13 What she did amazed me.
14 I never write what she tells me.
15 What he wrote was a lie.

VII • PRACTICA ORAL

A   DIALOGO COMPLEMENTARIO

(Una gira por Lima.)

ROBERTO   Espero que te guste la ciudad. Es mucho más pequeña que Chicago y sus calles no son tan anchas.

BETTY   Me gusta más que la mía pues las calles no parecen interminables. Uno se pierde muy fácilmente en Chicago.

ROBERTO   Los edificios de Lima no son tan altos como los de Norteamérica. Este es el Ayuntamiento. Es muy antiguo y data del siglo XVI.

BETTY   ¡Qué pintoresco es el paisaje! ¡Y qué altas son las cordilleras allá en el fondo!

ROBERTO   Hay picos más altos que los de Norteamérica. Tú sabes que en la cordillera de los Andes el Aconcagua llega a una altura de unos 23.000 pies sobre el nivel del mar.

(Llegan a casa de Roberto.)

BETTY   ¡Caramba! ¿Es tuya esta casa? Es mucho más grande que la mía.

ROBERTO   La casa no es mía, es de mis padres que están de vacaciones en Nueva York. Y hablando de vacaciones, mis dos primas, Dolores y Hortensia, pasan las suyas en esta ciudad. Son de Cuzco.

BETTY   Parece que dos muchachas se están acercando. ¿No son ellas tus primas?

ROBERTO   Sí. ¿Qué tal, Dolores? ¿Cómo estás, Hortensia? Quiero presentarles a Betty Anderson. Es de San Diego, California.

DOLORES Y HORTENSIA   Muchísimo gusto.

DOLORES   Pensaba que íbamos a pasar la tarde en la playa.

HORTENSIA   Tenemos una casa en el Callao.

ROBERTO   ¿Quieres ir, Betty?

BETTY   Sí, pero no traje traje. *(Todos ríen.)*

DOLORES   No importa. Puedo prestarte uno, si quieres.

BETTY   ¿Cuál es la temperatura del agua en esta época del año?

HORTENSIA   Creo que subirá a 68 grados Fahrenheit.

BETTY   Demasiado fría para mí. Pasa lo mismo en California, de modo que no nado muy a menudo. Otro día les aceptaré la invitación.

ROBERTO   Estoy de acuerdo contigo, Betty. Vamos a bailar un poquito.

BETTY   Con mucho gusto, Roberto.

B EXPRESION ORAL

Invite a un amigo (o amiga) a ayudarle en los preparativos de un programa especial, por ejemplo, una fiesta. ¿En qué fecha será? El programa—música, bailes, canciones. Las personas que se encargan de las varias partes de la fiesta: invitaciones, comida, baile, etc. ¿Quiénes van a tomar parte? Lo que hará cada persona.

C PLÁTICA ESPONTÁNEA

1 ¿Qué hace usted cuando está de vacaciones?
2 ¿A dónde prefiere ir para sus vacaciones?
3 ¿Por qué?
4 ¿Quién se encarga de la casa durante su ausencia?
5 ¿Cuando va usted de vacaciones?
6 ¿A qué juega usted cuando está de vacaciones?
7 ¿Quién le acompaña en sus vacaciones?
8 ¿Cómo viaja usted a su lugar favorito?
9 ¿Cuánto tiempo está de vacaciones?
10 ¿Cuánto tiempo hace que no ha estado usted de vacaciones?

VIII • COMPOSICION

Imagínese que usted va a llevar a un estudiante de Chile a visitar los lugares de interés de una ciudad norteamericana. Escriba sobre lo siguiente en forma de diálogo:

1 ¿Qué medio de transporte piensa Ud. usar?
2 ¿Qué sitios históricos y de diversión hay: edificios, museos, parques, bibliotecas, playas, montañas, hoteles, universidades, etc.?
3 ¿Qué estudia su amigo allí?
4 ¿Cuáles son sus intereses?
5 La familia de su amigo.

Lección octava

I • DIALOGO

(*Ricardo y José se acercan a la receptoría del hotel para inscribirse.*)

DEPENDIENTE   Buenos días, señores, ¿en qué puedo servirles?

RICARDO   Estamos aquí para el congreso del club panamericano y deseamos un cuarto con dos camas.

DEPENDIENTE   Tenemos uno en el quinto piso con cuarto de baño y ducha, y vista a la calle.

JOSÉ   ¿Hay televisión en el cuarto? Me gusta mucho ver el noticiario.

DEPENDIENTE   Sí, y no es necesario pagar nada por este servicio.

RICARDO   ¿Cuánto cuesta el cuarto?

DEPENDIENTE   Cinco pesos por día y treinta por semana. Pero hay un precio especial para los estudiantes que asisten al congreso: veinte pesos por semana.

JOSÉ   Está bien. Nos quedamos con la habitación. Que lleve el botones nuestro equipaje.

RICARDO   Quiero subir al cuarto en seguida para lavarme la cara y las manos.

JOSÉ   (*Al dependiente.*) ¿Dónde está el ascensor?

DEPENDIENTE   Allá a la derecha, por detrás.

JOSÉ   Gracias. (*A Ricardo.*) Hoy día en los hoteles de lujo el ascensor no está tan lejos de la oficina.

RICARDO   Oye, ¿cuándo llegan Rosario y Luisa?

JOSÉ   Llegaron la semana pasada. ¿No sabías?

RICARDO   No, pero creo que aquí vienen.

(*Llegan Rosario y Luisa antes de que puedan subir los muchachos.*)

ROSARIO   ¿Qué tal? ¿Ustedes por aquí? ¿Cuándo llegaron? El comité nos hospedó en el Hotel Cortés, el del famoso ascensor de vidrio que está fuera del edificio.

JOSÉ   Sí, ya recuerdo. Lo vi a lo lejos cuando veníamos de la estación.

RICARDO   ¿Cuánto tiempo hace que están aquí?

LUISA   Hace tres días. Llegamos con anticipación para ir de compras.

José La primera sesión del congreso será esta noche. Les sugiero que comamos pronto. Vamos al comedor.

Ricardo No te preocupes por eso. Parece que siempre piensas en el estómago.

Rosario No importa. Vamos pronto porque tengo hambre.

Luisa Y yo también. Vámonos.

(José no puede más y los cuatro entran en el comedor del hotel.)

Courtesy Spanish Tourist Office
Museo del Prado, Madrid

II • MODISMOS Y EXPRESIONES

a la derecha	*to the right*
a lo lejos	*in the distance*
lejos de	*far from*
de antemano	*beforehand*
¿En qué puedo servirles?	*What can I do for you?*
hoy día	*nowadays*
impacientarse por	*to be impatient to, anxious to*
la semana pasada	*last week*
no importa	*it doesn't matter*
no poder más	*to give up*
por detrás	*behind*
preocuparse por	*to worry about*

III • PRACTICA SOBRE MODISMOS Y EXPRESIONES

A USE LOS MODISMOS SIGUIENTES EN UNA FRASE COMPLETA Y TRADUZCA LAS FRASES AL INGLÉS:

1 la semana pasada
2 lejos de
3 por detrás
4 hoy día
5 ¿En qué puedo servirles?
6 a lo lejos
7 no importa
8 a la derecha

B DIGA EN ESPAÑOL:

1 John gives up because he's tired.
2 Elena gives up because she's tired.
3 They give up because they're tired.
4 We were impatient to leave.
5 They're impatient to see it.
6 I'm not impatient to return.
7 Why did they worry about paying the bill?
8 Why did she worry about telling me the truth?
9 Who worries about those things?

IV • REPASO DE VERBOS

A (REPASE LOS VERBOS **poner** Y **poder** EN EL APÉNDICE.)
CAMBIE LOS VERBOS

AL PLURAL:

1 Ella puso el libro en la mesa.
2 No puedo ir al cine hoy.
3 Pondré el diccionario en el estante.
4 No puede más.
5 He puesto el cojín en el sofá.
6 ¿Ha podido usted verlo?

AL SINGULAR:

7 Poníamos la televisión todas las noches.
8 ¿Pueden Vds. acompañarlos?
9 Pusimos el lápiz en el mostrador.
10 No pudieron ver bien.
11 ¿Pondrán la radio?
12 ¿Podrían venir temprano?

B CAMBIE LOS VERBOS A LOS TIEMPOS INDICADOS:

1 No he podido ayudarlos. (presente)
2 Lo pondremos allá. (perfecto)
3 Nosotros no podemos más. (pretérito)
4 Jorge puso un telegrama. (presente)
5 ¿Puede Ud. prestármelo? (imperfecto)
6 No se pone el sombrero. (perfecto)
7 No podían sacar el coche del garaje. (pretérito)
8 La dependienta ha puesto la cuenta en el mostrador. (futuro)
9 Gloria no puede venir. (imperfecto)
10 Se han puesto los guantes. (imperfecto)

C DÉ UNA SINÓPSIS DE:

(Vds.) no poder venir
(Yo) poner la radio

V • GRAMATICA Y EJERCICIOS ORALES

43 ADJECTIVES (ADJETIVOS)

a Es **un edificio alto.**
   It's a high building.

Es **una casa alta.**
It's a tall house.
Tengo **una bolsa gris.**
I have a gray purse.

Adjectives ending in **o** in the masculine change to **a** in the feminine. Adjectives ending in any other letter remain the same in the feminine.

b Es **española.**
She is Spanish.
Juana no es **holgazana,** sino **habladora.**
Juana is not lazy but talkative.
But
Ella es **menor** que él.
She is younger than he.

Adjectives of nationality ending in a consonant have feminine forms in **a.** Adjectives ending in **án, ón, or** (but not the comparatives **mayor** and **menor**) also have feminines in **a.**

c | blanco | blancos | blanca | blancas | *white* |
| --- | --- | --- | --- | --- |
| **difícil** | **difíciles** | **difícil** | **difíciles** | *difficult* |
| **andaluz** | **andaluces** | **andaluza** | **andaluzas** | *Andalusian* |

Adjectives ending in a vowel add **s** to form the plural. Those ending in a consonant add **es.** If the adjective ends in **z, z** is changed to **c** before adding **es.**

d **El paisaje y la gente** son **pintorescos.**
The landscape and the people are picturesque.

An adjective modifying two nouns of different genders is generally masculine plural.

EJERCICIO **A**

Sustituya y haga los cambios necesarios:

1 Es un coche blanco.
   (pluma, flores, comedor)
2 Tengo una cartera grande.
   (lápices, manzanas, palacio)
3 Vicente es español y Juanita es española.
   (portugués, holandés, francés, andaluz)
4 Carlos es hablador y Elena es habladora.
   (holgazán, joven, estudioso)
5 Alfonso y Gertrudis son simpáticos.
   (Rita, Samuel, las muchachas, Rita y Samuel)

44 POSITION OF ADJECTIVES (POSICION DE LOS ADJETIVOS)

a **Estos muchachos** son grandes.
These boys are big.
Mis padres están aquí.
My parents are here.
Quiero **dos manzanas.**
I want two apples.
Algunas personas le conocían.
Some persons knew him.
Mi coche está en el garaje.
My car is in the garage.
Hay **muchos libros** en la mesa.
There are many books on the table.

Nondescriptive adjectives (such as demonstratives, possessives, numerals, indefinites, articles, and quantitatives) usually precede the noun.

b Miguel es **un muchacho inteligente.**
Michael is an intelligent boy.
Me gustan **las casas pequeñas.**
I like (the) small houses.

Descriptive adjectives usually follow the noun when they emphasize, distinguish, or differentiate the noun from others of its class.

c mis amigos **ricos**   *my rich friends (not all are rich)*
mis **ricos** amigos   *my rich friends (all are rich)*

When the adjective is stressed, it usually comes after the noun; when the noun is stressed, the adjective comes before the noun.

d Es **un buen muchacho.**   *He's a good boy.*
Es **una mala costumbre.**   *It's a bad custom.*

Certain common descriptive adjectives **(bueno, malo, grande)** have lost their differentiating force and often precede the noun.

e **la blanca nieve**   *white snow*
un fiero tigre   *a fierce tiger*

An adjective describing an inherent or logical characteristic may precede the noun.

f un **pobre** muchacho   *a poor (unfortunate) boy*
un muchacho **pobre**   *a poor (penniless) boy*

un hombre **grande**	*a big (tall) man*
un **gran** hombre	*a great (important) man*

Some adjectives have a different meaning when they precede or follow the noun.

g Cervantes es un **famoso** autor **español.**
Cervantes is a famous Spanish writer.
Es un hombre **alto y delgado.**
He is a tall, thin man.

When two or more adjectives modify one noun, each is placed according to the rules given above; if both follow the noun, they are connected by **y.**

EJERCICIO **B**

Use el adjetivo dado antes o después del sustantivo y explique la razón de su selección:

1 (siete) Me dijo que tenía lápices.
2 (azul) Juan tiene corbatas.
3 (bello) ¿Visitó usted el Palacio de Artes?
4 (difícil) Me gustan los exámenes.
5 (pobre, *without money*) El hombre me lo agradeció mucho.
6 (bonito) Quiero comprar una casa.
7 (tercero) Manuel vive en el piso.
8 (joven) Las hermanas están aquí.
9 (pobre, *unfortunate*) La mujer tiene mala suerte.
10 (bueno) Nos bendijo el cura.
11 (famoso, americano) Byrd es un explorador.
12 (mucho) Han llegado hombres.
13 (inteligente) Ana es una muchacha.
14 (gordo y bajo) He visto al hombre.
15 (pequeño) Vivo en un cuarto.
16 (alguno) Tengo dinero.
17 (malo) María es una alumna.
18 (cualquiera) Ninguna persona sabe eso.
19 (mi) Tengo plumas.
20 (grande) Washington es un hombre.

45 SHORTENED FORM OF ADJECTIVES (FORMA ABREVIADA DE LOS ADJETIVOS)

a Es un **buen** libro.
It's a good book.
Llegamos el **tercer** día.
We arrived the third day.

No veo **ningún** error en el texto.
I don't see any errors in the text.
He leído **algunas** novelas.
I've read some novels.

Bueno, malo, uno, alguno, ninguno, primero, and **tercero,** lose the final **o** when used before a masculine singular noun. **Algún** and **ningún** acquire accents when **o** is lost.

b	
San Carlos	*Saint Charles*
Santo Tomás	*Saint Thomas*
Santa Teresa	*Saint Theresa*
la **gran** señora	*the great lady*
el **gran** capitán	*the great captain*
cualquier hombre	*any man*
cualquier cosa	*anything*
cien dólares	*one hundred dollars*
ciento diez mil estudiantes	*one hundred ten thousand students*

Santo becomes **San** before a masculine singular noun unless the noun begins with **To** or **Do**. **Grande** becomes **gran** before a singular noun of both genders. **Cualquiera** drops **a** before nouns of both genders. **Ciento** becomes **cien** before nouns.

EJERCICIO **C**

Reemplace los sustantivos y haga los cambios necesarios:

1 ¡Qué buen amigo es!
(muchacha, platos, frutas)
2 Tuve un mal ejemplo.
(semana, frenos, llantas)
3 Es un gran profesor.
(señores, mujer, persona)
4 Necesito la tercera línea.
(número, cuenta, libro)
5 Me gusta cualquier película.
(diccionario, maleta, baúl)
6 ¿Han mandado alguna carta?
(cosas, recado, tarjeta)
7 La visité el primer día.
(semana, años, meses)

46 SPECIAL USES OF ADJECTIVES (USOS ESPECIALES DE ADJETIVOS)

Viven **contentos.**
They live happily.
La rubia es mi hermana.
The blonde is my sister.

Adjectives may be used as adverbs and as nouns.

47 ADVERBS (ADVERBIOS)

a **rápido, –a** *rapid* **rápidamente** *rapidly*
    triste *sad* **tristemente** *sadly*

Adverbs are formed by adding **mente** to the feminine singular form of the adjective. If the adjective has an accent, it is retained in the adverb.

EJERCICIO **D**

Diga en español:

Modelo She walks slowly.
      Ella camina lentamente.

1 She walks lazily.
2 She walks easily.
3 She walks horribly.
4 She walks perfectly.
5 She walks lightly.
6 She walks rapidly.

b Habla **lenta** y **claramente.** *She speaks slowly and clearly.*

If two adverbs are connected by a conjunction, the first adverb loses **mente.**

EJERCICIO **E**

Diga en español:

Modelo They speak clearly and rapidly.
      Hablan clara y rápidamente.

1 They speak slowly and distinctly.
2 They speak clearly and easily.
3 They speak gravely and professionally.
4 They speak regularly and openly.
5 They speak beautifully and sonorously.
6 They speak lazily and sadly.

c   Me pegó **con violencia** (rather than **violentamente**).
He hit me violently.

In Spanish a prepositional phrase is frequently preferred to an adverb in **mente.**

EJERCICIO **F**

Diga en español:

Modelo   She studied it diligently.
Lo estudió diligentemente.
Lo estudió con diligencia.

1   She opened it carefully.
2   She said it frequently.
3   She read it rapidly.
4   She wrote it intelligently.
5   She learned it easily.
6   They did it carelessly.

EJERCICIO **G**

Diga en español:

Modelo   It's exactly the contrary.
Es exactamente lo contario.

1   It's precisely the contrary.
2   It's unfortunately the contrary
3   It's probably the contrary.
4   It's generally the contrary.
5   It's possibly the contrary.
6   It's clearly the contrary.

VI • PRACTICA ESCRITA

1   Can you see the tall towers in the distance?
2   Can they see the pretty girls in the distance?
3   Can we see the low buildings in the distance?
4   Can he see the beautiful park in the distance?
5   Can she see the green trees in the distance?
6   These women are English.
7   Those girls are Andalusian.
8   These maids are Spanish.
9   Those young women are talkative.
10   These women are lazy.

11 Goethe is a famous German author.
12 García is a short fat man.
13 Do you have seats in the fifth row?
14 Any man can say that.
15 Anything will please her.

VII • PRACTICA ORAL

A DIALOGO COMPLEMENTARIO

ANTONIO Bueno, Matilde, ¿a dónde quieres ir hoy?

MATILDE Puesto que hace mucho que estudio arte, quiero visitar el famoso Museo del Prado.

ANTONIO Está bien. No está muy lejos del hotel y podemos detenernos allí después de dar un corto paseo de unos veinte minutos.

MATILDE Tengo ganas de entrar en el salón principal para ver los magníficos cuadros de Velázquez.

ANTONIO Ah, sí. En un extremo está colgado el famoso cuadro de *La rendición de Breda* o *Las lanzas,* como se llama hoy día. ¿Sabes qué representa?

MATILDE ¡Hombre! ¡No he estudiado arte en vano! Representa el momento en que el vencido comandante holandés, Justín de Nassau, entrega las llaves de la ciudad a su generoso vencedor, el marqués de Espínola.

ANTONIO ¡Bravo! Y este marqués en actitud de suavizar la vergüenza de Justín de Nassau, le pone una mano sobre el hombro izquierdo como si le dijera «No se preocupe Ud. Ha sido un adversario muy valeroso.»

MATILDE ¡Cuánto sabes de la pintura española!

ANTONIO Y ¿por qué no? Hace dos años que estudio la historia del arte.

MATILDE ¡Ah!, otra cosa. Recuerdo que a la derecha del cuadro se pueden ver los soldados españoles con sus uniformes azules y sus lanzas en alto.

ANTONIO Sí. Y el hombre del extremo derecho lleva un sombrero grande y muchos creen que es un autorretrato de Velázquez.

MATILDE Me asombra tu conocimiento del arte.

ANTONIO Gracias.

MATILDE Otro cuadro de Velázquez que me gusta mucho es *Las meninas.*

ANTONIO La escena representa el taller del artista en el Palacio Real. Parece que Velázquez pintaba a los reyes, Felipe IV y Mariana, cuyas figuras se ven en el espejo grande al fondo de la pintura, cuando entró la princesa Margarita con sus meninas, dos enanos, una monja, el mayordomo y un perro.

MATILDE ¿Vamos ahora al Museo?

ANTONIO Sí, en un momentito. ¿Sabes que la princesa Margarita lleva un vestido grande llamado guardainfante?

MATILDE Basta. Tú sabes demasiado.

B EXPRESION ORAL

Una dramatización: Haga un estudiante el papel de dependiente. Llegan dos estudiantes y piden una habitación con cuarto de baño. Discuten precios, por día, por semana. ¿Hay ducha? ¿Televisión o radio? ¿Ascensor? ¿Comedor?

C PLATICA ESPONTANEA

1 ¿Cuánto cuesta hoy día un cuarto con baño en un hotel? ¿Sin baño?

2 ¿En qué piso prefiere Ud. vivir?

3 ¿Por qué?

4 ¿Cómo se llama su hotel favorito?

5 ¿Dónde está?

6 ¿Por qué son automáticos los ascensores?

7 ¿Quién sube el equipaje al cuarto?

8 ¿Por qué hay ascensor en el hotel?

9 ¿Por qué le gustan (o no le gustan) los grandes hoteles de lujo?

10 ¿Por qué son necesarios los hoteles?

VIII • COMPOSICION

Escriba una conversación sobre el arte español. Imagínese que visita con unos amigos el Museo del Prado en Madrid. Haga comentarios sobre:

1 cuánto dista el museo del hotel
2 si van Vds. en taxi o en autobús
3 las horas de visita del museo
4 los cuadros de El Greco, Velázquez, Murillo y Goya

Lección novena

I • DIALOGO

(Es la noche del gran baile panamericano. Beatriz viene vestida de largo y la acompaña Luis llevando smoking. Entran en el gran salón de baile del hotel.)

BEATRIZ ¡Qué dulce suena la música de la orquesta!

LUIS Sí, es la orquesta de Pancho González y sus diez picadores.

BEATRIZ ¿Por qué los llaman «picadores»?

LUIS No es más que un nombre.

BEATRIZ ¿Bailamos? No hay tanta gente aquí como esperaba.

LUIS Sí. ¿Te has fijado en aquella pareja al otro lado del salón?

BEATRIZ ¿No es ella la reina del baile?

LUIS ¡Ya lo creo! Fue elegida el mes pasado. La conocí por primera vez en mi clase de español.

BEATRIZ Cállate porque me das celos.

LUIS No te preocupes. Sólo quería señalártela. Tú eres más bonita que ella y bailas mejor.

BEATRIZ ¡Lisonjero! Vamos a sentarnos un rato. Empiezan a dolerme los pies un poco.

LUIS Si insistes en llamarme lisonjero, no voy a decirte la verdad de aquí en adelante. ¿Quieres que te traiga un vasito de limonada?

BEATRIZ Sí. Te espero aquí.

(Mientras Luis va por limonada, Beatriz queda sentada en un sofá. Después de unos cuantos minutos vuelve Luis con la limonada.)

BEATRIZ Gracias, tú eres tan amable como siempre.

LUIS Ya empieza el intermedio y va a cantar Elena Contreras, una estrella mexicana recién venida a los Estados Unidos.

BEATRIZ ¡Qué interesante! Allí está. Parece más joven de lo que creía.

LUIS Llegó a ser estrella por un disco que grabó para una compañía norteamericana. Luego hizo una película en Hollywood.

BEATRIZ Después que termine la canción, vamos a bailar junto al escenario para verla mejor. No me duelen los pies tanto como antes.

II • MODISMOS Y EXPRESIONES

al otro lado de	*on the other side of*
de aquí en adelante	*hereafter, henceforth*
dolerle a uno algo	*to ache, hurt*
el mes pasado	*last month*
no obstante	*nevertheless*
tener celos	*to be jealous*
dar celos	*to make jealous*

III • PRACTICA SOBRE MODISMOS Y EXPRESIONES

A USE LOS MODISMOS SIGUIENTES EN FRASES COMPLETAS, Y LUEGO TRADÚZCALAS AL INGLÉS:

1 tener celos
2 no obstante
3 dolerle a uno algo
4 dar celos
5 al otro lado de

B REEMPLACE LOS PRONOMBRES Y HAGA TODOS LOS CAMBIOS NECESARIOS:

1 A mí me duelen los pies.
(nosotros, ustedes, ella)
2 A ustedes les dolía la cabeza.
(mí, nosotros, él)
3 A nosotros nos dolió la garganta.
(ustedes, mí, ti, ellos)
4 A él le dolían los ojos.
(nosotros, mí, ellas, ti)

IV • REPASO DE VERBOS

A (REPASE LOS VERBOS **querer** Y **saber** EN EL APÉNDICE.)
CAMBIE LOS VERBOS

AL SINGULAR:

1 Quieren ver la feria.
2 No sabíamos eso.
3 No querrán oír la verdad.
4 ¡Que lo sepan perfectamente!
5 Querrían estudiarlo bien.
6 No sabrían eso.

AL PLURAL:

7 Quise subir la montaña.
8 Sé lo que han dicho.
9 Yo quería hacer un viaje a Barcelona.
10 Supe lo que quería decirme.
11 Ella ha querido al presidente.
12 Sabrá tocar el piano.

B CAMBIE LOS VERBOS A LOS TIEMPOS INDICADOS:

1 No quisieron asistir a la clase. (presente)
2 Me alegro de que lo sepa Beatriz. (imperfecto)
3 ¿Querrá ir Alberto al baile? (pretérito)
4 Yo no sabía que llegaban. (pretérito)
5 No queremos leer el periódico. (futuro)
6 No saben la verdad. (futuro)
7 Marta quiere ir mañana. (condicional)
8 Lo hemos sabido por radio. (imperfecto)
9 No quiero entrar allá. (perfecto)
10 Jorge sabía eso. (condicional)

C DÉ UNA SINOPSIS DE:

(Ella) querer trabajar aquí.
(Yo) saber la verdad.

V • GRAMATICA Y EJERCICIOS ORALES

48 COMPARISON OF ADJECTIVES AND ADVERBS (COMPARACION DE ADJETIVOS Y ADVERBIOS)

a Adjectives

POSITIVE		COMPARATIVE AND SUPERLATIVE	
claro	*clear*	**más claro**	*clearer, clearest*
cortés	*courteous*	**más cortés**	*more courteous, most courteous*

Es **claro.** (positive)
It's clear.
Es **más claro.** (comparative)
It's clearer.
Es **el más claro.** (superlative)
It's the clearest.
Es el punto **más claro.** (superlative)
It's the clearest point.

b Adverb

cerca	*near*	**más cerca**	*nearer, nearest*

El pueblo está **cerca.** (positive)
The town is near.
El otro pueblo está **más cerca.**
The other town is nearer (comparative), *nearest* (superlative).

The comparative and superlative degrees of adjectives and adverbs are formed by placing **más** before them. In Spanish the comparative and superlative have the same form. The definite article generally precedes the superlative.

49 IRREGULAR COMPARISON (COMPARACION IRREGULAR)

a Adjectives

POSITIVE	COMPARATIVE AND SUPERLATIVE
pequeño	**más pequeño**
small	*smaller, smallest* (size)
	menor
	smaller, smallest (importance)
	younger, youngest
grande	**más grande**
large, great	*larger, largest* (size)
	mayor
	greater, greatest (importance)
	older, oldest
malo	**peor**
bad	*worse, worst*
bueno	**mejor**
good	*better, best*

b Adverbs

mucho	*much*	**más**	*more, most*
poco	*little*	**menos**	*less, least*

bien	*well*	**mejor**	*better, best*
mal	*badly*	**peor**	*worse, worst*

50 COMPARISON OF EQUALITY (COMPARATIVOS DE IGUALDAD)

a   Tengo **tanto** dinero **como** usted.
I have as much money as you.
Hay **tantas** plumas **como** lápices aquí.
There are as many pens as pencils here.

Comparisons of equality are expressed by **tanto (–a, –os, –as)** **. . . como** *(so much . . . as, so many . . . as, as much . . . as, as many . . . as)*. **Tanto** stands before the noun and agrees with it in number and gender.

b   Es **tan** grande **como** yo.
He's as tall as I.
Anda **tan** despacio **como** yo.
He walks as slowly as I.
But
El no habla **tanto como** ella.
He doesn't talk as much as she.

The adverbial form **tan** *(so [as] . . . as)* is used before an adjective or an adverb.

EJERCICIO A

Sustituya:

1   Esta casa no es tan grande como la otra.
(interesante, amplia, bonita, fuerte)
2   Juan habla tan bien como Elena.
(mal, perfectamente, seriamente, admirablemente)
3   No debo exagerar tanto como mi mujer.
(comer, andar, ver, escribir)
4   Hay tantos profesores aquí como en Londres.
(problemas, coches, tranvías, robos)
5   Necesito tanto dinero como usted.
(plata, postre, libertad, consejos)
6   Me regalaron tantos pañuelos como medias.
(zapatos, blusas, faldas, camisas)
7   La señora Blanco tiene tanta fortuna como yo.
(dinero, pesetas, tocadiscos, sillas)
8   Como persona, la Sra. García es tan simpática como la señora González.
(seria, inteligente, amable, buena)

51 THAN (CONJUNCION COMPARATIVA)

a Tengo **más libros que** él.
I have more books than he.
Juan es **más inteligente que** María.
John is more intelligent than Mary.
El tiene **menos de** diez pesos.
He has less than ten dollars.

In comparison **que** is equivalent to *than*; before a number **de** is used.[1] After a superlative, **de** is equivalent to *in:*

Es el niño más rico **de** la clase.
He is the richest boy in the class.

b Era más listo **de lo que** creía usted.
He was more clever than you believed.

In a comparison involving two clauses, the second clause is introduced by **de lo que** *(than);* but if the comparison involves a noun, **del (de la, de los, de las)**[2] introduces the second clause:

Mi padre me compró más libros **de los que** yo necesitaba.
My father bought me more books than I needed.
He leído más novelas **de las que** hay en la biblioteca.
I have read more novels than there are in the library.

EJERCICIO **B**

Haga preguntas:

1 Tengo tanto interés en ir a California como usted.
2 María canta tan bien como Rita.
3 Jorge me dio tantos papeles como Ud.
4 El es tan grande como su hermano menor.
5 Este banco tiene tanto dinero como el otro.
6 Compramos tantas cosas como ellos.
7 Yo soy tan inteligente como la señorita González.
8 Ella es más hermosa de lo que usted piensa.
9 Ella habla tanto como yo.
10 Yo tengo menos pelo que ustedes.
11 Mateo tiene menos de doce pesos.
12 Marta es más rica de lo que creía.
13 El era el más grande de la clase.
14 Tengo más libros de los que hay en la librería.
15 Mi madre me compró más música de la que necesitaba.

[1] Note the expression **no . . . más que: No** tengo **más que** dos. *I have only two.*
[2] Depending on the gender and number of the antecedent noun.

EJERCICIO C

Diga en español:

Modelo She is prettier than I.
Ella es más bonita que yo.

1 She is more serious than I.
2 They are more intelligent than she.
3 She is more slender than we.
4 I am more industrious than he.
5 She has more coats than you.
6 I have more problems than you.
7 He has more opportunities than I.
8 She has more houses than we.

EJERCICIO D

Modelo Johnny spends more than ten dollars.
Juanito gasta más de diez dólares.

1 Charles spends more than five dollars.
2 Robert and Louis spend more than one hundred dollars.
3 We spend more than one thousand dollars.
4 She spends more than one million dollars.
5 She earns more than one hundred dollars.
6 She loses more than three hundred dollars.
7 She pays more than seven hundred dollars.
8 She invests more than seven hundred dollars.

EJERCICIO E

Modelo Helen is the richest girl in town.
Elena es la chica más rica del pueblo.

1 Helen is the richest girl in the class.
2 Mary is the poorest girl in the city.
3 Rose is the richest girl in the world.
4 Martha is the prettiest girl in the neighborhood.

EJERCICIO F

Modelo I am more industrious than you think.
Yo soy más aplicado de lo que usted piensa.

1 I am more intelligent than you think.
2 We are more serious than you think.
3 They are stronger than you think.
4 He is poorer than you think.

52 ABSOLUTE SUPERLATIVE (EL SUPERLATIVO ABSOLUTO)

Es **una casa muy alta.**
It's a very high house.
Es **una casa altísima.**
It's a very high house.
El tren marcha **lentísimamente.**
The train goes very slowly.

The absolute superlative does not indicate comparison but a quality in a very high degree. It is expressed in two ways: by using **muy** before the adjective (or adverb) or by adding **–ísimo, –ísima, –ísimos, –ísimas** to adjectives (**–ísimamente** to adverbs), dropping the final vowel of the adjective. Regardless of the accent in the original adjective, the accent of an absolute superlative is always on the **í** of **–ísimo.**

EJERCICIO G

Cambie la forma del superlativo:

Modelo   Es una casa muy alta.
           Es una casa altísima.

1 Es un cuento muy interesante.
2 Es un tren muy lento.
3 Es una flor muy bonita.
4 Es un hombre muy rico.
5 Es un libro muy pequeño.
6 Es una lección muy difícil.
7 Es una alumna muy inteligente.
8 Es un parque muy grande.
9 Es una línea muy larga.
10 Es una señora muy agradable.
11 Es un capítulo muy fácil.
12 Es un edificio muy alto.
13 Es una habitación muy amplia.
14 Es un capítulo muy sencillo.
15 Es una flor muy preciosa.

EJERCICIO H

Conteste:

1 ¿Por qué son estas casas tan bonitas como las otras?
2 ¿Quiénes son los muchachos más altos de la clase?
3 ¿Quién tiene tanta plata como yo?
4 ¿Por qué es dificilísima la lección?
5 ¿Dónde vive su hermano menor?

6 ¿Quién es la persona más pequeña de su familia?
7 ¿Cómo anda su coche?
8 ¿Por qué sabe que María es tan estudiosa como Ud?
9 ¿Por qué marcha tan lentamente el autobús?
10 ¿Quién es el estudiante más popular de la fraternidad?
11 ¿Quién tiene tanto dinero como Pedro?
12 ¿Cómo es la Gramática?
13 ¿Pagó usted más de lo que pensaba por la televisión?
14 ¿Quién es el alumno más inteligente del equipo de fútbol?
15 ¿Quién es la alumna más bonita de la clase?

VI • PRACTICA ESCRITA

1 My ears ache more than ever.
2 Her hands ache more than ever.
3 His feet ache more than ever.
4 My head aches more than ever.
5 She is smaller and younger than her brother.
6 I am shorter and older than my sister.
7 He is taller and thinner than his father.
8 He runs as fast as you do.
9 They walk as slowly as she does.
10 We eat as much as they do.
11 Mr. Guzmán is older than you think.
12 She wrote more letters than I.
13 Mrs. Moreno has more fruit than she can sell.
14 They sell more than they buy.
15 We eat more than we drink.

VII • PRACTICA ORAL

A DIALOGO COMPLEMENTARIO

PEPE Oye, Paco, me duelen tanto los ojos desde el mes pasado que me parece que necesito anteojos.

PACO Lamento oír eso. ¿Quieres que te lleve al oculista mañana?

PEPE Si me haces este favor, te lo agradeceré siempre.
(Al día siguiente.)

PACO   A causa de tanto tráfico tengo que manejar el coche
       lentísimamente. Además, este cochecito no es tan rápido
       como el tuyo.

PEPE   Me dicen que el oculista, el Dr. Murguía, es simpatiquí-
       simo.

PACO   Sí, y es el oculista más caro de la ciudad.

PEPE   No importa. Cuando se trata de los ojos no hay nada caro.

PACO   Tienes razón. ¿Por qué los usas tanto?

PEPE   En mi campo de especialización, que es la historia, hay
       que leer muchísimo.

PACO   ¿Qué piensas hacer después de graduarte?

PEPE   Espero ser profesor de historia uno de estos días.

PACO   ¿Por qué?

PEPE   Porque me interesa la gente, en primer lugar. Y porque
       creo que a través del estudio de la historia de otras épocas,
       se pueden comprender las faltas del pasado, evitando tales
       errores en el futuro.

PACO   Esta es una de las ventajas de una educación universitaria
       y, sobre todo, de estudiar la historia. Pero si quieres en-
       señar en una universidad, tendrás que esperar muchos
       años más para llegar a ser catedrático.

PEPE   No importa, seguiré con mi propósito. Me gusta la carrera
       de la enseñanza porque estimula el pensamiento y da más
       significado a la vida.

PACO   Si sacas buenas notas en tus estudios, vas a llegar a ser uno
       de los mejores profesores ¡Buena suerte!

B   EXPRESION ORAL

Invite a una muchacha a un baile. Dígale cuándo es, a qué
hora empieza y a qué hora termina, de quién es la orquesta,
si hay programa de variedades, qué piensa hacer antes y después del baile, qué debe llevar, a qué hora usted piensa reco-
gerla, dónde, y algo sobre el motivo del baile.

C   PLATICA ESPONTANEA

1   ¿Cuándo irá usted al baile?
2   ¿Con quién va usted a bailar?
3   ¿Dónde se celebra el baile?
4   ¿Qué hará usted antes del baile?

5 ¿Qué hace usted después del baile?
6 ¿Por qué va (o no va) usted muchas veces al baile?
7 ¿Cuál es su orquesta favorita?
8 ¿Cuántas parejas asisten al baile usualmente?
9 ¿Cuánto tiempo dura el baile?
10 ¿A qué hora se toman los refrescos?

VIII • COMPOSICION

Escriba un diálogo sobre su familia y la de otra persona. 1. ¿Quiénes son? 2. ¿Quién tiene más edad, usted, su(s) hermano(s) o su(s) hermana(s)? 3. ¿Quién es más alto? ¿Más aplicado? ¿Más rico? ¿Más inteligente?

Lección décima

I • DIALOGO

(*Pablo y Ana entran en un gran almacén donde piensan comprar lo necesario para la tertulia del día siguiente.*)

DEPENDIENTA ¿En qué puedo servirles?

PABLO Buscamos vasos y servilletas de papel.

DEPENDIENTA Están en el mostrador a la derecha.

ANA Gracias. (*A otra dependienta.*) Necesitamos doce vasos y dos paquetes de servilletas.

DEPENDIENTA Tres cincuenta.

PABLO Aquí tiene Vd. un billete de cinco dólares.

DEPENDIENTA He aquí el cambio: uno cincuenta, y muchas gracias. (*Continúan caminando los dos hasta llegar a otro mostrador donde se venden dulces.*)

ANA ¿A cómo se venden los dulces?

DEPENDIENTA A uno setenta y cinco la caja.

ANA Bueno, llevamos tres cajas. Pablo, haz el favor de pagar la cuenta.

PABLO ¿Cuánto es?

DEPENDIENTA Cinco veinte y cinco.

PABLO Le doy diez dólares.

DEPENDIENTA Y yo la vuelta: cuatro setenta y cinco, gracias. (*Pasan a otro departamento donde se venden sombreros para mujer.*)

ANA ¡Ay! ¡Qué bonitos están los sombreros! Pablo, espérate un rato. Quiero probarme uno.

PABLO (*sarcásticamente*) ¿Sólo uno? ¿No más?

DEPENDIENTA ¿Le interesa éste, señorita? Es la última moda.

ANA (*Probándose el sombrero y mirándose en el espejo.*) Me sienta bien. ¿Cuánto vale?

DEPENDIENTA Sólo quince dólares. ¡Es una verdadera ganga!

ANA ¿Qué te parece, Pablo?

By Pease from Monkmeyer
Pequeño almacén en México

PABLO   Francamente te digo que no entiendo nada de sombreros para mujer. Por ejemplo, ¿para qué sirve esa pluma tan larga? Y además, ¿para qué sirve tanta fruta: bananas, manzanas, uvas y piña?

ANA   Francamente, no te entiendo a ti. La fruta adorna el sombrero.

PABLO   ¿A cómo son las manzanas?

ANA   Cállate, hombre. Vámonos. *(A la dependienta.)* Muchas gracias.

II • MODISMOS Y EXPRESIONES

¿a cómo se venden?	*how much are they?*
en poco tiempo	*in a short time*
es decir	*that is to say*
haber de	*to be to; to have to*
lo necesario	*the necessary things*
¿para qué sirve?	*what's the good of?*
ponerse (más adjetivo)	*to become, get* (plus adjective)
quedarse con	*to take*
sentarle bien (a uno)	*to be becoming (to one)*

III • PRACTICA SOBRE MODISMOS Y EXPRESIONES

A   USE CADA MODISMO EN UNA FRASE INTERROGATIVA Y TRADÚZCALA AL INGLÉS:

1   quedarse con
2   haber de
3   lo necesario
4   ponerse (más adjetivo)

B   HAGA PREGUNTAS USANDO LOS SUSTANTIVOS SIGUIENTES:

Modelo   las naranjas
    ¿A cómo se venden las naranjas?

1   el trigo
2   las lentejas
3   el arroz
4   los huevos

C USE LOS PRONOMBRES O SUSTANTIVOS INDICADOS COMO SUJETOS:

1 Yo me quedo con el libro.
(nosotros, ellos, usted, tú)
2 Me sienta bien el sombrero.
(los guantes, el traje, los zapatos)
3 Juan se quedará con el reloj.
(yo, nosotros, ustedes, tú)
4 Yo me puse triste.
(ella, ustedes, tú, nosotros)

IV • REPASO DE VERBOS

A (REPASE LOS VERBOS **salir** Y **tener** EN EL APÉNDICE.) CAMBIE LOS VERBOS

AL SINGULAR:

1 Mañana saldremos para Boston.
2 Dudan que tengamos miedo del oso.
3 Ya han salido de la clase.
4 Tuvieron cinco casas.
5 Cuando salíamos de casa, estaba a punto de llover.
6 Si hubiera sol, tendrían una cosecha grande.

AL PLURAL:

7 Si supiera eso, yo saldría en seguida.
8 Tendrá la intención de no volver.
9 Ella sale temprano todos los días.
10 ¿Ha tenido usted catarro recientemente?
11 Al volver ella a casa, había salido él.
12 Ella se alegra de que yo haya comprado la casa.

B CAMBIE LOS VERBOS A LOS TIEMPOS INDICADOS:

1 Salgo para Burgos. (perfecto)
2 Tuvieron que pagar la cuenta. (condicional)
3 Hemos salido para Argel. (imperfecto)
4 [Dudo que] Tenemos cinco libros aquí. (presente de subjuntivo)
5 No salimos para Honduras. (futuro)
6 Los alumnos tienen que preparar sus lecciones. (pretérito)
7 Yo no salía de la casa. (pretérito)
8 No tenían nada que hacer. (futuro)

9   Hemos salido ya. (pluscuamperfecto)
10 ¿Tenía Vd. algo que decir? (presente)

C   DÉ UNA SINOPSIS DE:

(Yo) salir temprano.
(El) no tener cambio.

V • GRAMATICA Y EJERCICIOS ORALES

53 INTERROGATIVES (LOS INTERROGATIVOS)

¿qué?	*what?*
¿cuál? (¿cuáles?)	*which one (ones)?*
¿cómo?	*how?*
¿dónde?	*where?*
¿quién? (¿quiénes?)	*who?*
¿de quién? (¿de quiénes?)	*whose?*
¿a quién?	*whom? to whom?*
¿cuándo?	*when?*
¿por qué?	*why?*
¿cuánto?	*how much?*
¿cuántos?	*how many?*

Interrogative words bear written accents to distinguish them from relative pronouns and conjunctions they closely resemble.

a   **¿Quiénes** son esos niños?
Who are those children?
¿De quién es esta pluma?
Whose pen is this?
¿A quién habló usted?
To whom did you speak?

¿Quién? (¿quiénes?) refers only to persons.

b   **¿Qué** desea usted?
What do you want?
¿Qué libro desea usted?
What (which) book do you want?

¿Qué? is used as a pronoun or an adjective.

c **¿Cuál** es su oficina?
   Which (one) is your office?
   ¿Cuáles son sus libros?
   Which (ones) are your books?
   But
   ¿En qué casa vive usted?
   In which house do you live?

   ¿Cuál (¿cuáles?) is used usually as a pronoun *(which [one]?)*, referring to certain persons or things of a larger number mentioned or implied. **¿Qué?** is used as an adjective before a noun. However, in spoken Spanish, **cuál** is often used as an adjective.

d **¿Cuál** es la capital del Perú?
   What is the capital of Peru?
   ¿Cuáles son los elementos naturales?
   What are the natural elements?
   But
   ¿Qué es aire?
   What is air?

   ¿Cuál? is used in place of **¿qué?** before forms of **ser** followed by a noun, except when a mere definition is asked for.

e **¿Cómo** está usted?
   How are you?
   ¿Cómo se hace eso?
   How is that done?
   ¿Cómo le gusta el té, con limón o con leche?
   How do you like your tea, with lemon or with milk?

   ¿Cómo? is used to ask about the manner or way a thing is done.[1]

f **¿Cuántos** trajes tiene usted?
   How many suits do you have?
   ¿Cuánto vale?
   How much is it worth?

   ¿Cuánto (–a, –os, –as)? *(how much or how many?)* is used as an adjective or a pronoun.

[1] Compare:
   ¿Qué tal les parece la feria?
   How do you like (What do you think of) the fair?
   ¿A cómo se venden las naranjas?
   ¿For how much are oranges sold?

g **¿Quién** llegó anoche?
Who arrived last night?
Quiero saber **quién** llegó anoche.
I want to know who arrived last night.

In indirect questions, preceded by such verbs as **saber, decir, preguntar,** the pronoun retains the written accent.

EJERCICIO **A**

Conteste:

1 ¿Cuántos años tienes?
2 ¿Quién estudia más, el alumno o la alumna?
3 ¿Cuánto vale un buen coche?
4 ¿Qué quieres comer?
5 ¿Qué coche deseas comprar?
6 ¿A quién hablaste ayer?
7 ¿De quién es este reloj?
8 ¿Cuál es tu bicicleta?
9 ¿En qué edificio estudias?
10 ¿Cuál es la capital de la Argentina?
11 ¿Cuáles son tus libros?
12 ¿Qué es aire?
13 ¿Cómo estás?
14 ¿A cómo se venden los huevos?
15 ¿Cómo te gusta el café, negro o con leche?
16 ¿Cómo está usted hoy?
17 ¿Cómo le gustan los huevos, pasados por agua o revueltos?
18 ¿A cómo se venden las naranjas?
19 ¿Qué tal le pareció el programa?
20 ¿Cómo le gusta la casa, blanca o amarilla?

EJERCICIO **B**

Diga en español:

1 Which one is writing?
2 Which ones are writing?
3 Which student is writing?
4 Which students are writing?
5 Who *(pl.)* is eating?
6 When does one eat?
7 Why does one eat?
8 With whom is he eating?
9 With whom *(pl.)* is he eating?
10 Which one is eating?
11 Which ones are eating?

12 How many are eating?
13 How much is he eating?
14 How much does he eat?

EJERCICIO C

Haga preguntas a su amigo (o amiga) y espere la respuesta:

Modelo   Pregúntele a dónde va.
            ¿A dónde vas?
            Voy a casa.

1 Pregúntele con quién va.
2 Pregúntele por qué va.
3 Pregúntele cómo va.
4 Pregúntele cuándo va.
5 Pregúntele de dónde sale.

EJERCICIO D

Haga preguntas empleando los interrogativos siguientes:

1 ¿Qué?
2 ¿Cuánto?
3 ¿Cuántos?
4 ¿Cómo?
5 ¿Por qué?
6 ¿Cuándo?
7 ¿Con quién?
8 ¿A dónde?
9 ¿Quién?
10 ¿Quiénes?
11 ¿De quién?

54 INTERROGATIVES AS EXCLAMATIONS (INTERROGATIVOS USADOS COMO EXCLAMACIONES)

a **¡Qué** magnífico!
   How magnificent!
   ¡Qué cerca está la feria!
   How near the fair is!

   ¡Qué! means *How . . . !* before an adjective or adverb.

   ¡Qué hombre!
   What a man!
   ¡Qué famoso hombre!
   What a famous man!

¡Qué hombre tan (más) famoso!
What a famous man!

¡Qué means *What a . . . !* before a noun.

b   ¡Cuánto me alegro!
How glad I am!
¡Cuántos trenes hay allí!
How many trains there are there!

¡Cuánto! may be used as pronoun and adjective.[1]

EJERCICIO   **E**

Diga en español:

   1   What a book!
   2   What a watch!
   3   What a library!
   4   What a school!
   5   What a pen!
   6   What a pencil!
   7   What a record!
   8   What a man!
   9   What a girl!
  10   What a teacher!
  11   How far the fair is!
  12   How badly he speaks!
  13   How pretty she is!
  14   How glad I am!
  15   How many busses there are there!

EJERCICIO   **F**

Sustituya los adjetivos siguientes haciendo los cambios necesarios:

Modelo   What an interesting novel!
             ¡Qué novela tan (más) interesante!

   1   malo
   2   grande
   3   bueno
   4   aburrido
   5   serio
   6   famoso

---

[1] **Cuanto (–a, –os, –as)** in the sense of "all that," "all those who," "as much as," "as many as" is also used as adjective or pronoun:
Tengo cuantos libros tiene usted.
I have as many books as you.
Le di cuanto tenía.
I gave him all I had.

    7 horrible
    8 magnífico
    9 notable
  10 corto

55 RELATIVE PRONOUNS, ADJECTIVES, AND ADVERBS (PRONOMBRES, ADJETIVOS Y ADVERBIOS RELATIVOS)

a Esta es **la primera vez que** la he visto.
This is the first time (that) I've seen her.[1]
El estudiante que escogieron fue Alberto.
Albert was the student (that) they selected.

The most common relative pronoun is **que,** which may be used as subject or object and refers to persons or things (except as indicated in **b**, below). **Que** is also used as the object of a preposition:

La residencia en que (donde) vivo es vieja.
The dorm (that) I live in is old.

Note that the preposition immediately precedes **que.** In spoken Spanish **en que** is often replaced by **donde.**

b **El hombre con quien** hablaba era casado.
The man with whom I was talking was married.

After a preposition when referring to persons, **quien(es)** must be used. The combination **a quien,** however, is often replaced in spoken Spanish by **que:**

La mujer a quien (que) vi anoche está aquí.
The woman whom I saw last night is here.
El que (Quien) estudia, aprende.
He who studies, learns.

Quien or **el (la, los, las) que** is equivalent to *he who, the one who,* etc.

EJERCICIO G

Sustituya las palabras siguientes haciendo los cambios necesarios:

1 Es la persona de quien hablábamos.

    Son _____.
    _____ libros _____.
    _____ niñas _____.
    _____ muchacha _____.

---

[1] The relative pronoun is normally not omitted in Spanish, as it may be in English.

_____ cuento _____.
_____ hombre _____.
_____ niños _____.

2 La señora con quien estudiábamos no está en casa.

_____ muchachas _____.
_____ libros _____.
_____ texto _____.
_____ alumno _____.

c Llegaron **muchas señoritas,** entre **las cuales** (entre **las que**)
estaba Lolita.
Many young women came, among whom was Lolita.
Vi **al padre** de Josefina, con **el cual** (con **el que**) hablé un rato.
I saw Josephine's father, with whom I spoke a while.

El (la) cual, los (las) cuales, or **el (la, los, las) que,** may be used
as a substitute for **que** or **quien** after prepositions or to avoid
ambiguity.

d **Lo que** hizo usted me sorprendió mucho.
What you did surprised me greatly.

The neuter pronoun **lo que**[1] refers to an idea, not to a specific
noun.

e **Aquella casa cuya** puerta está abierta es bonita.
That house whose door is open is pretty.

The relative adjective **cuyo (–a, –os, –as)** *(whose)* comes immediately before the noun it modifies, agreeing with it in number
and gender.

f Me quedo **donde** estoy.
I'll stay where I am.
Me voy al pueblo **donde** vive Juan.
I'm going to the town where (in which) John lives.

Donde functions as a relative adverb.

EJERCICIO **H**

Diga en español:

Modelo   The book I lost belonged to the library.
             El libro que perdí pertenecía a la biblioteca.

---

[1] The corresponding form **lo cual** is used only in referring to a complete preceding
statement, from which it is always set off by a comma:
No quiso hacerlo, **lo que (lo cual)** me enfadó mucho.
He refused to do it, which made me very angry.

1 The watch I found was gold.
2 The notebook she bought cost seventy-five cents.
3 The handkerchief he gave her was silk.
4 The coat I was wearing was wool.
5 The table I sold was of wood.

Modelo   The boy who lives in that residence hall is my best friend.
El muchacho que vive en esa residencia es mi mejor amigo.

1 The girl who lives in this house is my cousin.
2 The students who were eating in the dining room were making a lot of noise.
3 The man who was crossing the street was my father.
4 The professors who were advising students were also doing research.
5 The man who works for my father died.

Modelo   The person I was speaking about was my daughter.
La persona de quien hablaba era mi hija.

1 The man I was explaining the problem to was my Spanish teacher.
2 The students we gave the books to were from Kansas.
3 The girl I met was not married.
4 The clerk I paid is Spanish.
5 I brought the girl's father, whom I first knew in Madrid.

Modelo   What you said was the truth.
Lo que dijo era la verdad.

1 What you heard was the truth.
2 What you saw was an illusion.
3 What he wrote was the truth.
4 What we read was false.
5 What they said was the truth.

Modelo   Whose hat is that?
¿De quién es ese sombrero?

1 Whose book is that?
2 Whose paper is that?
3 Whose records are these?
4 Whose office is that?
5 Whose socks are these?

Modelo   The man whose pen I have is not here.
El hombre cuya pluma tengo no está aquí.

1 The boy whose hat I picked up is from Brazil.
2 The student whose wife is working does not have to worry.
3 The girls whose courses are expensive often have to work for a living.

4 The professors whose classes were large received the same salary.

5 The children whose parents were from Mexico became Americans.

VI • PRACTICA ESCRITA

1   I want the one (f.) that was here yesterday.
2   What an answer!
3   Which house did you buy?
4   I'm not one of those who speak a lot.
5   What is the matter with John?
6   I'll ask Paul, whose opinions are good.
7   It's the man I spoke with.
8   Who are you and what do you want?
9   Here is the house in which they signed the document.
10 What's a fair?
11 Whose hat is this?
12 Mary's mother, who was here last night, is forty-five.
13 How glad I am to see you!
14 Which train are you going to take?
15 What a woman! I want to know where she lives.
16 This is the town where I was born.
17 The young lady I brought the novel for is absent.
18 Will you sell me all the eggs you have?
19 What you said was the truth.
20 This is the student whose father is ill.

VII • PRACTICA ORAL

A   DIALOGO COMPLEMENTARIO

DEPENDIENTA   Hola, señor Beltrán. Mucho gusto en verlo. ¿Cómo está usted?

SR. BELTRÁN   Pues, bien, gracias. Estaba muy cansado ayer, lo que no me sorprende, porque había hecho muchos preparativos para mi viaje a Oregón. Y esta noche tengo invitados.

DEPENDIENTA	Pues, ¿en qué puedo servirle?
SR. BELTRÁN	¿A cómo se venden las naranjas?
DEPENDIENTA	A ochenta centavos la docena.
SR. BELTRÁN	Bueno, favor de darme dos docenas. También quiero diez libras de papas, un kilo de café, tres botellas de leche, dos panes y una cajita de fresas.
DEPENDIENTA	¿Lo meto todo en una caja?
SR. BELTRÁN	No, póngalo en dos paquetes, por favor. *(En casa más tarde.)*
JUANITA	Oye, Tomás, ¿cuándo vas a tener otra cita con tu novia?
TOMÁS	No seas indiscreta, hermana, pues puedes sufrir una paliza.
SR. BELTRÁN	Hijos, basta de eso. Recuerden que esta noche tenemos invitados. Quiero que tengan más respeto cuando se sienten a la mesa.
SRA. DE BELTRÁN	Sí, recuerden que en boca cerrada no entran moscas. *(Entran el Sr. Peña y su esposa.)*
SR. PEÑA	Buenas noches.
SRA. DE PEÑA	Buenas noches, ¿cómo están?
SR. BELTRÁN	Muy bien, gracias. Y ¿ustedes?
SR. PEÑA	Nosotros muy bien, pero nuestra hijita Marta se enfermó el otro día y guarda cama.
SRA. DE BELTRÁN	¡Qué lástima! Y ¿cómo se encuentra ahora?
SRA. DE PEÑA	Un poquito mejor. ¡Qué susto nos dio cuando regresó a casa la semana pasada, pálida y con fiebre! Mi esposo fue por el médico el cual dijo que tenía la gripe. Nos dejó una receta y hemos hecho cuanto nos pidió.
TOMÁS	¡Cuánto lo siento! ¿Me permite visitarla mañana por un rato?
SR. PEÑA	Sí. A menudo pregunta por ti, Tomás. Creo que se pondrá contenta al verte y se mejorará en poco tiempo. Una visita del novio es la mejor medicina.

B EXPRESION ORAL

1 Dos estudiantes toman parte en la conversación. Están en una sastrería. Uno es el cliente, el otro el sastre. El cliente

desea saber el precio de los trajes. Hablan de un traje ya hecho y de uno hecho a la medida. Discuten la diferencia: la hechura, el precio, la tela (lana o seda) y el estilo.

2 Dos muchachas entran en una sombrería a probarse los sombreros. Discuten la última moda, los adornos, el precio y los colores.

C PLATICA ESPONTANEA

1 ¿Por qué le gusta (o no le gusta) ir de compras?
2 ¿Cuál es su tienda favorita? ¿Por qué?
3 ¿Cuándo va Vd. de compras usualmente?
4 ¿Qué desea Vd. comprar para mañana?
5 ¿Dónde comprará Vd. un sombrero?
6 ¿Cuánto vale un buen sombrero?
7 ¿Qué clase de sombrero le gusta más?
8 ¿Cómo es el sombrero que acaba de comprar?
9 ¿Cómo son los precios en el gran almacén?
10 ¿Por qué es más barato ir de compras a un gran almacén?

VIII • COMPOSICION

Escriba una conversación en que intervienen varios turistas norteamericanos en un mercado mexicano. Preguntan los precios de los sarapes, botijas, encajes y de las demás cosas que se venden. Se prueban los sombreros y las chaquetas y regatean con los vendedores.

Lección once

I • DIALOGO

(José, estudiante universitario, descuelga el receptor del teléfono para llamar a su consejero. Suena el teléfono en el despacho del profesor Sánchez y contesta la secretaria.)

SECRETARIA ¡Diga!

JOSÉ ¿Con el despacho del profesor Sánchez?

SECRETARIA Sí. ¿En qué puedo servirle?

JOSÉ Quiero hablar con el profesor sobre un problema. ¿Podría tener una cita con él pronto?

SECRETARIA Estará aquí hoy a eso de las dos de la tarde.

JOSÉ Bueno. Estaré allí sin falta. Adiós.

SECRETARIA Adiós.

(José cuelga el receptor y sale de la casilla de teléfono. Más tarde, en el despacho del profesor.)

SÁNCHEZ Buenas tardes, José. La secretaria me dijo que quería verme hoy.

JOSÉ Sí. He tratado varias veces de llamarle a su despacho y siempre me decían que el número estaba ocupado. Tengo un problema que deseo discutir con usted.

SÁNCHEZ ¿No va bien su trabajo? En la clase de español va recibiendo una nota de «A».

JOSÉ No es eso, señor Sánchez. Es otra cosa de mucha más importancia.

SÁNCHEZ Pues, ¿qué será? ¿Qué pasa?

JOSÉ Que he ganado una beca para estudiar el próximo año en la Universidad de Madrid.

SÁNCHEZ ¡Felicitaciones! No sabía eso. Pero no comprendo todavía el problema.

JOSÉ El problema, señor Sánchez, es que no quiero separarme por tanto tiempo de mi novia.

SÁNCHEZ Pues, es un problema que usted mismo tendrá que resolver. Por consiguiente, lo único que puedo de-

163

By Henle from Monkmeyer
Plaza de España en Madrid: estatuas de Don Quijote, Sancho Panza y Cervantes

cirle es que lo piense bien antes de llegar a una decisión. Por mi parte, si fuera usted, yo continuaría mi educación. Eso es lo más importante. Si ella le quiere bien, a mi parecer, le esperará hasta que vuelva usted a este país.

JOSÉ   Creo que tiene mucha razón. Ha sido usted muy amable conmigo y me ha dado muy buenos consejos. Mis padres me han dicho lo mismo. Le agradezco muchísimo su ayuda, señor profesor. Hasta luego.

SÁNCHEZ   Hasta luego.

II • MODISMOS Y EXPRESIONES

a eso de	*at about (used only with expressions of time)*
a la sombra de	*in the shade of*
a mi parecer	*in my opinion*
al aire libre	*in the open air*
alrededor de	*around*
consistir en	*to consist of*
dar consejos	*to give advice*
decir para sí	*to say to oneself*
parar, detenerse	*to stop*
por consiguiente	*consequently*
tener razón	*to be right*
tratar de (más infinitivo)	*to try to* (plus infinitive)

III • PRACTICA SOBRE MODISMOS Y EXPRESIONES

A   ESCOJA EL MODISMO DE LA LISTA ANTERIOR QUE MEJOR COMPLETE LA FRASE:

1   El tren _____ aquí.
2   El profesor Sánchez siempre me _____.
3   Me hace falta dinero, _____ no puedo ir al cine con usted esta noche.
4   Mi profesor me _____.

5 _____ que no podría trabajar más.
6 ¿_____ llamarme ayer?
7 El profesor dijo que _____ .
8 Mañana vamos a comer _____ .
9 Espero llegar _____ las ocho de la noche.
10 El problema _____ saber la causa del fracaso.

B USE LOS MODISMOS SIGUIENTES EN UNA FRASE COMPLETA:

1 alrededor de
2 detenerse
3 a la sombra de
4 a eso de
5 a mi parecer

C DIGA EN ESPAÑOL:

1 Were you right when you spoke to the student?
2 I'm sure he was wrong.
3 I know she's right. She's always right.
4 They arrived around one o'clock.
5 There was a crowd around the statue.
6 Try to call me around seven.

IV • REPASO DE VERBOS

A (REPASE LOS VERBOS **traer** Y **valer** EN EL APÉNDICE.) CAMBIE LOS VERBOS

AL SINGULAR:

1 No traíamos pan.
2 Valdrían mucho si fueran buenos.
3 Traerán los libros la semana que viene.
4 No valemos mucho.
5 Trajimos la plata al banco.
6 Han valido pocos dólares.

AL PLURAL:

7 Les traigo discos.
8 Espera que valga mucho el coche.
9 ¿Quieres que te traiga un vaso de vino?
10 La casa vale treinta mil dólares.
11 He traído la carne.
12 Valió mucho.

B CAMBIE LOS VERBOS SIGUIENTES A LOS TIEMPOS INDICADOS:

1   Traerían mucha plata. (presente)
2   Valía poco. (condicional)
3   Habían traído el traje de baño. (pretérito)
4   He valido mucho. (presente)
5   Traen sus libros. (futuro)
6   ¿Valdrían diez pesos? (imperfecto)
7   Traigamos la leche. (perfecto)
8   Valían cien pesos. (futuro)
9   Yo no traje el reloj. (imperfecto)
10 Ha valido demasiado. (pretérito)

C DÉ UNA SINOPSIS DE:

(Vd.) traer la ropa.
(Yo) valer por ciento.

V • GRAMATICA Y EJERCICIOS ORALES

56   REFLEXIVE VERBS (LOS VERBOS REFLEXIVOS)

Me lavo.
I wash myself.

A reflexive verb expresses an action in which the subject and the recipient of the action are the same.

57   REFLEXIVE PRONOUNS (LOS PRONOMBRES REFLEXIVOS)

	WITH A VERB	AFTER A PREPOSITION
me	*(to) myself*	**mí**
te	*(to) yourself*	**ti**
se	*(to) himself, herself, yourself, itself*	**sí**
nos	*(to) ourselves*	**nosotros, −as**
os	*(to) yourselves*	**vosotros, −as**
se	*(to) themselves, yourselves*	**sí**

a   Ellos **se engañan.**
They deceive themselves.
They are mistaken.

Sentándose, se puso a estudiar.
Seating himself, he began to study.
Nos compramos guantes.
We bought gloves for ourselves.
Vio venir el tren **hacia mí**.
He saw the train coming toward me.

There are two types of reflexive pronouns—those used with a verb and those used after a preposition. The former may function as direct or indirect object.

b Ella se lo llevó **consigo.**
She took it with her.

Mí, ti, and **sí,** when used with the preposition **con,** become **conmigo, contigo,** and **consigo.**

EJERCICIO **A**

Sustituya haciendo todos los cambios necesarios:

1 El se lo llevó consigo.
(Yo, nosotros, tú, Vd.)
2 Roberto lo vio venir hacia sí.
(Vd., yo, tú, él)
3 Levantándome, me puse el sombrero.
(Nosotros, tú, yo, ella)

c Nos escribimos.
We write to each other.
Se ayudan (uno a otro).
They help each other.

The plural forms of the reflexive pronoun **(nos, os, se)** may have reciprocal meaning. **Uno a otro, el uno al otro** may be added for clearness.

EJERCICIO **B**

Conteste:

Modelo ¿Vds. se conocen?
Sí, nos conocemos.

1 ¿Vds. se escriben a menudo?
2 ¿Vds. se veían muchas veces?
3 ¿Vds. se ayudaron en el trabajo?

4 ¿Vds. se entendían bien?
5 ¿Vds. se enviarán libros?
6 ¿Vds. se hablarán?
7 ¿Vds. se parecen?
8 ¿Vds. se querían?
9 ¿Vds. se encontraron?
10 ¿Vds. se miraron?

d Se quejó.
He complained.
Se quejó de la comida.
He complained about the meal.

Some verbs are always used reflexively in Spanish (while their English counterparts are not): **apresurarse (a)** *to hurry;* **atreverse (a)** *to dare;* **arrepentirse (de)** *to repent;* **quejarse (de)** *to complain.*

e			
acostar	*to put to bed*	**acostarse**	*to go to bed*
alegrar	*to cheer*	**alegrarse**	*to rejoice, be glad*
casar	*to marry (off)*	**casarse**	*to get married*
levantar	*to raise*	**levantarse**	*to rise, get up*

Many verbs acquire a different meaning when reflexive.

EJERCICIO **C**

Diga en español:

Modelos She washes herself.
Ella se lava.

She washes the child.
Ella lava al niño.

1 My name is John. They call me John.
2 They went to bed. They put the children to bed.
3 We are happy. We cheered the sad (ones).
4 You get up. You get the child up.
5 John and Mary are getting married.
The father marries off his daughter.
6 The students will not deceive themselves. They will not deceive their parents.
7 I shave myself. The barber shaves me.

f ¿Cómo **se escribe** eso?
How do you (does one) write that?

Se prohibe fumar.
One is forbidden to smoke.
Smoking prohibited.
Se sale por aquí.
Exit here. (People get out here.)
Escríbase en inglés.
Write in English.

Spanish uses an indefinite reflexive construction with the pronoun **se** where English uses *one, they, people, you* (indefinite), often in a passive construction. **Se** is also used in directions.

EJERCICIO **D**

Sustituya usando los verbos entre paréntesis:

1 ¿Cómo se dice eso?
(deletrea, pronuncia, entiende, toma)
2 Se prohibe fumar.
(hablar, entrar, subir, pescar)
3 Se sale por aquí.
(entra, marcha, corre, pasa)

EJERCICIO **E**

Un alumno hace la pregunta y otro contesta:

Modelo ¿Cuándo se reunió el club?   Se reunió ayer.

1	pintó la casa	el año pasado.
2	escribió el libro	en el siglo pasado.
3	organizó el baile	anoche.
4	firmó el documento	en 1967.
5	compró el libro	anteayer.

Modelo ¿Dónde se compraron los libros?   Se compraron en la librería.

1	publicó el poema	en Chile.
2	fundó la biblioteca	en Wáshington.
3	vendieron los muebles	en Los Angeles.
4	pintaron las sillas	en casa.
5	reúne la clase	en la universidad.

Modelo ¿Como se organizó la fiesta?   Se organizó bien la fiesta.

1	preparó el discurso	mal.
2	hizo el curso	bien.
3	pintó la casa	lindamente.
4	aprendió la lección	fácilmente.
5	publicó la novela	recientemente.

**58 THE REFLEXIVE IN FORTUITOUS EVENTS
(EL REFLEXIVO EN SUCESOS FORTUITOS)**

Se me olvidó el libro.
I forgot the book.
Se me olvidaron los libros.
I forgot the books.

To express an occurrence that happens fortunately or acci-
dentally such as "I forgot it," Spanish employs the reflexive
se and adds an indirect object pronoun referring to the
person concerned.

EJERCICIO **F**

Sustituya usando los sustantivos indicados:

1 Se les olvidó la carta.
   (lápices, dirección, número, panes)
2 Se me quedó el sobre en casa.
   (paraguas, pañuelos, peine, pluma)
3 Se me ocurre un chiste.
   (idea, cambio, los mismos pensamientos, picardía)
4 Se le murió el perro.
   (gatita, perros, conejo, canario)
5 Se me cayó la botella.
   (tazas, platos, reloj, pulsera)

EJERCICIO **G**

Diga en español:

Modelo He forgot his handkerchief.
            Se le olvidó el pañuelo.

1 He forgot his hat.
2 He forgot his money.
3 He forgot his paper.
4 He forgot his number.
5 He forgot his book.

EJERCICIO **H**

Diga en español:

Modelo I broke a tooth (or my tooth got broken).
            Se me rompió un diente.

1 My window got broken.
2 My shirt got torn.
3 My tie got torn.

4 My record got broken.
5 My plate got broken.

EJERCICIO I

Diga en español:

Modelo We dropped the cups.
    Se nos cayeron las tazas.

1 We dropped the hats.
2 We dropped the books.
3 We dropped the spoons.
4 We dropped the dictionaries.
5 We dropped the cards.

59 PASSIVE VOICE (LA VOZ PASIVA)

Active:
El muchacho pintó la silla.
The boy painted the chair.
Passive:
La silla fue pintada (por el muchacho).
The chair was painted (by the boy).

In an active construction, the subject performs the act. In a passive construction, the subject is acted upon.

a Los pueblos **fueron destruidos por** los españoles.
The towns were destroyed by the Spaniards.
La comida **fue preparada (por** la cocinera).
The meal was prepared (by the cook).
Edison **es estimado de** todo el mundo.
Edison is esteemed by everybody.

The "true" passive voice in Spanish consists of **ser** plus past participle (which agrees in number and gender with the subject). The agent is expressed by **por.** After verbs of mental action, **por** is sometimes replaced by **de.**

b La novela **está** bien **escrita.** (condition)
The novel is well written.
Los montes **están cubiertos** de nieve. (condition)
The mountains are covered with snow.
Las puertas **estaban abiertas.** (condition)
The doors were open.
But

La puerta **fue abierta por** Juan. (action: true passive)
The door was opened by John.

An "apparent" passive expresses a resultant condition and consists of **estar** plus the past participle (which agrees in number and gender with the subject). The instrument or agent *(by, with)* is expressed usually by **de.**

EJERCICIO J

Cambie las oraciones de pasivas a activas y vice versa:

Modelo   La constitución fue establecida por el gobierno.
La constitución está establecida.

1   La puerta fue abierta por Juan.
2   Las sillas fueron pintadas por el hombre.
3   Las manifestaciones fueron prohibidas por la ley.
4   Los documentos fueron firmados por el gobernador.
5   El pueblo fue destrozado por los indios.

Modelo   La nieve cubrió la montaña.
La montaña está cubierta de nieve.

6   Los faroles alumbraron la calle.
7   El polvo cubrió el camino.
8   Las hojas cubrieron los campos.
9   El agua inundó la casa.
10   Mucho humo llenó el cuarto.

60   SUBSTITUTE CONSTRUCTIONS FOR THE PASSIVE (EL SUSTITUTO REFLEXIVO)

a   **Se abren** las puertas a las once.
The doors are opened at eleven.
Se esperó el ataque.
The attack was expected.

If the subject of a passive verb is a thing and the agent is not expressed, Spanish prefers a reflexive construction (called the "reflexive substitute") to the passive.

EJERCICIO K

Cambie las frases al plural:

Modelo   Se abrió la puerta.
Se abrieron las puertas.

1   Se cerró la ventana.
2   Se vio la estrella.

3 Se celebró la fiesta.
4 Se comió la legumbre.
5 Se oyó la canción.
6 Se necesitó la tarjeta.

b **Se eligió** a Juan.
John was elected. (One elected John.)
Se le eligió.
He was elected. (One elected him.)

An impersonal reflexive construction in the third person singular may be substituted for the passive if the agent is not expressed.

EJERCICIO **L**

Sustituya los sustantivos por pronombres:

Modelos Se eligió a Juan
Se le eligió.
Se eligió a María.
Se la eligió.

1 Se libertó a Jorge.
2 Se nombró a María.
3 Se escogió al jefe.
4 Se mandó a la Sra. Peralta.
5 Se llamó al prisionero.
6 Se vio al general.
7 Se llevó a Anita.
8 Se quiere a Carmen.
9 Se espera al profesor.
10 Se entiende a José.

c **Mataron los toros.**
The bulls were killed. (They killed the bulls.)
Nombraron capitán a Juan.
John was named captain. (They named John captain.)

If the subject of the passive verb is a person or living object and an agent is not expressed, Spanish often employs an active construction.

EJERCICIO **M**

Cambie las frases al pasivo:

Modelo El hombre pintó la casa.
La casa fue pintada por el hombre.

1 Cervantes escribió la novela.
2 Juan abrirá las puertas.
3 El dependiente vendió los muebles.
4 Los estudiantes escribieron las lecciones.
5 Los amigos lavarán los platos.
6 María cerró la ventana.
7 Los moros atacaron la ciudad.
8 El jefe organizó el grupo.
9 El muchacho preparó el programa.
10 El agente vendió la casa.

EJERCICIO N

Imite el modelo, usando las frases del ejercicio M:

Modelo   El hombre pintó la casa.
           Se pintó la casa.

VI • PRACTICA ESCRITA

1 Pistols are forbidden here.
2 The story was told by the teacher.
3 The streets were filled with people.
4 John was named chief of the group.
5 The doors close at twelve o'clock.
6 The furniture was sold.
7 I was given a present.
8 Four cows were killed.
9 The road is covered with snow.
10 He was elected by his friends.
11 Spanish and Portuguese are spoken in this store.
12 I don't want to bring it with me today.
13 God helps those who help themselves.
14 Getting up, we took leave of our friends.
15 How does one say that in Spanish?
16 My mother set (poner) the table. The table was set by my mother.
17 The table is well set.
18 We were given the examination yesterday.
19 They cheer me, and I'm glad.
20 They send each other books.

VII • PRACTICA ORAL

A DIALOGO COMPLEMENTARIO

MARGARITA ¡Qué ameno es este parque!

RAFAEL Sí, me gusta venir aquí con mis amigos para comentar las noticias de los Estados Unidos, tomar refrescos, dar un paseo o leer un libro.

MARGARITA ¿Por qué detuvo la policía a aquel señor? Parece que hay mucha gente alrededor de esa estatua.

RAFAEL Creo que mi profesor va a pronunciar un discurso en honor del gran escritor español Miguel de Cervantes.

MARGARITA Ahora puedo ver mejor. Es una estatua de Don Quijote montado en Rocinante y acompañado de su escudero Sancho Panza en el rucio.

RAFAEL Me dijeron que había una feria de libros y que un estudiante de esta ciudad había ganado el premio «Cervantes» por haber escrito el mejor ensayo sobre la famosa novela.

MARGARITA Ya me acuerdo. La noticia fue recibida ayer con mucho aplauso por la gente.

RAFAEL Bajo la estatua hay un estante abierto con libros de conocidos autores como Shakespeare, Goethe, Poe y otros—una especie de biblioteca al aire libre para los que quieran leer un rato a la sombra de los árboles.

MARGARITA ¡Qué agradable es la vida aquí en esta ciudad! Al volver al hotel voy a comprarme un ejemplar de *Don Quijote.*

RAFAEL En la librería de la esquina, en el barrio donde vivimos, hay un cartel que dice—«Aquí se venden libros de toda clase.» Quiero entrar para averiguar si tienen un ejemplar usado.

MARGARITA El otro día estaba abierta la puerta, y yo entré. Pero no había ninguna edición barata del *Quijote.* Cuando estaba a punto de salir sucedió algo extraordinario; tembló la tierra. Todos fuimos sorprendidos por un breve terremoto. El edificio en donde se encuentra la librería está bien construido y, por consiguiente, nada le pasó. Pero me dio un susto tremendo.

B EXPRESION ORAL

1 Telefonee Vd. al despacho de su consejero y pídale una cita para pasado mañana a las diez.

2 Solicite Vd. una entrevista con su consejero para hablar acerca de sus notas. Explíquele Vd. por qué no sale bien en sus estudios.

C PLATICA ESPONTANEA

1 ¿Por qué tiene usted que ver a su consejero?
2 ¿En qué edificio tiene su oficina?
3 ¿Cuál es el número de su oficina?
4 ¿A qué hora puede verlo?
5 ¿Cómo se llama su secretaria?
6 ¿Cuándo piensa graduarse?
7 ¿En qué materia se especializa Vd?
8 ¿Tiene usted planes para continuar sus estudios en la escuela graduada?
9 ¿Para qué estudia usted?

VIII • COMPOSICION

Sugerencias para un tema: un paseo por el parque:

1 quién le acompañó
2 lo que vieron ustedes
3 dónde se pararon a tomar refrescos
4 cuánto tiempo pasaron ustedes en el parque

Lección doce

I • DIALOGO

PROFESOR ¿Por qué tardó Vd. tanto en llegar a la clase hoy?

PAQUITA Porque anoche fui a un concierto de la orquesta sinfónica y volví tarde a casa. También tuve que preparar mi lección de español para hoy.

PROFESOR ¿A qué hora se levantó Vd. esta mañana?

PAQUITA Me levanté a las siete en punto. Tengo que ayudar a mi hermana menor que asiste a la escuela superior.

PROFESOR Además de eso, no tiene nada que hacer, ¿verdad?

PAQUITA No, excepto despertar a mi hermana y recordarle las cosas que debe hacer antes de que yo vuelva a casa por la tarde.

PROFESOR Por ejemplo, ¿qué tiene que hacer su hermana?

PAQUITA Tiene que lavar los platos después de las comidas, barrer la casa, hacer las camas e ir de compras.

PROFESOR ¿Vuelve Vd. a casa para el almuerzo?

PAQUITA Sí, porque puedo regresar a casa en quince minutos. Mi hermana vuelve antes que yo, y tiene preparado el almuerzo para las doce en punto. Sabe cocinar muy bien y siempre sirve buenas comidas.

PROFESOR ¿Puede Vd. contar con ella para todo?

PAQUITA Sí. Me ayuda con la limpieza del fin de semana.

PROFESOR ¿Cuándo se separa usted de su hermana por la tarde?

PAQUITA A eso de la una porque tengo clase a la una y media. Entonces la llevo a la escuela en mi coche. Al bajar ella, le digo que se porte bien y estudie mucho.

PROFESOR Y ¿la obedece a usted siempre?

PAQUITA Sí, porque es muy buena muchacha.

II • MODISMOS Y EXPRESIONES

además de	*in addition to, besides*
alejarse (de)	*to go away (from)*

bajar	to take down; to get out
contar con	to count on, to rely on
cuidar de (a)	to take care of
despedirse de	to take leave of
darse la mano	to shake hands
hace fresco	it is cool
no dejar de	not to fail
sacar la cabeza por	to stick one's head out of
la ventana	the window

III • PRACTICA SOBRE MODISMOS Y EXPRESIONES

A ESCOJA UN MODISMO DE LA LISTA ANTERIOR QUE COMPLETE LA FRASE:

1 _____ papeles, tengo muchos libros que comprar.
2 ¿Por qué _____ usted de sus padres?
3 Cuando _____, me gusta dar un paseo.
4 Mañana yo _____ los niños.
5 ¡_____ escribirme pronto!
6 Al conocerme, Juan me _____ la mano.
7 ¡_____ durante el viaje en tren!
8 ¡_____ usted la valija del desván!
9 El tren _____ lentamente.
10 ¿Puedo _____ usted?

B USE CADA MODISMO EN UNA FRASE COMPLETA Y LUEGO TRA-DÚZCALA AL INGLÉS:

1 alejarse de
2 contar con
3 no dejar de
4 darse la mano
5 hace fresco

IV • REPASO DE VERBOS

A (REPASE LOS VERBOS **venir** Y **ver** EN EL APÉNDICE.) CAMBIE LOS VERBOS

AL PLURAL:

1 Vengo temprano.
2 Me vio en la calle.
3 Vendría yo si pudiera.
4 ¿Ha visto Vd. el nuevo coche?
5 He venido a felicitarte.
6 Yo veía que iba a llover.

AL SINGULAR:

7 Vinimos a ver la feria.
8 No vieron mucho.
9 Vienen de Francia.
10 Es posible que veamos la exposición de libros en Madrid.
11 Vendríamos mañana si pudiéramos.
12 Vendrán el año que viene.

B CAMBIE LOS VERBOS A LOS TIEMPOS INDICADOS:

1 Vendré si puedo.   (presente)
2 Vieron el tranvía en la esquina.   (perfecto)
3 Vengo a saludarte.   (pretérito)
4 Hemos visto el océano.   (imperfecto)
5 Vinieron de Nogales.   (No creía que + imperfecto de subjuntivo)
6 Vea Vd. mi cartera.   (pretérito)
7 Hemos venido a aprender portugués.   (condicional)
8 Veo a mi novia.   (futuro)
9 Vinimos a la feria.   (futuro)
10 Veían el centro de Barcelona.   (condicional)

C DÉ UNA SINOPSIS DE:

(Vds.) venir temprano.
(Nosotros) ver la playa.

V • GRAMATICA Y EJERCICIOS ORALES

61 SUBJUNCTIVE IN INDEPENDENT CLAUSES
(EL SUBJUNTIVO EN CLAUSULAS PRINCIPALES)

a **Déme** (usted) el lápiz.
Give me the pencil.
No se lo **dé** a él.
Don't give it to him.

Hagámoslo esta tarde.
Let's do it this afternoon.
No lo **hagamos** esta tarde.
Let's not do it this afternoon.

The subjunctive is used in a conventional affirmative command (with or without **usted, ustedes**); a negative command, both conventional and familiar; and a first person plural command (English *let us* . . .).[1]

EJERCICIO **A**

Cambie al imperativo:

Modelo   El señor Sánchez come la carne.
                    Señor Sánchez, coma (Vd.) la carne.

1 La señorita Fagundo escribe la carta.
2 Alberto lee el libro.
3 María sale pronto.
4 Enrique abre el cuaderno.
5 El señor hace los preparativos.
6 Marta se sienta en el banco.
7 Roberto se acuesta en el catre.
8 Betty se lava bien.
9 El señor Morales toma la silla.
10 El Dr. Romeralo cierra la ventana.

EJERCICIO **B**

Cambie al imperativo:

Modelo   Juan y María comen en casa.
                    Juan y María, coman Vds. en casa.

1 Los señores escriben la carta.
2 Los profesores explican la lección.
3 Los alumnos dicen la verdad.
4 Las muchachas estudian la lección para mañana.
5 Enrique y Carlos abren los cuadernos.
6 Las mujeres hacen los vestidos.
7 Marta y María se ponen delante de la clase.
8 Los niños juegan en casa.
9 Ellos se lavan la cara.
10 Los niños se quitan los zapatos.

---

[1] A common substitute for this construction is **vamos a** plus infinitive. This substitute is always used to avoid a double **s**:
Vamos a dárselos. (not **Démosselos**). *Let's give them to him.*

EJERCICIO C

Cambie las frases:

Modelo   La señorita Castillo come la carne.
Señorita Castillo, no coma la carne.

1   La señorita Alonso escribe la carta.
2   Juan lee el libro.
3   María sale pronto.
4   El señor Uceda abre el cuaderno.
5   El señor Ruiz hace los preparativos.
6   Marta se sienta en el banco.
7   Roberto se acuesta en el catre.
8   El señor Román se levanta tarde.
9   La señora Rosaldo prepara la comida.
10   La señorita Fernández se quita los guantes.

EJERCICIO D

Cambie las frases:

Modelo   Juan y María comen en casa.
Juan y María, no coman en casa.

1   Los señores escriben la carta.
2   Los profesores explican la lección.
3   Los alumnos dicen mentiras.
4   Las muchachas van al cine.
5   Enrique y Carlos vienen mañana.
6   Las mujeres hacen las maletas.
7   Marta y María se ponen delante de la clase.
8   Las señoras se levantan tarde.
9   Adela y Rosario son malas.
10   Ellos se lavan las manos.

EJERCICIO E

Diga en forma negativa:

1   Démelo en seguida.
2   Hágame la cama.
3   Dígame la verdad.
4   Explíqueselo ahora.
5   Sígalos por esta calle.
6   Préstenselos ahora mismo.
7   Escríbanmelo Vds. la semana que viene.
8   Mándenselos mañana.
9   Háganmelo, por favor.
10   Pónganme la mesa.

EJERCICIO **F**

Diga en forma afirmativa:

1 No me lo dé ahora.
2 No se lo preste hoy.
3 No se los regale la semana próxima.
4 No nos la explique en la clase.
5 No se las diga aquí.
6 No me los escriban hoy.
7 No se las manden la semana que viene.
8 No se lo quiten ahora.
9 No se las lean en la clase.
10 No nos lo den en seguida.

EJERCICIO **G**

Diga en español:

Modelo   Let's study it!
¡Vamos a estudiarlo!
¡Estudiémoslo!

1 Let's eat it!
2 Let's send it!
3 Let's hear it!
4 Let's touch it!
5 Let's construct it!

b **Vistámonos.**
Let's get dressed.

When **nos** is attached to the first person plural of the present subjunctive (to express English *let us . . .*), the final **s** is dropped before **nos** is added.

EJERCICIO **H**

Diga en forma afirmativa:

1 No nos acostemos tarde.
2 No nos durmamos aquí.
3 No nos peinemos en la peluquería.
4 No nos lavemos allá.
5 No nos pongamos el sombrero.
6 No nos vayamos al cine.
7 No nos escribamos a menudo.
8 No nos expliquemos la lección.
9 No nos veamos por aquí.
10 No nos marchemos juntos.

EJERCICIO I

Diga en forma negativa:

1 Vámonos al cine esta noche.
2 Levantémonos temprano.
3 Acostémonos a las once.
4 Durmámonos ahora.
5 Sentémonos aquí.
6 Lavémonos la cara.
7 Despertémonos tarde.
8 Escribámonos a menudo.
9 Peinémonos bien.
10 Quitémonos el sombrero.

62 SUBJUNCTIVE IN DEPENDENT CLAUSES WITH MAIN VERB SUPPRESSED (EL SUBJUNTIVO EN CLAUSULAS SUBORDINADAS)

The subjunctive is used in two types of dependent clauses where the main verb has been suppressed.

a **Que Carlos lo haga.**   (Deseo **que Carlos lo haga.**)
Let Charles do it.   *(I wish that Charles do it.)*

The subjunctive is used in indirect third-person commands introduced by **que.**[1] In this case the object pronoun precedes the verb.

EJERCICIO J

Diga en español:

Modelo   Let George do it!
            ¡Que lo haga Jorge!

1 Let George sing it!
2 Let George write it!
3 Let George say it!
4 Let George read it!
5 Let George bring it!

EJERCICIO K

Diga en español:

Modelo   Let me eat!
            ¡Déjeme comer!

1 Let me see!
2 Let me count!

[1] But: **Déjeme ir.** *Let me go.*

3 Let me return!
4 Let me cook!
5 Let me serve!

EJERCICIO L

Diga en español:

Modelo Let them enter!
¡Que pasen!

1 Let them study!
2 Let them work!
3 Let them come!
4 Let them speak!
5 Let them write!

b **¡Ojalá que tenga** la oportunidad!
Would that (I wish that) I might have the opportunity!
¡Ojalá que tuviera (tuviese) la oportunidad que tuvo usted!
Would that (I wish that) I had the chance you had!
¡Ojalá que hubiera (hubiese) tenido la misma oportunidad!
Would that (I wish that) I had had the same chance!

The subjunctive expresses a wish in a sentence introduced by
ojalá que. The present subjunctive is used if the wish is possible of fulfillment; the imperfect subjunctive (**r** or **s** form) if the
wish is impossible of fulfillment in the present; and the
pluperfect subjunctive (**r** or **s** form of the auxiliary verb) if the
wish was impossible of fulfillment in the past.

EJERCICIO M

Cambie los verbos al imperfecto de subjuntivo:

Modelo ¡Ojalá que tenga la oportunidad!
¡Ojalá que tuviera la oportunidad!

1 ¡Ojalá que vea el horario!
2 ¡Ojalá que haga el viaje a España!
3 ¡Ojalá que tenga mucho dinero!
4 ¡Ojalá que diga la verdad!
5 ¡Ojalá que me vista pronto!
6 ¡Ojalá que duerma bien!
7 ¡Ojalá que me pida el diccionario!
8 ¡Ojalá que salga temprano!
9 ¡Ojalá que venga a vernos!
10 ¡Ojalá que ponga la mesa!

63 IMPERATIVE (IMPERATIVO)

a AFFIRMATIVE COMMANDS

IMPERATIVE

Toma (tú).	*Take.*
Tomad (vosotros).	*Take.*
Escríbelo.	*Write it.*
Escribidlo.	*Write it.*

NEGATIVE COMMANDS

SUBJUNCTIVE

No tomes.	*Do not take.*
No toméis.	*Do not take.*
No lo escribas.	*Do not write it.*
No lo escribáis.	*Do not write it.*

The imperative is used as an affirmative familiar command (with or without **tú, vosotros**). The singular of the imperative is usually the same as the third person singular indicative. The plural is formed by changing the **r** of the infinitive to **d**. In negative commands, subjunctive forms are used. (See section 61, above.)

b

Lávate.	**No te laves.**
Wash yourself.	*Don't wash yourself.*
Lavaos.	**No os lavéis.**
Wash yourselves.	*Don't wash yourselves.*

With reflexive verbs the final **d** is dropped before adding **os** in the plural imperative. The only exception is **irse: idos.** *Go away.*

c Irregular Imperatives

decir	**di**	ir	**ve**
hacer	**haz**	poner	**pon**
salir	**sal**	tener	**ten**
ser	**sé**	venir	**ven**

These verbs are irregular in the singular only. There are no irregular imperative forms in the plural.

VI • PRACTICA ESCRITA

1 Write him a letter; write it to him.
2 Send us the books. Don't send them to us.
3 Let George do it.
4 Would that he were here!
5 I would like to go to the movies.
6 Let the boys study it.
7 Please wait a moment.
8 Would that I had had the money!
9 Let us explain it to them.
10 Have the men bring down the piano.
11 Go to the board at once.
12 I hope that (would that) I have the money next year.
13 May we know the truth!
14 John, leave the room.
15 Let's wash ourselves.
16 They would like to sing today.
17 Mary, don't come with me.
18 Let her bring up the dress.
19 Would that I had studied more!
20 Boys, sit here; don't sit there.

VII • PRACTICA ORAL

A DIALOGO COMPLEMENTARIO

(En el tren de Guadalajara: Entran los señores García y sus cinco hijos: Renato de veinte y un años; Chato de diez y nueve; Alicia de diez y siete; Anita de doce; y Chucho, el menor, de diez años. Entra también un profesor de español, el Dr. Ernesto Martín.)

SR. GARCÍA ¡No te alejes mucho, Chucho, y no pierdas el sombrero nuevo que te compramos en El Paso!

SRA. GARCÍA ¡Ojalá que estuviéramos en casa! No me gusta viajar cuando hace tanto calor. Además, no puedo encontrar mi abanico en la bolsa.

ALICIA ¿Por qué no se sienta Vd. junto a mí, mamá? Aquí hace fresco. Anita, ¡no saques la cabeza por la ventanilla!

COBRADOR ¡Favor de darme los boletos!

DR. MARTÍN Quisiera presentarme. Me llamo Ernesto Martín. Soy profesor de español en los Estados Unidos.

SR. GARCÍA Yo soy Pablo García. Soy médico y vivo en Guadalajara. Mamá, ¡ven a charlar con nosotros! ¡Que Alicia cuide a los niños!

DR. MARTÍN ¡Ojalá que hubiera traído alguna cosa para comer! Hoy tengo un apetito canino.

RENATO Tengo algo en la maleta que está debajo del asiento. Tome este sandwich. Yo no quiero nada ahora.

SR. GARCÍA Aquí en mi maleta tengo una botella de vino, el mejor de todo México. ¿Quiere un trago? ¡Caracoles! No puedo destaparla.

RENATO Démela. He tenido mucha experiencia en estas cosas.

SR. GARCÍA Vamos a beber a la salud y buena fortuna de nuestro amigo.

SRA. GARCÍA ¡Que se divierta mucho durante sus vacaciones en México! Y si viene a Guadalajara, no deje de visitarnos.

B EXPRESION ORAL

Diga Vd. cómo pasa el día: a qué hora se levanta, con quién se desayuna, qué hace por la mañana; por qué vuelve (o no vuelve) a casa para el almuerzo, quién lo prepara usualmente, qué se sirve, cómo pasa Vd. la tarde, dónde come Vd. y lo que hace por la noche.

C PLATICA ESPONTANEA

1 ¿Cuándo ayuda Vd. a sus padres con los quehaceres de la casa?

2 ¿Qué hace Vd?

3 ¿Cuándo va Vd. de compras?

4 ¿Qué cosas compra Vd. en el supermercado?

5 ¿Quién limpia su casa?

6 ¿A qué hora se levantó Vd. esta mañana?

7 ¿Qué se sirve en su casa para el desayuno? ¿Para el almuerzo? ¿Para la comida?

8 ¿Por qué no conduce Vd. el coche al centro?

    9 ¿Quién sabe manejar mejor el coche, el hombre o la mujer? ¿Por qué?

  10 ¿Por qué toma Vd. el autobús en vez del coche para llegar a la universidad?

VIII • COMPOSICION

Sugerencias para un tema. Supóngase que usted conoce a una familia en el tren que va de Madrid a Irún, en la frontera francesa:

1 ¿De dónde es la familia?
2 ¿Quiénes comprenden la familia?
3 ¿Qué edad tienen los chicos?
4 ¿Qué hacen?
5 ¿Por qué van a la frontera?
6 ¿Qué hace el padre?

Lección trece

I • DIALOGO

CARLOS Perdóneme, señorita, pero ¿por dónde se va a la biblioteca?

ANITA Tiene que bajar la colina y al llegar a la calle State, siga derecho por dos cuadras hasta llegar a la fuente. Luego vaya a la izquierda donde se encuentra la entrada principal.

CARLOS Gracias. Usted es muy amable. Soy estudiante de primer año y todavía no sé dónde están muchos edificios principales. Permítame presentarme: me llamo Carlos Zapata y soy de San Francisco.

ANITA Mucho gusto en conocerle. Me llamo Anita García y soy de Nueva York. Soy de tercer año.

CARLOS Mi profesor de español quiere que escribamos un ensayo sobre la cultura hispánica en los Estados Unidos y tengo que ir a la biblioteca a buscar los libros necesarios.

ANITA Yo también voy a la biblioteca. ¿Quiere que le acompañe?

CARLOS Sí, con mucho gusto. Vámonos.
(Charlan mientras caminan hacia la biblioteca.)

ANITA Siempre preparo mis asignaturas en el salón de lectura donde todo el mundo tiene que guardar silencio y así no me interrumpe nadie.

CARLOS Comprendo lo que quiere decir. En la residencia donde vivo, mi compañero de cuarto pone discos de música clásica todo el tiempo y nunca me deja en paz.

ANITA Le sugiero que de aquí en adelante estudie usted también en la biblioteca. No está muy lejos de la residencia.

CARLOS Gracias.
(Llegan a las gradas de la biblioteca.)

ANITA ¿Se ha fijado Vd. en el gran número de estudiantes que están sentados en las gradas?

CARLOS Parece que todos charlan animadamente.

ANITA   Está prohibido hablar dentro.

CARLOS   ¿Tendría usted inconveniente de encontrarse conmigo a las cuatro para tomar refrescos?

ANITA   De ninguna manera, encantada. Discúlpeme por haberle quitado tanto tiempo charlando. De todos modos me alegro mucho de conocerle y espero que goce de sus cuatro años de estudios aquí.

Courtesy American Airlines
Biblioteca de la Universidad de México

II • MODISMOS Y EXPRESIONES

a medida que, mientras	*while*
alegrarse de	*to be glad*
dar una vuelta	*to take a walk*
dedicarse a	*to devote oneself to*
de ninguna manera	*by no means*
derecho	*straight ahead*
de todos modos	*at any rate*
disculparse por	*to apologize (for)*
el año que viene	*next year*
gozar de	*to enjoy*
guardar silencio	*to keep silent*
¿Por dónde se va a . . ?	*How does one get to . . ?*
tener inconveniente (de)	*to have an objection, to object (to)*
tener sed	*to be thirsty*
todo el mundo	*everybody*

III • PRACTICA SOBRE MODISMOS Y EXPRESIONES

A   USE CADA MODISMO EN UNA FRASE COMPLETA Y LUEGO TRA-
DÚZCALA AL INGLÉS:

1   todo el mundo
2   ¿por dónde se va a . . . ?
3   a medida que
4   gozar de
5   de todos modos
6   el año que viene
7   tener inconveniente
8   dar una vuelta

B   ESCOJA UN MODISMO QUE COMPLETE LA FRASE:

1   Yo _____ estudio de las humanidades.
2   ¿Por qué _____ en hacerlo?
3   ¿Piensa usted ir al parque? ¡_____!
4   Juan _____ por haberse tomado la libertad de
pedirle prestado su coche.
5   ¿Quiere usted _____ conmigo por la Quinta
Avenida?

6 La señorita García decía que había bebido mucha agua porque _____.

7 ¿Siempre _____ usted de buena salud?

8 Vaya _____ hasta llegar a la biblioteca.

9 Nosotros _____ haberla visto en Madrid.

10 No dijimos nada durante la discusión, sino que _____.

IV • REPASO DE VERBOS

A USE LOS SUSTANTIVOS O PRONOMBRES INDICADOS COMO SU-
JETOS. (REPASE LOS VERBOS **pensar, sentir, volver** Y **dormir**
EN EL APÉNDICE.):

1 Pienso ir a México.
(Carlos, Vds., tú, nosotros)

2 Pensé ir a Colombia.
(nosotros, tú, Vds., Carlos)

3 Lo siento mucho.
(Vds., nosotros, Carlos, tú)

4 Lo sentí mucho.
(María y yo, tú, ellos, Vds.)

5 Vuelven mañana.
(yo, tú, Alberto, nosotros)

6 Volvieron ayer.
(nosotros, yo, tú, las muchachas)

7 No duermo bien.
(Vds., nosotros, Jorge, tú)

8 No dormí bien.
(nosotros, Vds., tú, Margarita)

B CAMBIE LOS VERBOS

AL PLURAL:

1 Pensé en la película.
2 Vuelvo en seguida.
3 Yo lo sentía mucho.
4 Anoche durmió mal.
5 Pensará en su falta.
6 He vuelto a California.
7 Siento no haberlo hecho.
8 Duerme como un tronco.

AL SINGULAR:

9 Pensaron que habíamos llegado.

10 Habían vuelto antes de las tres.

11 Sentimos que no lo hagan.

12 Dormirán aquí.

13 Pensábamos que iba a llover.

14 Vuelven con su hermano.

15 Sintieron el accidente.

16 Dudaban que durmiésemos.

C CAMBIE LOS VERBOS A LOS TIEMPOS INDICADOS:

1 Pienso ir a Acapulco.   (imperfecto)

2 Volvió temprano.   (presente)

3 Ella duda que lo sintamos.   (Ella dudó + imperfecto de subjuntivo)

4 Era imposible que durmiera Vd.   (presente)

5 Hemos pensado en ello.   (imperfecto)

6 Volverán las golondrinas.   (perfecto)

7 Ha sentido la falta.   (pretérito)

8 No dormirán allá.   (pretérito)

9 Pensó nadar en el lago.   (presente)

10 Volveré a tiempo.   (imperfecto)

11 Sentíamos el choque.   (presente)

12 Durmió en el pajar.   (Es necesario que + presente de subjuntivo)

13 Piensan en el viaje.   (futuro)

14 Vuelvan Vds. mañana.   (condicional)

15 Ella sintió que su novio no estuviera aquí.   (presente)

D DÉ UNA SINOPSIS DE:

1 (Yo) pensar viajar.

2 (El) volver pronto.

3 (Vds.) sentir la falta.

4 (Ella) dormir bien.

V • GRAMATICA Y EJERCICIOS ORALES

64 SUBJUNCTIVE IN DEPENDENT CLAUSES (EL SUBJUNTIVO EN CLAUSULAS SUBORDINADAS)

The indicative mood states facts and expresses reality. The subjunctive mood, especially in dependent clauses, expresses what is merely possible or probable, what is indefinite or doubtful, or what is unreal.

In Spanish, the subjunctive is commonly used in dependent clauses that express the moods described above. Such clauses are usually introduced by the conjunction **que,** by a relative pronoun, or by a conjunctive adverb.

65 CLAUSES INTRODUCED BY THE CONJUNCTION QUE (CLAUSULAS INTRODUCIDAS POR LA CONJUNCION QUE)

a **Deseo que usted escriba** la carta en español.
I want you to write the letter in Spanish.
No quería consentir en que yo entrara.[1]
He would not consent to my coming in.
But
Prefiero salir solo.
I prefer to go out alone.

The subjunctive is used after verbs and expressions of command, request, demand, desire, permission. Note that a subjunctive **que** clause is used only if there is a change of person. Otherwise, a dependent infinitive is used (last example).

Common verbs requiring subjunctive in dependent clauses are:

aconsejar[2]	*to advise*	**pedir**	*to request*
consentir en	*to consent*	**permitir**	*to permit*
desear	*to desire*	**preferir**	*to prefer*
impedir	*to prevent*	**prohibir**	*to forbid*

---

[1] A preposition precedes **que** if it is required by the main verb or if the clause is dependent on a noun in the main clause:
Insisto en que usted me lo dé.
I insist that you give it to me.
Da la orden de que cerremos los libros.
He orders us to close our books.

[2] **Aconsejar** *(to advise),* **rogar** *(to beg),* **dejar** *(to allow),* **hacer** *(to make),* **mandar** *(to order),* **permitir** *(to permit),* **prohibir** *(to forbid)* allow an infinitive construction even if the subject is changed, but the subjunctive construction is preferred if the subject of the subordinate clause is a noun or a stressed pronoun:
Le permite fumar de vez en cuando.
He allows him to smoke once in a while.
But
Su padre **no permite que Carlos** fume nunca.
Charles's father never allows him to smoke.

Such idiomatic English constructions as *I want him to read the book* are not possible in Spanish. Compare: **Quiero que lea el libro.**

insistir en	to insist	querer	to wish
mandar	to order	rogar	to beg

EJERCICIO **A**

Conteste las preguntas:

Modelo   ¿Qué prefiere? (explicar la lección)
   Prefiero que usted explique la lección.

1   ¿Qué desea?   (ir al cine)
2   ¿Qué aconseja?   (estudiar la lección)
3   ¿Qué pide?   (darme una limonada)
4   ¿Qué ruega?   (llevarnos al circo)
5   ¿En qué insiste?   (en hacerlo pronto)
6   ¿Qué quiere?   (explicarme el problema)
7   ¿Qué prohibe?   (fumar cigarrillos)
8   ¿Qué manda?   (quedarse en casa)
9   ¿Qué impide?   (entrar en la casa)
10   ¿En qué consiente?   (en casarse pronto)

b   **Siento que no esté** en casa **mi padre.**
   I'm sorry my father isn't at home.
   Me alegraba de que ustedes no lo hubieran hecho.
   I was glad that you hadn't done it.
   But
   Siento llegar tarde.
   I'm sorry to be late.

The subjunctive is used after verbs and expressions of feeling
and emotion.

EJERCICIO   **B**

Comience cada frase por «Siento que»:

Modelo   Ella no está en casa.
      Siento que ella no esté en casa.

1   Ustedes lo hacen.
2   Ellos no saben la lección.
3   Tú vuelves tarde a casa.
4   Vd. se levanta tarde.
5   Vd. nunca dice la verdad.
6   Jorge no se cepilla los dientes.
7   Ana no barre la casa.
8   Tú no vienes temprano.
9   Ellas no alcanzan el coche.
10   La criada no pone la mesa.

c   **Dudo que sea** verdad.
I doubt that it is true.
But
No creo poder hacerlo hoy.
I don't think I can do it today.

The subjunctive is used after verbs and expressions of doubt and denial. Common verbs and expressions of this type are **no creer** *(not to believe)*, **dudar** *(to doubt)*, **negar** *(to deny)*.

EJERCICIO   C

Comience cada frase con las palabras indicadas:

Modelo   La señorita Moreno está aquí. (Dudo que)
Dudo que la señorita Moreno esté aquí.

1   Don Rodrigo conoce a Elena.
(Dudo que, Niego que, No creo que)
2   Los González vienen mañana.
(Me alegro de que, Siento que, Temo que)
3   Carlos va con su tío.
(Es posible que, No es verdad que, Es probable que)
4   Piden un vaso de limonada.
(Prefiere que, Sugiere que, Aconseja que)
5   Sigo cursos en la universidad.
(Mandan que, Insisten en que, Permiten que)
6   Duermen bien todas las noches.
(Espero que, Ojalá que, Me alegro de que)
7   Hay muchos edificios principales aquí.
(Es probable que, Es fácil que, Es imposible que)
8   Escribo un ensayo sobre la cultura hispánica.
(Mi profesor quiere que, Prefieren que, Sugieren que)
9   Los alumnos hablan en la biblioteca.
(Prohiben que, Se oponen a que, No permiten que)
10   Gozo de buena salud.
(Dudan que, No creen que, Niegan que)

d   **Es necesario que Carlos vaya** con su padre.
It's necessary (that Charles go) for Charles to go with his father.

The subjunctive is used with impersonal expressions denoting possibility, uncertainty, necessity, and the like. If, however, an impersonal expression indicates certainty, the indicative is used:

Es verdad que Carlos lo hizo.
It's true that Charles did it.

EJERCICIO **D**

Comience cada oración con las siguientes palabras:

Es preciso que, Es verdad que, Es lástima que

1 Gloria aprovecha la ocasión.
2 Gozan de sus ratos de ocio.
3 Asisto a las clases de francés.
4 Llegan a tiempo.
5 Lolita va a España.
6 El no viene mañana.
7 Hacemos los preparativos.
8 La criada pone la mesa.
9 Los niños están en casa.
10 Mi padre se acuesta temprano.

66 CLAUSES INTRODUCED BY A RELATIVE PRONOUN (CLAUSULAS INTRODUCIDAS POR UN PRONOMBRE RELATIVO)

Two common types of adjective clauses require the subjunctive.

a Busco un sitio que sea más ameno.
I'm looking for a place that's more pleasant.
Quiero encontrar un mozo que pueda ayudarme.
I want to find a porter who can help me.
Compare:
Busco al mozo que me ayudaba antes.
I'm looking for the porter who helped me before.

The subjunctive is used in a relative clause if a characteristic or quality is desired but not yet found or if the relative clause refers to no specific person.

b No conozco a nadie que hable portugués.
I'm not acquainted with anyone who speaks Portuguese.

The subjunctive is used in a relative clause if the person or thing is considered to be nonexistent.[1]

EJERCICIO **E**

Cambie las frases (subjuntivo):

Modelos Busco a la criada que habla español.
Busco una criada que hable español.

---

[1] If a question implies a general negative answer, the verb may be subjunctive:
¿Hay alguien que no le guste?
Is there anyone whom you don't like?

Hay una señorita que sabe cantar.
No hay ninguna señorita que sepa cantar.

1 Buscamos al hombre que vende legumbres.
2 Invitamos a las personas que dicen la verdad.
3 Compremos la novela que es interesante.
4 Van a escoger las frutas que están maduras.
5 Vamos al teatro donde dan una película mexicana.
6 Conozco al profesor que sabe ocho lenguas.
7 Buscan el vapor que va a Sud América.
8 Hay alguien aquí que habla ruso.
9 Hay algo que se puede usar.
10 Hay un alumno que sabe hacerlo.
11 Hay un hombre que es perfecto.
12 ¿Cuándo nos das el coche que anda bien?
13 ¿Dónde puedo encontrar el chófer que maneja bien?
14 Vamos al restaurante que sirve buenas comidas.
15 Invitamos a los alumnos que sacan buenas notas.

67 SEQUENCE OF TENSES IN THE SUBJUNCTIVE (CORRELACION DE LOS TIEMPOS)

In general, if the verb of the main clause is in the present or future tense or expresses a command, the dependent verb is in the present subjunctive. If the verb of the main clause is in any other tense, the subordinate verb is in the imperfect subjunctive (either **r** or **s** form).

68 TABLE OF TENSE SEQUENCE (TABLA DE CORRELACION)

VERB OF MAIN CLAUSE	DEPENDENT VERB
Present Indicative ⎫ Future Indicative ⎬ Command Form ⎭	Present Subjunctive or Perfect Subjunctive
Imperfect Indicative ⎫ Preterit Indicative ⎬ Conditional ⎭	Imperfect Subjunctive or Pluperfect Subjunctive

Quiero que usted me lo **diga.**
I want you to tell me.
Querré que usted me lo **diga.**
I'll want you to tell me.
Dígale que lo **haga** ahora mismo.
Tell him to do it at once.

Siento que no **venga.**
I'm sorry he's not coming.
Siento que no **haya venido** todavía.
I'm sorry he hasn't come yet.

Quería (Quise) que me lo **dijera.**
I wanted you to tell me.
No **querría** que me lo **dijera.**
I wouldn't want you to tell me.

The rules for sequence may be broken when the sense of the sentence requires it. Note, however, that only the verb in the dependent clause is then affected:

Siento que no **viniera** ayer.
I'm sorry that he didn't come yesterday.
Siento que no **hubiera venido** la semana pasada.
I'm sorry that he hadn't come last week.

EJERCICIO **F**

Cambie al tiempo pasado:

1 Pides que yo les dé los libros.
2 Busco una muchacha que hable portugués.
3 Creo que es la verdad.
4 Es imposible que lo sepa María.
5 ¿Tiene V. miedo de que ellos vengan?
6 Conviene que vayamos a la tienda.
7 Es lástima que no llegara ayer el alumno.
8 Deseo un libro que sea interesante.
9 Dudo que lean la lección.
10 Insisten en que yo venga todos los días.
11 Espero que Vds. lo hayan hecho.
12 No es verdad que me lo hayan dicho.
13 ¿Hay algo que le guste?
14 No hay nadie que me conozca.
15 Es probable que ella se haya dormido.

VI • PRACTICA ESCRITA

1 I insist that you study.
2 Is there anyone here who knows him?
3 He regrets that I lost it.
4 They doubted that she would come.

5 It's certain that he went away.

6 We forbid him to leave.

7 I hope I'll be able to do it.

8 It's possible that they are there.

9 Do you believe that the students will return?

10 She wanted me to send it to you.

11 We are looking for a novel that is interesting.

12 It was a pity that she couldn't sing.

13 They ordered Charles to help the soldiers.

14 Tell them to enter the house now.

15 I was afraid that they had bought the book.

16 She knows the man who said that.

17 Nobody doubts that he's a doctor.

18 They advised me to open the store.

19 We were glad that they took the train.

20 Do you prefer a room that is large?

VII • PRACTICA ORAL

A DIALOGO COMPLEMENTARIO

Víctor	Oye, Gloria, ¿quieres ir a la corrida de toros hoy? Los señores Estrada insisten en que yo los acompañe.
Gloria	Sí, con mucho gusto.
	(*Más tarde en la plaza de toros.*)
Sr. Estrada	Hoy el famoso torero El Cordobés estará en la plaza. ¿Hay alguien que no reconozca que es el mejor torero del mundo?
Gloria	¿Cree V. que Antonio Ordóñez sea mejor que El Cordobés?
Sr. Estrada	Me sorprende que los norteamericanos sepan tanto de tauromaquia.
Víctor	Es que he leído *Los toros* de José María de Cossío.
Sra. de Estrada	Me alegro mucho de que haya tanta gente aquí hoy. La semana pasada hubo poca asistencia. Se temía que cayera un aguacero. Nosotros no teníamos ni impermeable ni paraguas.

VÍCTOR   Veo acercarse a un mozo vendiendo refrescos y tortillas.

GLORIA   Pídele que venga. Tengo sed. Hace mucho calor aquí.

SR. ESTRADA   Allá entra El Cordobés en la plaza. Después del desfile el presidente le tirará la llave del toril. Bueno, Víctor, ya que usted sabe tanto, ¿puede decirme las varias fases del toreo?

VÍCTOR   Primero los capeadores capean al toro por unos minutos para cansarle un poquito. Luego llega el picador montado a caballo el cual está protegido contra los cuernos del toro por un viejo colchón. Después siguen los banderilleros que ponen seis banderillas en el cuello del animal. Por fin el matador lo capea un ratito.

SRA. DE ESTRADA   Y antes de matar al toro, honrará a una señorita, ofreciéndole la faena y rogándole que guarde la montera. Es muy probable que usted, Gloria, sea la señorita.

GLORIA   Es lástima que sea ésta la última corrida de la temporada.

SRA. DE ESTRADA   Espero que vuelvan Vds. a México el próximo año para ver más corridas.

SR. ESTRADA   Ahora quiero que guarden silencio porque la primera corrida está a punto de empezar.

B   EXPRESION ORAL

1   Explique a alguien por dónde se va a la casa de correos, a la biblioteca, al edificio de la Unión Estudiantil.

2   Pregunte a alguien por qué va a la biblioteca, a la casa de correos, a la librería.

C   PLATICA ESPONTANEA

1   ¿Por qué prefiere Vd. estudiar en la biblioteca?
2   ¿Por dónde se va a la biblioteca?
3   ¿Para cuándo quiere su profesor que escriba Vd. un tema en español?
4   ¿Cuál es el tema de su composición?
5   ¿Para qué tiene Vd. que ir a la biblioteca?

6 ¿A qué quiere Vd. dedicarse en la vida?
7 ¿Dónde está su residencia?
8 ¿Por qué no se permite hablar en la biblioteca?
9 ¿Cuánto tiempo hace que estudia Vd. español?
10 ¿Cuántos estudiantes viven en su casa?

VIII • COMPOSICION

Sugerencias para un tema: Escriba un diálogo sobre una corrida de toros.

1 ¿Dónde se compran las localidades?
2 ¿Qué clase de localidades hay?
3 ¿Cuánto cuestan?
4 ¿A qué hora empieza la corrida?
5 ¿Cuántas personas van a asistir?
6 ¿Quiénes torean hoy?
7 ¿Qué refrescos se sirven?
8 ¿Quiénes toman parte en la corrida?
9 ¿Qué hace el capeador?
10 ¿Qué hace el banderillero?
11 ¿Qué hace el picador?
12 ¿Quién mata al toro?

Lección catorce

I • DIALOGO

RITA   ¿Por qué tienes que volver a casa tan temprano?

JORGE   Porque mañana vuelo a Albuquerque para visitar a mis tíos que tienen una hacienda allí.

RITA   ¿De dónde sales?

JORGE   Del aeropuerto O'Hare en Chicago. Es un vuelo de cinco horas. Siempre paso todas mis vacaciones de verano e invierno en Nuevo México.

RITA   ¿Cómo es la hacienda?

JORGE   Es muy grande. Hay vacas, ovejas, caballos y mulas. Me gusta montar a caballo todos los días.

RITA   ¿Está la hacienda cerca de la ciudad?

JORGE   No, está bastante lejos, en las montañas, a una altura de 6.000 pies.

RITA   ¿Qué haces todo el día?

JORGE   Algunas veces voy a visitar a los pastores que cuidan las ovejas. Tienen un perro enorme, un San Bernardo. Otras veces un amigo mío y yo cazamos pumas. Soy muy aficionado a la caza.

RITA   ¿Hay otras maneras de divertirse?

JORGE   Sí, cuando hace calor en el verano, nado y pesco en el riachuelo donde me divertía tanto siendo niño.

RITA   ¿Cómo pasas los días de lluvia?

JORGE   Pues, paso largos ratos leyendo mi novela favorita, *Don Quijote*. Cuando me canso, me tiendo en un diván cerca de la chimenea para mirar las llamas que bailan sobre la leña.

RITA   ¿Qué haces por la noche?

JORGE   Si no tengo ganas de leer, voy a casa de un amigo. El invita a otros amigos y tenemos música y baile. Alguna que otra vez jugamos al bridge.

RITA   ¿Piensas pasar la Navidad allí?

JORGE   Sí. Me gusta esquiar. Salimos por la mañana llevando los esquíes encima del coche. Después de dos horas llegamos a un caserío, donde almorzamos y tomamos varias tazas de café. Figúrate si nos divertimos o no. Bajamos a una velocidad de setenta millas por hora, zigzagueando por entre los pinos cubiertos de nieve.

RITA   Basta, por favor. Si continúas así, me darás ganas de aprender a esquiar. Y debo confesarte que hace tiempo que tengo este deseo. También quisiera ir contigo a la hacienda de tus tíos.

By Hans Mann from Monkmeyer
Finca en el Perú

II • MODISMOS Y EXPRESIONES

al día siguiente	*on the following day*
alguna que otra vez	*sometimes, once in a while*
divertirse	*to enjoy oneself*
encima de, arriba de	*on, on top of*
hace tiempo que (más presente)	*for a long time* (plus present tense)
ser aficionado a	*to be fond of*

III • PRACTICA SOBRE MODISMOS Y EXPRESIONES

A USE CADA MODISMO EN UNA FRASE COMPLETA Y LUEGO TRADÚZCALA AL INGLÉS:

1 ser aficionado a
2 alguna que otra vez
3 hace tiempo
4 al día siguiente
5 divertirse

B DIGA EN ESPAÑOL:

1 I have been here for a long time.
2 Have you been here for a long time?
3 We haven't seen her for a month.
4 They have been studying Spanish for a year and a half.
5 Did you enjoy yourself last night?
6 I had a wonderful time at the party.
7 They won't enjoy themselves studying all day.
8 We are enjoying ourselves very much on the beach.
9 Imagine my surprise on seeing her here!
10 I imagine that they are not studying.
11 He imagined that they would not come.
12 She imagines that they are here.

IV • REPASO DE VERBOS

A (REPASE LOS VERBOS **empezar, conocer, dirigir, vencer** Y **pedir** EN EL APÉNDICE.) CAMBIE LOS VERBOS

AL PLURAL:

1 El hombre dirige la orquesta.
2 No pido nunca nada a nadie.
3 Se alegra de que yo empiece la lección.
4 Vencí al rival.
5 Yo conocía a la señora Mendoza.
6 Dirigiré el grupo.
7 Ha empezado a estudiar.
8 La muchacha pidió la fotografía.
9 Venzo a los enemigos.
10 No conozco a las muchachas.

AL SINGULAR:

11 Empezamos a estudiar.
12 Vencían a los enemigos.
13 Dudan que conozcamos a María Elena.
14 Dirigimos la banda.
15 Le pidieron agua a la señorita.
16 Sentimos que empiecen a salir tan temprano.
17 Habrán conocido al presidente.
18 Queremos que dirijan el tránsito.
19 Venceríamos si fuéramos héroes.
20 Se alegran de que pidamos el favor.

B CAMBIE LOS VERBOS A LOS TIEMPOS INDICADOS:

1 Pedimos pan. (perfecto)
2 Empezaré el trabajo mañana. (presente)
3 He conocido al jefe. (presente)
4 Se alegra de que hayamos vencido. (imperfecto + plus-cuamperfecto de subjuntivo)
5 Dirijo la casa de correo. (pretérito)
6 Pedirá más pan. (pretérito)
7 Hemos empezado la nueva tarea. (pretérito)
8 Vencí a mi rival. (futuro)
9 Deseaban que conociésemos al decano. (presente + presente de subjuntivo)
10 Habían dirigido el coro. (pretérito)
11 Insisten en que pidamos más sueldo. (imperfecto + imperfecto de subjuntivo)
12 Empecé la carta. (imperfecto)
13 Quiero que venzan a sus enemigos. (imperfecto + imperfecto de subjuntivo)
14 No conocimos el caso. (perfecto)
15 Dudan que yo dirija bien. (imperfecto + imperfecto de subjuntivo)

C DÉ UNA SINOPSIS DE:

(Ellos) no pedir dinero.
(Yo) no conocer a María.
(Yo) dirigir la orquesta.
(Yo) vencer muchas dificultades.
Empezar a llover.

V • GRAMATICA Y EJERCICIOS ORALES

69 SUBJUNCTIVE IN DEPENDENT CLAUSES (CONTINUED) (EL SUBJUNTIVO EN CLAUSULAS SUBORDINADAS)

The subjunctive is required in certain temporal clauses, in clauses of purpose, and in clauses of concession or proviso.

a Se lo daré **cuando le vea.**
I'll give it to him when I see him.
Dije que se lo daría **cuando le viera.**
I said that I would give it to him when I saw him.

The subjunctive is used in temporal clauses in which the time is future with reference to the main verb.[1] Common introductory words and phrases are:

cuando	when
en cuanto	as soon as, when
hasta que	until
antes (de) que	before
después (de) que	after

EJERCICIO A

Conteste:

Modelo —¿Cuándo veré a las muchachas?
　　　　　—Cuando vengan.

1 ¿Cuándo veré a Elena?
2 ¿Cuándo veré al general?
3 ¿Cuándo veré a los soldados?
4 ¿Cuándo veré a las actrices?

Modelo —¿Cuánto tiempo va a escribir Lolita?
　　　　　—Hasta que termine.

---

[1] The indicative is used if definite present or past time is expressed:
Cuando llegó a México, me escribió una carta.
When he reached Mexico, he wrote me a letter.

1 ¿Cuánto tiempo van a escribir tus alumnos?
2 ¿Cuánto tiempo va a escribir su hijo?
3 ¿Cuánto tiempo vamos a escribir?
4 ¿Cuánto tiempo voy a escribir?

Modelo   —¿Vas a comer con él?
           —Sí, antes de que se vaya.

1 ¿Vas a comer con ella?
2 ¿Vas a comer con nosotros?
3 ¿Vas a comer conmigo?
4 ¿Vas a comer con los profesores?

b Hablo despacio **para que usted pueda** entenderme mejor.
   I speak slowly so that you can understand me better.

The subjunctive is used in adverbial clauses expressing
purpose. Common introductory words and phrases are **para
que,**[1] **a fin de que** *(in order that, so that)*.

c Repítalo tantas veces **de modo que no lo olvide** nunca.
   Repeat it so many times that you will never forget it.

The subjunctive is used in clauses introduced by **de modo que**
(so that) and **de manera que** *(so that)*, but only if the action of
the dependent clause occurs after the time of the main verb.[2]

d Lo hizo **sin que nadie lo supiera.**
   He did it without anyone's knowing it.

The subjunctive is used after certain conjunctions or conjunctive phrases:

a menos que	*unless*
a no ser que	*unless*
antes (de) que	*before*
con tal que	*provided that*
para que	*in order that*
sin que	*without*

[1] If there is no change of subject, **para** (**a** after verbs of motion) plus infinitive is
used:
Compré papel **para escribir** una carta.
I bought paper to write a letter.
Vienen a verme.
They are coming to see me.
[2] If the clause states an accomplished fact, the indicative is used:
Habló despacio, **de modo que le entendí.**
He spoke slowly, so that I understood him.

e Voy al mercado **aunque llueva.**
I'm going to the market even if it rains.

The subjunctive is used in clauses of concession referring to a future action or when the speaker does not concede a fact.[1] The most common introductory word is **aunque** *(although, even if).*

f Se lo pediré **con tal que le vea.**
I'll ask him for it, provided that I see him.

The subjunctive is used after conjunctive expressions denoting proviso. The most common introductory phrase is **con tal que** *(provided that).*

EJERCICIO **B**

Cambie las frases, usando cláusulas subjuntivas:

Modelo Hágalo antes de partir.
Hágalo antes de que Elena parta.

 1 No podemos ayudarle sin trabajar.
_____ sin que él mismo _____.
 2 Compremos boletos para ir al teatro.
_____ para que Pedro y Anita _____.
 3 Voy a preparar el programa antes de volver a casa.
_____ antes de que los alumnos _____.
 4 No queremos salir sin verla.
_____ sin que ellos _____.
 5 Vamos a jugar bien para ganar el partido.
_____ para que el equipo _____.
 6 Van a escribirla antes de mandársela.
_____ antes de que Jorge _____.
 7 No podré ir hasta terminar la carta.
_____ hasta que ellos _____.
 8 Ellos entran sin saberlo.
_____ sin que Juan _____.
 9 Lo voy a repetir para no olvidarlo.
_____ para que Vds. _____.
10 Nos marchamos después de hacerlo.
_____ después de que ellos _____.

EJERCICIO **C**

Cambie los verbos al tiempo presente (nótese el uso del subjuntivo):

---

[1] If the concession is stated as an actual fact, the indicative is used:
Voy al teatro **aunque llueve.**
I'm going to the theater even though it is raining.

Modelo   Se lo dio cuando le vio.
Se lo va a dar cuando le vea.

1   Lo repitió tantas veces que no lo olvidó nunca.
2   Esperó hasta que vinieron.
3   Tan pronto como lo hizo, volvió a casa.
4   Cuando viajó en avión, tenía miedo.
5   Llegó a casa aunque llovió a chuzos.
6   Habló mientras estaba yo estudiando.
7   En cuanto hubo sublevación, me la contó.
8   La invitó aunque no quería venir.
9   Vendió frutas tan pronto como necesitó dinero.
10   Lo cantó después que Carlos salió.

EJERCICIO   **D**

Cambie las frases siguientes al pasado:

Modelos   Se lo diré cuando llegue.
Se lo dije cuando llegó.

Lo hace sin que nadie lo sepa.
Lo hizo sin que nadie lo supiera.

1   Se lo daré con tal que él venga.
2   Cuando Juan reciba la carta, estará en el Japón.
3   Leo despacio, de modo que me entiendan todos los estudiantes.
4   Con tal que vengan, se lo daré.
5   Vengo temprano para que me puedan ver.
6   Aunque llueve, voy al teatro.
7   Aunque venga, no le veré.
8   Se lo diré a él, con tal que lo vea.
9   Me darán las cartas cuando me vean.
10   Es posible que salgan ellos.
11   Es verdad que llega ella.
12   Busco un mozo que me ayude con el equipaje.
13   No conozco a nadie que lo haga.
14   Voy a la Universidad aunque nieve.
15   Se marchan sin que Juan los vea.

70   CONDITIONAL SENTENCES (ORACIONES CONDICIONALES)

A conditional sentence consists of a conclusion and of a
supposition usually introduced by **si** *(if)*. Conditional sentences may be classified as (**a**) certain, (**b**) uncertain, or
(**c**) contrary to fact.

a Si **viene** hoy, se lo **daré.**
If he comes today, I'll give it to him.
Si **vino** ayer, no le vi.
If he came yesterday, I did not see him.

If conditional sentences indicate certainty or fact, the indicative is used both in the **si** clause and in the conclusion.

b Si **viniera (viniese),** se lo **daría.**
If he should come, I would give it to him. (His coming is uncertain.)

A conditional sentence expressing uncertainty about a future act requires the imperfect subjunctive (either **r** or **s** form) in the **si** clause, and the conditional in the conclusion.[1]

c **Si estuviera (estuviese)** aquí, se lo **daría.**
If he were here, I'd give it to him.   (He is not here.)

A supposition stating what is contrary to fact at the present time requires the imperfect subjunctive (**r** or **s** form) in the **si** clause, and the conditional in the conclusion.[2]

Si hubiera (hubiese) venido, se lo **habría dado.**
If he had come, I would have given it to him.   (He did not come.)

A supposition stating what was contrary to fact in past time requires the pluperfect subjunctive. The conditional perfect is used in the conclusion.[3]

Note: A **si** clause can never be in present subjunctive or in future or conditional indicative.

d **De (A)** no **llover** hoy, iría a la feria.
If it shouldn't rain today, I'd go to the fair.
De (A) no **haberle** conocido, diría que era ladrón.
If I hadn't known him, I'd say he was a thief.

The infinitive preceded by **de** or **a** may replace a **si** clause, especially if the **si** clause suggests a situation contrary to fact.

EJERCICIO **E**

Cambie los verbos poniendo el verbo principal en el condicional y el verbo dependiente en el imperfecto de subjuntivo:

---

[1] The imperfect subjunctive (**r** form only) may be substituted for the conditional: Si viniera (viniese), se lo **diera.**

[2] The imperfect subjunctive (**r** form only) may be substituted for the conditional: Si estuviera (estuviese) aquí, se lo **diera.**

[3] The pluperfect subjunctive (**r** form only) may be substituted for the conditional perfect: Si hubiera (hubiese) venido, se lo **hubiera dado.**

Modelo   Si le veo, se lo daré.
   Si le viera, se lo daría.

1   Si tienen plata, la gastarán.
2   Si viene, me lo dará.
3   Si es preciso, nos lo dirán.
4   Si me lo pide, se lo entregará.
5   Si lo decimos, nos lo creerán.
6   Si está el alumno, aprenderá la lección.
7   Si viene, se lo diré.
8   Si estamos de acuerdo, no habrá inconveniente.
9   Si digo la verdad, la sabrán.
10   Si tengo dinero, haré un viaje a Venezuela.

EJERCICIO   **F**

Cambie los verbos poniendo el verbo principal en el condicional perfecto y el verbo dependiente en el pluscuamperfecto de subjuntivo:

Modelo   Si han aprendido la lección, la sabrán.
   Si hubieran aprendido la lección, la habrían sabido.

1   Si hemos enviado la carta, ellos la recibirán.
2   Si ella ha cosido los vestidos, los tendrán.
3   Si yo he depositado el cheque, tendré el dinero.
4   Si han tomado la medicina, no estarán enfermos.
5   Si ha llovido, Juan estará mojado hasta los huesos.
6   Si hemos aceptado la oferta, vendrán a vernos.
7   Si mi mujer ha pagado la cuenta, no le deberemos nada.
8   Si él ha conducido con cuidado, no habrá accidente.
9   Si han dicho la verdad, serán libertados.
10   Si ha volado el avión de prisa, llegará a tiempo.

e   **Quisiera** acompañarle.   (that is, **Quisiera** acompañarle si tuviera tiempo.)
   I would like to go with you.   (I would like to go with you if I had the time.)
   Compare:
   Quiero acompañarle.
   I want to go with you.

The imperfect subjunctive in the **r** form is used in so-called softened statements with **deber, poder,** and **querer.** These forms are in fact the conclusions of conditional sentences in which the **si** clause has been suppressed.

EJERCICIO G

Cambie las frases al imperfecto de subjuntivo:

Modelo ¿Puede V. verme mañana?
¿Pudiera V. verme mañana?

1 ¿Puedes prestarme diez dólares?
2 ¿Quiere V. pasarme el pan?
3 ¿Debes visitar el hospital?
4 ¿Podemos asistir al teatro hoy?
5 ¿Quieres pedirle el coche?
6 ¿Debemos estudiar esta noche?
7 ¿Pueden venir a verme esta tarde?
8 Quiero acompañarlos a la universidad.
9 No debes hacer eso.
10 Podemos ir mañana.

71 COMO SI CLAUSES (CLAUSULAS CON COMO SI)

Lo manda **como si fuera** rey.
He orders it as if he were king.
Me saludó **como si no me hubiera visto** por mucho tiempo.
He greeted me as if he hadn't seen me for a long time.

Como si *(as if)* may be followed only by the imperfect or pluperfect subjunctive, regardless of the sequence of tenses.

EJERCICIO H

Sustituya usando los sujetos indicados y haciendo los cambios necesarios:

1 Tomás lo hace como si fuera profesor.
(nosotros, tú, ellas)
2 Los pasajeros lo describieron como si hubieran estado allá.
(yo, tú, nosotros, Vd.)
3 Se lo dijo como si lo hubiera visto.
(ella, nosotros, tú, ellos)

VI • PRACTICA ESCRITA

SUSANA   I hear there's an exhibit of Mexican art in the museum. Have you seen it?

ARTURO   No, but I would like to. Why don't we ask the art instructor to take the class there next week and give us a
lecture on it?

SUSANA   That's a good idea. Here's Mariana. Maybe she's seen
it. Let's ask her.
(Mariana approaches and greets the two.)

MARIANA   How are you? What are you two talking about?

ARTURO   A trip to the museum . . .

MARIANA   *(interrupting him)* You mean the Mexican art exhibit?
I've seen it; it's excellent.

SUSANA   What else is there besides paintings?

MARIANA   There are Aztec idols and ceramics. In addition, there
are examples of folkloric art: skeletons and skulls. It
was very impressive. If I have time next week, I'll go
visit it again.

ARTURO   As soon as I speak to Dr. Holmes, I'm sure he'll be in
favor of taking the entire class there.

MARIANA   How long has it been since you visited the museum?

ARTURO   I haven't been there for two years at least.

SUSANA   I don't want to wait until next week. I'll go tomorrow,
provided it doesn't rain.

ARTURO   Splendid. I'll accompany you, if you have no objection.

SUSANA   After my mother returns home, I'll meet you at the
fountain a little after three. So long.

ARTURO   See you later.

VII • PRACTICA ORAL

A   DIALOGO COMPLEMENTARIO

MANUEL   ¡Qué día tan caluroso!

LUIS   ¿Por qué no vamos a la casa de campo de los
abuelos? Allá en las montañas hace fresco.

MANUEL   ¡Linda idea! Tú, Luis, ¿quieres manejar la
camioneta?

LUIS   Sí. Pondré las maletas en ella en seguida.
Siempre recuerdo con nostalgia el paisaje que
se veía cuando subíamos las colinas. Tan pronto

como llegábamos a lo alto, podíamos ver la hacienda donde vivían los abuelos.

MANUEL   Y ¡cuánto se alegrarán de que vayamos, porque hace tiempo que se sienten solos!

LUIS   Lástima que no vivan allí los primos, pues con ellos pudiéramos divertirnos más. Se han trasladado a la ciudad para que los abuelos vivan en paz y sin apuros económicos.

(Más tarde.)

MANUEL   Serán las once. ¡Lo cansado que estoy! Me acuesto en seguida.

LUIS   Si hubieran estado aquí los primos, se hubieran reído de vernos tan cansados.

(Al día siguiente.)

ABUELO   Queridos nietos, vengan a desayunarse.

ABUELA   Sí, deben de tener un apetito formidable. Siento que no estén aquí Carlota y Jorge, pero van a llegar uno de estos días.

ABUELO   ¿Cómo van tus estudios de medicina, Manuel?

MANUEL   Muy bien, gracias. Ya he terminado los cursos y voy a trabajar de interno en el hospital San Juan de Dios en septiembre.

ABUELO   ¿Dónde está la abuela?

LUIS   Mientras comían y charlaban, se retiró sin ser vista. Alguien llamaba a la puerta y salió hace un momento.

ABUELA   *(desde otra habitación)* ¡Aquí están Carlota y Jorge! ¡Qué reunión más agradable! ¡Qué sorpresa tan grande!

LUIS Y MANUEL   ¡Bienvenidos! *(Se abrazan con los recién llegados.)*

LUIS   ¡Ya podemos ir a caballo por la sierra todos juntos! Es decir, si los abuelos no tienen inconveniente.

ABUELA   ¡Qué alegría! ¡Los cuidaremos como si fueran nuestros propios hijos!

B   EXPRESION ORAL

Diga a un amigo por qué va Vd. a esquiar en las montañas. ¿Qué lleva consigo? ¿Cómo viaja? ¿Cuánto tiempo tarda en llegar? ¿Cuánto tiempo piensa quedarse allá? ¿Quién le acompaña? ¿Cómo pasa la noche? ¿Dónde hay bailes? ¿A quiénes conoce allí?

C PLATICA ESPONTANEA

1 ¿Le gusta viajar en avión?
2 ¿Viaja Vd. mucho en avión? ¿Por qué? (¿Por qué no?)
3 ¿Dónde se divierte Vd. más?
4 ¿Qué libro ha leído Vd. recientemente?
5 ¿Quiénes son sus autores favoritos?
6 ¿Por qué tiene Vd. inconveniente de mirar televisión?
7 ¿Cómo se divirtió Vd. anoche?
8 ¿Cuánto cuesta un buen par de esquíes?
9 ¿Por qué le gusta (o no le gusta) esquiar?
10 ¿En qué estación del año se esquía en Colorado?

VIII • COMPOSICION

Sugerencias para un tema: Un verano en una casa de campo.

1 ¿Dónde está?
2 ¿Cómo se llega allí?
3 ¿Quiénes limpian la casa?
4 ¿Cuántos huéspedes se invitan allí?
5 ¿Quiénes llegan?
6 ¿Qué piensan hacer?
7 ¿Cuánto tiempo piensan quedarse?

Lección quince

I • DIALOGO

CARLOS ¡Uf, qué calor hace! Pronto terminan las clases y estaremos de vacaciones.

ANITA Sí. Cuando hace tanto calor, hago muy poco.

ELENA El calor me recuerda un refrán de Avila en donde hablando del clima se dice: «nueve meses de invierno y tres de infierno.»

CARLOS ¡Qué gracia! Ya estamos en pleno verano, y para este calor no hay remedio. A propósito, Anita, ¿has hecho planes para las vacaciones?

ANITA Pensaba ir a México con dos señoritas de Chicago, pero cuando mis padres se enteraron de mis planes, decidieron enviarme a pasar el verano con mi abuela, que vive en Seattle.

CARLOS ¡Qué lástima! No tendrás la oportunidad de conversar en español.

ANITA No, pero voy a leer unas novelas y muchas comedias. Soy muy aficionada al drama y allí pienso asistir a varias funciones de teatro durante el verano.

ELENA Pues, yo voy a California a visitar a mis tíos y a mis primos que viven en San Diego.

CARLOS Eso me acuerda de cuando, estando yo allí en la marina, visité el monumento a Cabrillo, el navegante portugués que fundó la ciudad de San Diego.

ELENA Y tú, Carlos, ¿qué piensas hacer durante las vacaciones?

CARLOS Desgraciadamente, no tengo tanta suerte como ustedes. Tengo que trabajar como de costumbre en una cervecería en Milwaukee.

ANITA Si no me equivoco, tú trabajaste de salvavidas en la playa de Milwaukee el verano pasado, ¿verdad?

CARLOS Sí, pero este verano tendré que ahorrar más dinero porque al volver a la Universidad, en el otoño, seré alumno de cuarto año y no quiero trabajar sino en mis estudios.

225

By Bloom from Monkmeyer
Monumento al navegante portugués Cabrillo: San Diego, California

II • MODISMOS Y EXPRESIONES

acordarse de	*to remember*
celebrarse	*to take place*
coger del brazo	*to catch by the arm*
enterarse de	*to find out about, be informed of*
entre tanto	*meanwhile*
equivocarse	*to be mistaken*
no había remedio	*it couldn't be helped*
¡qué gracia!	*how funny!*
según	*according to*

III • PRACTICA SOBRE MODISMOS Y EXPRESIONES

A USE CADA MODISMO EN UNA FRASE COMPLETA Y LUEGO TRADÚZCALA AL INGLÉS:

1 entre tanto
2 coger del brazo
3 ¡Qué gracia!
4 según
5 equivocarse

B DIGA EN ESPAÑOL:

1 I fell and broke my leg; it couldn't be helped.
2 When did you find out that the plane wouldn't arrive on time?
3 Meanwhile, the students attended class every day.
4 Why don't you feed the animals in the park?
5 According to the professor, the entire class failed the exam.
6 Catching her by the arm, I asked her why she missed the meeting of the student council yesterday.
7 James is always telling jokes in class. How funny!
8 The instructor said that the student was mistaken.
9 They don't remember where we left the timetable.
10 The meeting took place in the gym.

C HAGA PREGUNTAS A UN COMPAÑERO (O A UNA COMPAÑERA) DE CLASE:

Modelo Pregúntele qué comió ayer.
¿Qué comiste ayer?

1 Pregúntele cuándo se enteró del accidente de su amigo.
2 Pregúntele por qué no da de comer a los pájaros.
3 Pregúntele qué hace cuando se equivoca.
4 Pregúntele cuándo empieza el curso de verano en la universidad.
5 Pregúntele cómo se acuerda de hacer todas sus tareas.

IV • REPASO DE VERBOS

CAMBIE LOS VERBOS AL TIEMPO INDICADO. (REPASE LOS VERBOS **sacar, pagar** Y **averiguar** EN EL APÉNDICE.):

1 He sacado el lápiz. (pretérito)
2 ¿Pagará Vd. la cuenta? (Quiero que + presente de subjuntivo)
3 Habíamos averiguado la causa del choque. (Dudan que + presente de subjuntivo)
4 Sacaré el reloj. (presente)
5 ¿Ha pagado el diccionario? (presente)
6 Averiguamos la razón del fracaso. (imperfecto)
7 Siempre sacaron buenas notas. (Dudo que + imperfecto de subjuntivo)
8 Pagaríamos la renta una vez al año. (pretérito)
9 Nos alegramos de que lo averigüen. (imperfecto + imperfecto de subjuntivo)
10 Saca el coche todos los días. (imperfecto)

V • GRAMATICA Y EJERCICIOS ORALES

72 INFINITIVE (EL INFINITIVO)

a **Vivir** en el campo **es** para mí una gran satisfacción.
To live in the country is a great pleasure to me.
Recuerdo haberle visto antes.
I recall having seen him before.

The infinitive may be used as a noun and function as the subject or object of another verb.

Además de **ser** rica, **la muchacha** es bonita e inteligente.
In addition to the girl's being rich, she is also pretty and intelligent.

An infinitive may have a noun or pronoun subject.

EJERCICIO **A**

Use las palabras indicadas y haga los cambios necesarios:

1 Leer es interesante.
(comer, necesario / estudiar, útil / caminar, saludable / charlar, agradable)
2 Pepe recuerda haberme ayudado a mí.
(a ti, a nosotros, a ellos, a Marta)
3 Además de ser inteligente, la muchacha es rica.
(los niños, Luisa, tú, Mariana y Josefina)

b **Después de terminar** esta carta, tengo que escribir otra.
After finishing this letter, I have to write another.

The infinitive is used as object of a preposition (commonly equivalent to an English present participle).

Note that the Spanish present participle is rarely used with any preposition.

EJERCICIO **B**

Diga en español:

Modelo   Before entering, let's buy some tacos.
            Antes de entrar, vamos a comprar tacos.

1 Before leaving, let's sell the car.
2 Before visiting him, let's call him.
3 After walking, let's sit down.
4 After working, let's eat at home.
5 After running, let's rest a while.

c Compré una revista **para leerla** en el tren.
I bought a magazine to read on the train.

Para (sometimes **a** after verbs of motion) is used with an infinitive to express purpose. The infinitive alone cannot express purpose.

d **Al entrar** en la casa Juan vio a Carlos.
(On entering) When he entered the house, John saw Charles.

Al with an infinitive is equivalent to English *on, upon* plus present participle, though English normally prefers a clause.

EJERCICIO C

Use las expresiones siguientes con «al»:

Modelo ver su nota
Al ver su nota, Juan se puso triste.

1 llegar al aeropuerto
2 bajar del coche
3 subir al avión
4 perder su boleto
5 despedirse de su novia

e **A (De) no hacer** mal tiempo, le acompañaría a usted.
If the weather weren't bad, I would go with you.

A (De) plus infinitive is frequently used as a substitute for the **si** clause of a conditional sentence. (See Section 70 **d**.)

EJERCICIO D

Cambie las cláusulas subordinadas de acuerdo con el modelo:

Modelo Si no hiciera mal tiempo, le acompañaría a V.
De (A) no hacer mal tiempo, le acompañaría a V.

1 Si no fuera así, lo haría.
2 Si no lo hiciera Juan, lo haría yo.
3 Si no llegaran a tiempo, no los vería.
4 Si no tuviéramos bastante dinero, no haríamos el viaje.
5 Si no hubiera sol, no saldría yo.

f La **oyó cantar** muchas veces.
He heard her sing(ing) many times.

The infinitive is required after verbs of sense perception, such as **oír** and **ver**. The infinitive must immediately follow such verbs.

EJERCICIO E

Sustituya «cantar« por las expresiones siguientes:

Modelo La oímos cantar muchas veces.

1 tocar el piano
2 hablar con sus niños
3 silbar en casa
4 gritar a voces
5 escribir a máquina

g **Le aconsejo estudiar.**
I advise you to study.

The infinitive may be used after **aconsejar, dejar, hacer, mandar, permitir,** and **prohibir,** even when there is a change in the subject of the dependent verb.

EJERCICIO F

Sustituya los verbos siguientes por «aconsejo»:
Modelo   Le aconsejo salir.

1   permitir
2   mandar
3   prohibir
4   hacer
5   dejar

73   PARTICIPLES (LOS PARTICIPIOS)

a   **comprar**   *to buy*   **comprando**   *buying*
    comer   *to eat*   **comiendo**   *eating*
    vivir   *to live*   **viviendo**   *living*

The present participle in Spanish is formed in verbs of the first conjugation by adding **–ando** to the stem; in verbs of the second and third conjugations, by adding **–iendo** to the stem.[1]

b   **comprar**   *to buy*   **comprado**   *bought*
    comer   *to eat*   **comido**   *eaten*
    vivir   *to live*   **vivido**   *lived*

The past participle is formed in verbs of the first conjugation by adding **–ado** to the present stem; in verbs of the second and third conjugations, by adding **–ido** to the present stem.[2]

74   PRESENT PARTICIPLES (LOS GERUNDIOS)

a   **Hablando** se puede aprender a hablar.
    By speaking one can learn to speak.

The present participle is used to express manner, means, cause, or condition.

---

[1] Common irregular present participles are **diciendo (decir), durmiendo (dormir), pudiendo (poder), sintiendo (sentir), viniendo (venir), yendo (ir).**
Verbs of the second and third conjugations with stems ending in a vowel change the **i** of the ending **–iendo** to **y: leyendo (leer).**

[2] Common irregular past participles are: **abierto (abrir), dicho (decir), puesto (poner), escrito (escribir), cubierto (cubrir), hecho (hacer), roto (romper), vuelto (volver), muerto (morir), visto (ver).**

EJERCICIO G

Use la forma del gerundio de los verbos que siguen:

Modelo Hablando se aprende a hablar.

1 escribir
2 cantar
3 correr
4 saltar
5 leer
6 volar

b **Está (va) corriendo** por la calle.
He is (goes) running down the street.
Voy entendiendo la lección.
I'm getting to understand the lesson.
Vienen haciendo mejor su papel en la comedia.
They're playing their roles better in the play.
Sigo jugando al tenis.
I'm still playing tennis.

The present participle is used with **estar (ir, venir, seguir)** to express an act in definite progress.

EJERCICIO H

Cambie el verbo al gerundio como se indica en el modelo:

Modelo Tomo el autobús.
         Estoy tomando el autobús.

1 Juego al tenis.
2 Comen fruta.
3 Escribimos la lección.
4 El estudiante lee el periódico.

Modelo Caminan por la calle.
         Siguen caminando por la calle.

5 La criada prepara la cena.
6 Estudio el problema.
7 Traemos legumbres del mercado.
8 Duermen en el catre.
9 Los alumnos dicen la verdad.

75 PAST PARTICIPLES (LOS PARTICIPIOS PASADOS)

a Ella **ha hablado**.
She has spoken.

The past participle is combined with the auxiliary verb **haber** to form the compound tenses. The past participle never changes in form when thus used.

b El muchacho **fue alabado** por el maestro.
The boy was praised by the teacher.

The past participle is combined with **ser** to form the true passive voice.

c La ventana **estaba abierta.**
The window was open.

The past participle used as an adjective may be combined with **estar** to denote a condition or state.

d Tengo muchos **libros encuadernados.**
I have many bound books.

The past participle is used as an adjective modifying a noun or pronoun.

e Allí está su **sombrero colgado** en la percha.
There is your hat hanging on the rack.
Ella está sentada a la mesa.
She is sitting at the table.

Several Spanish past participles are equivalent to English present participles. The most common are:

acostado	*lying (down)*
atrevido	*daring*
colgado	*hanging*
divertido	*amusing*
dormido	*sleeping*
sentado	*sitting*

EJERCICIO **I**

Diga en español:

Modelo I found them sitting in the park.
Los hallé sentados en el parque.

1 I saw them sleeping in the classroom.
2 She found me lying on the floor.
3 We saw them hanging on the rack.
4 They left me standing at the corner.
5 He found them stretched out on the grass.

EJERCICIO **J**

Use las palabras indicadas y haga los cambios necesarios:

1 El perro estaba sentado en la cocina.
(la criada, Ramón, ellas)
2 Elena está dormida.
(nosotros, yo, tú, ellos)
3 El cuento era divertido.
(historia, novelas, comedia, drama)
4 Había un abrigo colgado en la percha.
(bufanda, camisas, chaqueta)

f **Hecho esto,** se acostó.
When he had done this, he went to bed.
Abiertas las ventanas, no hará tanto calor.
If (When) the windows are open, it won't be so warm.

The past participle is frequently used in Spanish in a so-called absolute construction.

EJERCICIO **K**

Use la forma del participio pasado de los verbos siguientes:

Modelo   Dicho esto, se marchó.

1 escribir
2 cubrir
3 hacer
4 ver
5 preparar
6 arreglar

g **Los heridos** no llegaron al hospital.
The wounded did not reach the hospital.
Los recién casados salieron para Nueva York.
The newlyweds left for New York.

The past participle, like an adjective, may be used as a noun.

EJERCICIO **L**

Cambie los sujetos de acuerdo con el modelo:

Modelo   Los alumnos matriculados no querían asistir a clases.
Los matriculados no querían asistir a clases.

1 Los amigos invitados no llegaron.
2 Los jóvenes aceptados se alistaron en el ejército.
3 Los señores defendidos no podían salir.

4 Las mujeres despedidas rehusaron volver a casa.
5 Los niños perdidos finalmente llegaron a casa.

h **Entre lo dicho y lo hecho** hay gran trecho.
There's a great difference between saying and doing.
Lo escrito no es siempre la verdad.
What's written is not always true.

Lo plus past participle functions as a noun.

VI • PRACTICA ESCRITA

On returning to my hotel one afternoon to take a nap, I found the door open. After examining my room carefully and discovering that I had been robbed, I went down to inform the manager of what had happened. Before answering my questions, he said he wanted to see the room, for «seeing is believing.» The manager, convinced of the robbery, telephoned the police.

After he had gone downstairs, I went out into the hall, where I saw a young man going away somewhat rapidly. I made him stop. While I was talking (use a participle) to him, he tried to escape, but I caught him by the arm. I took him to my room and made him sit down at the desk. A few moments later he confessed having stolen my money, saying that he had to support his family, since his father was dead and his aged mother was unable to work.

VII • PRACTICA ORAL

A DIALOGO COMPLEMENTARIO

(*Robo en el hotel.*)

VICENTE Despiértate, Ramón. He oído ruido en el cuarto.

RAMÓN (*medio dormido*) No es nada. Será el viento, no más.

VICENTE Hay alguien aquí con nosotros. Despiértate, pronto.

RAMÓN (*Incorporándose en la cama*) ¿Qué hay? No oigo nada. ¿Tú has dejado la ventana abierta?

VICENTE No, de ningún modo. ¿Ves? Eso prueba que ha entrado alguien.

RAMÓN   Enciende la luz.

VICENTE   Ya está encendida.

RAMÓN   No veo a nadie. Pero mira, la ropa está esparcida por toda la alcoba. Me han robado la cartera con todo el dinero.

VICENTE   Se ha escapado ya el ladrón. Voy a llamar al gerente y a la policía.

(Un poco más tarde.)

GERENTE   Acabo de prender al ladrón. Trató de huir, pero le cogí del brazo y le hice confesar el motivo de su delito.

POLICÍA   Parece que muerta la esposa, él mismo tiene que cuidar a sus cuatro hijos. Además, no tiene empleo y los niños casi se están muriendo de hambre.

LADRÓN   De no creerme, venga a mi casa y convénzase de la verdad de lo que estoy diciendo. Ver es creer.

POLICÍA   Ya no hay remedio.

RAMÓN   Voy a investigar su situación. Si es verdad lo que nos cuenta, le regalaré dinero para que dé de comer a la familia.

VICENTE   Además, le podemos prometer dos cosas: una, no entregarle a la policía, y otra, ayudarle a buscar trabajo en la ciudad.

RAMÓN   Pero si nos engaña, tendrá que ir a la cárcel y devolverme la cartera con todo el dinero que me ha robado.

B   EXPRESION ORAL

Cuente a su amigo (o amiga) sus planes para el verano. ¿A dónde piensa ir? ¿Y por qué? ¿Cuánto tiempo piensa quedarse allí? ¿Con quién piensa vivir? ¿Qué hará usted? ¿Cuánto dinero espera juntar para el viaje y cuánto dinero gastará en él?

C   PLATICA ESPONTANEA

1   ¿Por qué le gusta estar de vacaciones?
2   ¿Dónde pasa Vd. las vacaciones?
3   ¿Qué estación del año le gusta más?
4   ¿Por qué?
5   ¿Cómo pasa Vd. el verano?

6 ¿Le gusta más el teatro o el cine?
7 ¿Por qué?
8 ¿A quién le gusta oír cantar?
9 ¿Por qué lleva (o no lleva) Vd. sombrero?

VIII • COMPOSICION

Tema para un diálogo escrito: Robo en la casa de la fraternidad.

1 ¿Cuándo pasó?
2 ¿Qué se llevaron?
3 ¿A quiénes pertenecían los artículos robados?
4 ¿Cuánto costaban?
5 ¿Cómo entró el ladrón?
6 ¿Quién descubrió el robo?
7 ¿Qué hora era cuando se llamó a la policía?
8 ¿Qué preguntas hizo el detective?
9 ¿A quiénes?

Lección diez y seis

I • DIALOGO

MARÍA   Hola, Roberto. Acabo de presentar mi primer examen final.

ROBERTO   ¿En qué curso?

MARÍA   El español de segundo año. Ya sé por qué dicen que el Dr. González da los exámenes más difíciles del departamento.

ROBERTO   ¿Cuándo sales para casa?

MARÍA   El veinticuatro de este mes. El otro día me detuve en una agencia de turismo y reservé el boleto de avión para esa fecha.

ROBERTO   ¿Sabes? La encargada de nuestra residencia va a darnos una fiesta de despedida el veintitrés a las ocho. Te invito.

MARÍA   Gracias, pero como necesito levantarme temprano al día siguiente para llegar al aeropuerto a tiempo, no sé. ¿Podrías llevarme al aeropuerto en tu coche?

ROBERTO   Creo que sí. ¿Por qué no haces las maletas la víspera? Al llegar al aeropuerto no te olvides de facturarlas.

MARÍA   Sí, y además voy a mandar mi sombrerera y baúl por tren porque resulta más barato.

ROBERTO   ¿A qué hora sale el avión?

MARÍA   A las nueve y cuarto. Si tienes inconveniente de llevarme al aeropuerto, puedo tomar un taxi.

ROBERTO   De ningún modo. Y hablando de otra cosa, ¿sabes que Juana y Martín se casan a fines de junio?

MARIA   ¡Qué sorpresa tan agradable! ¿Dónde tiene lugar la boda?

ROBERTO   En Chicago, en casa de Juana. Creo que van a mandar las invitaciones muy pronto.

MARÍA   ¿Dónde piensan pasar la luna de miel?

ROBERTO   Martín dijo que irían a México, pero no estoy seguro.

MARÍA   ¿Sabes qué? Judit ha ganado una beca para pasar un año en España estudiando en Salamanca. Va a vivir con

una familia española. El padre es vice-rector de la
Universidad. Hay cinco hijos en la familia.

ROBERTO A ver si Judit pesca marido allá.

MARIA ¡Cállate, sinvergüenza! Es tarde y tengo que volver a
la residencia. ¡Buena suerte en tu próximo examen!
Hasta mañana.

ROBERTO Hasta mañana.

II • MODISMOS Y EXPRESIONES

a menudo	*often*
de ningún modo	*by no means*
hacer las maletas	*to pack suitcases*
por el estilo	*of that kind*
saltar a la vista	*to come into view, to be obvious*
tener lugar	*to take place*
tratarse de	*to be a question of*

III • PRACTICA SOBRE MODISMOS Y EXPRESIONES

Use cada modismo en una frase completa y luego tradúzcala al inglés:

1 de ningún modo
2 tener lugar
3 tratarse de
4 saltar a la vista
5 hacer las maletas
6 por el estilo

IV • REPASO DE VERBOS

A (REPASE LOS VERBOS **reír, enviar** Y **continuar** EN EL APÉNDICE.)
CAMBIE LOS VERBOS

AL PLURAL:

1 Río cuando habla el niño.
2 Ella continúa contando el dinero.
3 El me envió una carta.
4 Ría Vd. si quiere.
5 Ha continuado el plan de ella.
6 Le enviaré la cuenta pronto.

AL SINGULAR:

7 Ellos rieron a carcajadas.
8 Continuamos hablando por media hora.
9 Vds. enviarán fotografías a las chicas.
10 Habíamos reído demasiado.
11 Ellas no continuarían estudiando si supieran bien las lecciones.
12 Cuando llegó el tren, enviábamos el taxi a la estación.

B CAMBIE AL TIEMPO INDICADO:

1 Nos reímos con los chistes del payaso.   (futuro)
2 Continúo leyendo.   (Quieren que + presente de subjuntivo)
3 Le enviaba V. cartas a ella.   (pretérito)
4 Ellas han reído mucho.   (presente)
5 Continuaremos con el plan actual.   (perfecto)
6 Reí un poco en la clase.   (presente)
7 Vds. enviarían regalos, si tuvieran dinero.   (presente)
8 El continuó escribiendo su tema.   (presente)
9 Yo le enviaba cartas.   (Dudan que + presente de subjuntivo)
10 El público se rió mucho del payaso.   (presente)

C DÉ UNA SINOPSIS DE:

(Yo) reír poco.
(Ellos) enviar tarjetas postales.
(Vd.) continuar estudiando la lección.

V • GRAMATICA Y EJERCICIOS ORALES

76 CONJUNCTIONS (LAS CONJUNCIONES)

a Compraron pan **y** mantequilla.
They bought bread and butter.

Padre **e** hijo entraron.
Father and son came in.

The conjunction **e** is used instead of **y** before a word beginning with **i** or **hi.**

b ¿Quiere usted limonada **o** leche?
Do you want lemonade or milk?
Tiene siete **u** ocho hermanos.
He has seven or eight brothers.

The conjunction **u** is used instead of **o** before a word beginning with **o** or **ho.**

c Viene Isabel, **pero** no la veré.
Isabel is coming, but I will not see her.
No le gusta estudiar **sino** jugar.
He doesn't like to study but to play.

Pero is equivalent to English *but;* **sino** must be used, however, to introduce a contrary idea after a negative statement.[1]

77 PREPOSITIONS (PREPOSICIONES)

a Salió **después de comer.**
He left after eating.

Remember that prepositions in Spanish are normally followed by an infinitive, not a present participle. (See Lección Quince.)

b Siéntese usted **entre Juan y yo.**
Sit down between John and me.
Lo repartieron **entre sí.**
They divided it among themselves.

The preposition **entre** is followed by the subject form of a pronoun, with the exception of **sí.**

78 USES OF THE PREPOSITION POR (USOS DE LA PREPOSICION POR)

Por generally refers to source, cause, or means. It may be associated with the question **¿por qué?** *why?*

---

[1] If a finite verb (one with a personal ending) follows, **sino que** is used:
El no dijo nada **sino que** guardó silencio.
He did not say anything, but kept silent.

a Lo hice **por mi madre.**
I did it for (the sake of) my mother.

Por means *for* in the sense of "for the sake of," "on behalf of."

b Rafael ganó el campeonato de tenis **por su destreza.**
Rafael won the tennis championship because of his skill.

Por means *for* in the sense of "because of."

c Lo vendí **por seis pesos.**
I sold it for six dollars.

Por means *for* in the sense of "in exchange for."

d Lo echamos **por la ventana.**
We threw it out the window.
Caminamos **por la calle.**
We walked along the street.
Entraron **por el laboratorio.**
They entered through the laboratory.

Por means *for* in the sense of "through," "along," "out."

e Me quedé aquí **por el verano.**
I stayed here for (during) the summer.

Por expresses duration of time.

f La casa fue construida **por Juan.**
The house was built by John.
El correo llegó **por vapor.**
The mail arrived by steamship.

Por expresses the agent or means.

g Fue **por el médico.** *He went for the doctor.*

Por is used with the object of an errand (especially with **ir, venir, mandar, enviar,** and **volver**).

h ¡**Por Dios,** no lo haga!
For Heaven's sake, don't do it!

Por is used in exclamations.

i Common expressions with **por:**

por ahora	*for the time being*
por ejemplo	*for example*
algo por el estilo	*something like that*

por eso	*therefore, for that reason*
estar por	*to be in favor of*
por favor	*please*
por fin	*at last, finally*
por lo visto	*obviously, evidently*
por lo menos	*at least*

79 USES OF THE PREPOSITION <u>PARA</u> (USOS DE LA PREPOSICION <u>PARA</u>)

Para usually refers to purpose or destination. It may be associated with the question **¿para qué?** (*why?* in the sense of "for what purpose?").

a Los boletos son **para la corrida.**
The tickets are for the bullfight.

Para expresses purpose.

b Estudio **para aprender.**
I study in order to learn.

Para is used before an infinitive in the sense of "in order to."

c La lección **para mañana.**
The lesson for tomorrow
Termínelo **para el viernes.**
Finish it by Friday.

Para indicates a point in time as in a deadline.

d Salgo **para México.**
I'm leaving for Mexico.

Para indicates destination or direction.

e **Para norteamericano** habla muy bien el español.
For an American he speaks Spanish very well.

Para connotes comparison usually of inequality—one part of the comparison being different from what the other would lead us to expect.

f **una taza para té** *a teacup*

Para indicates the use to which something is put.

g Common expressions with **para:**

estar para	*to be about to*
Estoy para salir.	*I am about to leave.*

¿Para qué?	*Why?, For what reason?*
¿Para qué estudias?	*What are you studying for?*
Estudio **para** abogado.	*I am studying to be a lawyer.*

EJERCICIO **A**

*Use **por** o **para** y justifique su selección:*

1 Siempre trabajo _____ mi profesora de español.
2 Pasamos _____ el parque.
3 Están _____ salir.
4 Este dólar es _____ las entradas.
5 Leí _____ cuatro horas.
6 Luis lo hizo _____ su madre.
7 El drama fue escrito _____ Buero Vallejo.
8 _____ estudiante del segundo año habla español muy bien.
9 Nos prometieron la fotografía _____ hoy.
10 Mis tíos salieron _____ México ayer.
11 Los viejos caminaban _____ la calle.
12 Pagué cinco dólares _____ la caja de dulces.
13 La educación es _____ todos.
14 Jorge estudia _____ dentista.
15 Venían _____ la biblioteca.

EJERCICIO **B**

Diga en español:

1 We left for Spain.
  We left by way of Spain.
2 He did it for me (a favor).
  He did it for me (in my behalf).
3 I sold it to buy a house.
  I sold it for ten dollars.
4 I bought a ticket for the game.
  I bought a ticket because of the game.
5 The mail arrived for the plane.
  The mail arrived by plane.
6 She headed for (went in the direction of) the café.
  She went for the coffee.
7 They're going to Colombia for (to spend) their vacation.
  They're going to Colombia on account of their vacation.
8 He plays the piano well for his age.
  He plays the piano well because of his age.
9 I gave him money for (to buy) the car.
  I gave him money for (in exchange for) the car.
10 He did it for (as a favor to) his sister.
  He did it because of his sister.

80 INFINITIVE AFTER VERBS (EL INFINITIVO DESPUES DEL VERBO)

a **Esperamos ir** a España.
We hope to go to Spain.
Sírvase sentarse.
Please sit down.

The following are common verbs that take an infinitive without preposition:

conseguir	*to succeed in*
decidir	*to decide*
esperar	*to hope*
impedir	*to prevent*
lograr	*to succeed in*
necesitar	*to need*
olvidar	*to forget*
poder	*to be able*
procurar	*to try*
prometer	*to promise*
querer	*to want*
recordar	*to remember*
servirse	*to be so kind as*

b **Aprendo a** hablar español.
I'm learning to speak Spanish.
Me **invitan a** cenar.
They invite me to supper.

The following are common verbs that require the preposition **a** before an infinitive:

aprender	*to learn*
atreverse	*to dare*
ayudar	*to help*
comenzar	*to begin*
decidirse	*to decide*
empezar	*to begin*
enseñar	*to teach*
invitar	*to invite*
ir	*to go*
persuadir	*to persuade*
principiar	*to begin*

c **No deje de decirle** la verdad.
Don't fail to tell him the truth.

Me olvidé de traer el libro.
I forgot to bring the book.

The following are common verbs that require the preposition
de before an infinitive:

acabar	*to have just*
acordarse	*to remember*
alegrarse	*to be glad*
cesar	*to stop*
concluir	*to end*
no dejar	*not to fail to*
olvidarse	*to forget*
tratar	*to try*

d **Consentí en acompañarla.**
I consented to accompany her.
Nos empeñamos en leerlo.
We insisted on reading it.

The following are common verbs that require the preposition
en before an infinitive:

consentir	*to consent*
convenir	*to agree*
empeñarse	*to insist*

EJERCICIO **C**

Diga en español:

1   He knows how to read Japanese.
2   She decides to sell it.
3   They need to have it.
4   We forget to write it.
5   I promise to study it.
6   He wants to eat it.
7   We must remember to invite him.
8   She hopes to see him soon.
9   They are learning to swim.
10   We are beginning to understand her.
11   They dared to enter.
12   They are going to leave today.
13   I am teaching her to speak Spanish.
14   They invited him to learn Portuguese.
15   He persuaded her to study more.

81 VERBS WHICH INCLUDE THE PREPOSITION (VERBOS QUE INCLUYEN LA PREPOSICION)

buscar   *to look for*
Buscamos la casa.
We are looking for the house.

esperar   *to wait for*
Esperábamos el tren.
We were waiting for the train.

pagar   *to pay for*
Pago la cena.
I pay for the meal.
But
Pago dos dólares **por** la cena.
I pay two dollars for the meal.

If the price is given, **por** must be used.

pedir   *to ask for, ask a favor, request*
Le **pedimos** el periódico.
We ask him for the newspaper.
Me **piden** que estudie.
They ask me to study.
But
preguntar por   *to ask for, inquire about*
Dígale que **preguntamos por** ella.
Tell her we asked for her.

agradecerle a uno   *to be grateful (for)*
Le agradezco su ayuda.
I'm grateful to you for your help.

EJERCICIO **D**

Traduzca al español:

1 He asked us a favor.
2 He asked me where she lives.
3 The professor asks me to learn a lesson.
4 The woman teacher asks me why I'm not studying more.
5 We paid for the dinner.
6 We paid six dollars for the dinner.
7 Do you want to wait for her here?
8 No, she is waiting for me.
9 Are you looking for something?
10 I looked for Mrs. Torres.

11   We are grateful to you for your advice.

12   I am grateful to them for the use of their car.

82   ADVERBS (LOS ADVERBIOS)

a   La universidad está **cerca.**   (adverb)
The university is near(by).
Vivo **cerca de** la universidad.   (preposition)
I live near the university.

Distinguish carefully between adverbs and prepositional phrases:

ADVERBS		PREPOSITIONS	
antes	*beforehand*	**antes de**	*before (time)*
después	*afterwards*	**después de**	*after (time)*
cerca	*near by*	**cerca de**	*near*
detrás	*at the back*	**detrás de**	*behind*

EJERCICIO **E**

Diga en español:

Modelos   He ate before going to bed.
Comió antes de acostarse.

He ate before.
Comió antes.

1   She ate after doing it. She ate afterwards.
2   There is a school near the park. There is a school nearby.
3   A truck came behind the car. A truck came behind.

b   Viven **aquí** en esta casa.
They live here in this house.
El alumno viene **acá.**
The student is coming here.
¿No tienen tocadiscos **allá?**
Don't you have a record player there?

In general, **aquí** and **allí** are more definite as to location than **acá** and **allá.** After verbs of motion, **acá** and **allá** are preferred.

c   **Ya** vuelven los marineros.
The sailors are returning now.
Ya no están aquí.
They are no longer here.
Ya pasó.
It has already passed.

Ya volverá.
He will return later.

With a present tense, **ya** means *now*, unless the sentence is negative. In the latter case it means *no longer*. With a past tense **ya** means *already*. With a future tense **ya** means *later*.

d Duerme **todavía (aún).**
He is still asleep.
La novela era excelente, **aún** con todas las faltas.
The novel was excellent, even with all its mistakes.

Todavía and **aun** both mean *still* or *yet*. **Aun** bears a written accent if placed after the word it modifies.

83 DIMINUTIVES AND AUGMENTATIVES (DIMINUTIVOS Y AUMENTATIVOS)

a

libro	*book*	**librito**	*little book*
madre	*mother*	**madrecita**	*dear mother*
joven	*young man*	**jovencito**	*young fellow*
campana	*bell*	**campanilla**	*little bell*
casa	*house*	**casita**	*little house*

Diminutives are frequently used in Spanish to indicate smallness or affection. The most common diminutive endings are **ito (cito, ecito)** and **illo.** If a word (usually a noun or an adjective) ends in a vowel, the vowel is dropped before adding a diminutive suffix beginning with a vowel.

b

libro	*book*	**librote**	*big book*
muchacho	*boy*	**muchachazo**	*big boy*
hombre	*man*	**hombrón**	*big man*

The most common augmentative endings (to indicate large size or derogation) are **ote, azo, ón.**

EJERCICIO **F**

Cambie las frases usando diminutivos o aumentativos:

Modelo ¿Tienes un momento?
¿Tienes un momentito?

1 ¿Hay un libro?
2 ¿Hay una casa?
3 ¿Hay un jardín?
4 ¿Hay un amigo?
5 ¿Hay una pluma?

Modelo Se ve un muchacho.
Se ve un muchachazo.

1 Se ve un hombre.
2 Se ve una mujer.
3 Se ve una muchacha.
4 Se ve un libro.

VI • PRACTICA ESCRITA

No longer is it necessary to travel by ship from the United States
to Mexico City. They have just completed the Pan American
Highway, which runs from Laredo to Mexico City through forests
and over high mountains, offering beautiful scenes for the tourist.
One can make this trip from the border to Mexico City in three
days. If one wishes to travel more rapidly, there is always the airplane. After crossing the border, one forgets everything American
and tries to remember those few Spanish words learned in high
school or at the university. One is always happy to hear a Mexican
say, "For an American, you speak Spanish very well."
If you succeed in reaching Taxco, by all means visit the little
market behind the cathedral, where for only a few dollars one can
purchase gifts for every member of the family. Before leaving for
the United States, don't fail to see the palace built by the Spaniards
in Cuernavaca.

VII • PRACTICA ORAL

A DIALOGO COMPLEMENTARIO

(La última clase de español.)

DR. LÓPEZ Algunos de Vds. me han pedido que organice un
grupo de estudiantes para hacer una excursión de
tres o cuatro semanas a México.

DOROTEA Se puede llegar fácilmente a la capital en coche por
las varias rutas nuevas que se han construído. En
poco tiempo van a terminar la carretera panameri-

cana, de modo que se podrá ir desde Alaska a Patagonia en automóvil.

RICARDO Sé que la carretera atraviesa bosques de pintorescos valles tropicales y altas sierras desiertas donde saltan a la vista escenas y panoramas estupendos.

DR. LÓPEZ Yo pensaba llevar un grupo de quince personas en dos autobuses pequeños de fabricación extranjera. Podríamos armar tiendas por la noche y así ahorrar mucho dinero que de otra manera gastaríamos en hoteles y moteles. Va mi esposa y, por lo tanto, pienso llevar muchachos y muchachas.

ROBERTA He estado en México varias veces, pero siempre tengo ganas de volver lo antes posible porque México me encanta.

JUAN A mí también. Al cruzar la frontera se nota un ambiente distinto y muy pronto hay que hablar español aunque sólo se use el vocabulario aprendido en la escuela superior o en la universidad.

ROBERTA Se alegra uno de oír decir: «Para notreamericano, habla usted muy bien.»

DR. LÓPEZ Cada turista norteamericano desea traer a casa recuerdos de su viaje. Para conseguir una ganga, hay que ir al mercado y saber regatear. Si no se sabe regatear, se sale a menudo desilusionado, pues hay picarones que desean explotarle a uno.

JUAN Recuerdo que hay en Toluca un mercado en que todos los viernes, por unos cuantos pesos, se pueden comprar regalos para la familia y los amigos.

ROBERTA Hay cestas, sarapes, chaquetas, cinturones, corbatas, objetos de plata y otras cosas por el estilo.

DR. LÓPEZ Pero, ¡mucho ojo! Recuerden el refrán del *Quijote:* «Muchos van por lana y vuelven trasquilados.»

B EXPRESION ORAL

Cuente Vd. a su amigo (o amiga) algo de sus planes para el fin del semestre: ¿Cuántos exámenes tiene que sufrir? ¿Cuáles son? ¿Cuándo tienen lugar? ¿Cuándo piensa hacer las maletas y cuándo piensa irse de viaje? ¿Por qué tendrá que facturar el equipaje? ¿Vuelve Vd. a casa en coche, avión, tren o autobús? ¿Con quién? ¿Habrá fiesta de despedida? ¿Dónde? ¿Quién se encargará de ella?

C PLATICA ESPONTANEA

1 ¿Para quiénes son las becas?
2 ¿Por qué son necesarias las becas?
3 ¿Qué sabe Vd. de las becas de su universidad?
4 ¿Por qué son necesarios los exámenes finales?
5 ¿Por qué prefiere Vd. no viajar en avión?
6 ¿Cuándo piensa Vd. casarse?
7 ¿A qué edad debe uno casarse?
8 ¿Debe trabajar la esposa?
9 ¿Cuánto dinero debe uno tener antes de casarse?
10 ¿Qué se prefiere hoy, una familia grande o pequeña?

VIII • COMPOSICION

Tema para un diálogo escrito: «Haciendo planes para las vacaciones.»

1 ¿Qué se propone Vd. hacer?
2 ¿Cuándo sale Vd.? ¿Con quién(es)?
3 ¿A dónde va?
4 ¿Qué piensa Vd. ver?
5 ¿Por cuánto tiempo va Vd. a ausentarse?
6 ¿Cómo piensa Vd. viajar?
7 ¿Cuánto va Vd. a gastar?

Appendix

• VERB TABLES

REGULAR VERBS (VERBOS REGULARES)

I **-ar**   II **-er**   III **-ir**

INFINITIVE (INFINITIVO)
tomar *to take*   **comer** *to eat*   **vivir** *to live*

PRESENT PARTICIPLE (GERUNDIO)
tomando *taking*   **comiendo** *eating*   **viviendo** *living*

PAST PARTICIPLE (PARTICIPIO PASADO)
tomado *taken*   **comido** *eaten*   **vivido** *lived*

SIMPLE TENSES (TIEMPOS SIMPLES)

INDICATIVE MOOD (MODO INDICATIVO)

PRESENT (PRESENTE)

I take, do take, am taking	*I eat, do eat, am eating*	*I live, do live, am living*
tom**o**	com**o**	viv**o**
tom**as**	com**es**	viv**es**
tom**a**	com**e**	viv**e**
tom**amos**	com**emos**	viv**imos**
tom**áis**	com**éis**	viv**ís**
tom**an**	com**en**	viv**en**

IMPERFECT (IMPERFECTO)

I was taking, used to take, took	*I was eating, used to eat, ate*	*I was living, used to live, lived*
tom**aba**	com**ía**	viv**ía**
tom**abas**	com**ías**	viv**ías**
tom**aba**	com**ía**	viv**ía**
tom**ábamos**	com**íamos**	viv**íamos**
tom**abais**	com**íais**	viv**íais**
tom**aban**	com**ían**	viv**ían**

PRETERIT (PRETERITO)

I took, did take	*I ate, did eat*	*I lived, did live*
tomé	comí	viví
tomaste	comiste	viviste
tomó	comió	vivió
tomamos	comimos	vivimos
tomasteis	comisteis	vivisteis
tomaron	comieron	vivieron

FUTURE (FUTURO)

I will take	*I will eat*	*I will live*
tomaré	comeré	viviré
tomarás	comerás	vivirás
tomará	comerá	vivirá
tomaremos	comeremos	viviremos
tomaréis	comeréis	viviréis
tomarán	comerán	vivirán

CONDITIONAL (CONDICIONAL)

I would take	*I would eat*	*I would live*
tomaría	comería	viviría
tomarías	comerías	vivirías
tomaría	comería	viviría
tomaríamos	comeríamos	viviríamos
tomaríais	comeríais	viviríais
tomarían	comerían	vivirían

IMPERATIVE (IMPERATIVO)

take	*eat*	*live*
toma	come	vive
tomad	comed	vivid

SUBJUNCTIVE MOOD (MODO SUBJUNTIVO)

PRESENT (PRESENTE)

(that) I may take	*(that) I may eat*	*(that) I may live*
tome	coma	viva
tomes	comas	vivas
tome	coma	viva
tomemos	comamos	vivamos
toméis	comáis	viváis
tomen	coman	vivan

IMPERFECT, S FORM (IMPERFECTO, FORMA EN S)

(that) I might (would) take	*(that) I might (would) eat*	*(that) I might (would) live*

tomase	comiese	viviese
tomases	comieses	vivieses
tomase	comiese	viviese
tomásemos	comiésemos	viviésemos
tomaseis	comieseis	vivieseis
tomasen	comiesen	viviesen

r FORM (FORMA EN r)

(that I might	*(that) I might*	*(that) I might*
(would) take	*(would) eat*	*(would) live*
tomara	comiera	viviera
tomaras	comieras	vivieras
tomara	comiera	viviera
tomáramos	comiéramos	viviéramos
tomarais	comierais	vivierais
tomaran	comieran	vivieran

FUTURE (FUTURO)

(that) I will	*(that) I will*	*(that) I will*
(may) take	*(may) eat*	*(may) live*
tomare	comiere	viviere
tomares	comieres	vivieres
tomare	comiere	viviere
tomáremos	comiéremos	viviéremos
tomareis	comiereis	viviereis
tomaren	comieren	vivieren

COMPOUND TENSES (TIEMPOS COMPUESTOS)

INDICATIVE MOOD (MODO INDICATIVO)

PERFECT (PERFECTO)

I have taken	*I have eaten*	*I have lived*
he ⎫	he ⎫	he ⎫
has ⎬tomado	has ⎬comido	has ⎬vivido
ha ⎭	ha ⎭	ha ⎭
hemos⎫	hemos⎫	hemos⎫
habéis⎬tomado	habéis⎬comido	habéis⎬vivido
han ⎭	han ⎭	han ⎭

PLUPERFECT (PLUSCUAMPERFECTO)

I had taken	*I had eaten*	*I had lived*
había ⎫	había ⎫	había ⎫
habías⎬tomado	habías⎬comido	habías⎬vivido
había ⎭	había ⎭	había ⎭

habíamos ⎤
habíais ⎬ tomado
habían ⎦

habíamos ⎤
habíais ⎬ comido
habían ⎦

habíamos ⎤
habíais ⎬ vivido
habían ⎦

PRETERIT PERFECT (PRETERITO ANTERIOR)

I had taken

hube ⎤
hubiste ⎬ tomado
hubo ⎦

hubimos ⎤
hubisteis ⎬ tomado
hubieron ⎦

I had eaten

hube ⎤
hubiste ⎬ comido
hubo ⎦

hubimos ⎤
hubisteis ⎬ comido
hubieron ⎦

I had lived

hube ⎤
hubiste ⎬ vivido
hubo ⎦

hubimos ⎤
hubisteis ⎬ vivido
hubieron ⎦

FUTURE PERFECT (FUTURO PERFECTO)

I will have taken

habré ⎤
habrás ⎬ tomado
habrá ⎦

habremos ⎤
habréis ⎬ tomado
habrán ⎦

I will have eaten

habré ⎤
habrás ⎬ comido
habrá ⎦

habremos ⎤
habréis ⎬ comido
habrán ⎦

I will have lived

habré ⎤
habrás ⎬ vivido
habrá ⎦

habremos ⎤
habréis ⎬ vivido
habrán ⎦

CONDITIONAL PERFECT (CONDICIONAL PERFECTO)

I would have taken

habría ⎤
habrías ⎬ tomado
habría ⎦

habríamos ⎤
habríais ⎬ tomado
habrían ⎦

I would have eaten

habría ⎤
habrías ⎬ comido
habría ⎦

habríamos ⎤
habríais ⎬ comido
habrían ⎦

I would have lived

habría ⎤
habrías ⎬ vivido
habría ⎦

habríamos ⎤
habríais ⎬ vivido
habrían ⎦

SUBJUNCTIVE MOOD (MODO SUBJUNTIVO)

PERFECT (PERFECTO)

(that) I may have taken

haya ⎤
hayas ⎬ tomado
haya ⎦

hayamos ⎤
hayáis ⎬ tomado
hayan ⎦

(that) I may have eaten

haya ⎤
hayas ⎬ comido
haya ⎦

hayamos ⎤
hayáis ⎬ comido
hayan ⎦

(that) I may have lived

haya ⎤
hayas ⎬ vivido
haya ⎦

hayamos ⎤
hayáis ⎬ vivido
hayan ⎦

PLUPERFECT, **s** FORM (PRETERITO PLUSCUAMPERFECTO, FORMA EN **s**)

(that) I might (would) have taken	*(that) I might (would) have eaten*	*(that) I might (would) have lived*
hubiese hubieses }tomado hubiese	hubiese hubieses }comido hubiese	hubiese hubieses }vivido hubiese
hubiésemos hubieseis }tomado hubiesen	hubiésemos hubieseis }comido hubiesen	hubiésemos hubieseis }vivido hubiesen

r FORM (FORMA EN **r**)

hubiera hubieras }tomado hubiera	hubiera hubieras }comido hubiera	hubiera hubieras }vivido hubiera
hubiéramos hubierais }tomado hubieran	hubiéramos hubierais }comido hubieran	hubiéramos hubierais }vivido hubieran

FUTURE PERFECT (FUTURO PERFECTO)

(that) I will (may) have taken	*(that) I will (may) have eaten*	*(that) I will (may) have lived*
hubiere hubieres }tomado hubiere	hubiere hubieres }comido hubiere	hubiere hubieres }vivido hubiere
hubiéremos hubiereis }tomado hubieren	hubiéremos hubiereis }comido hubieren	hubiéremos hubiereis }vivido hubieren

RADICAL-CHANGING VERBS
(VERBOS QUE CAMBIAN LA RAIZ)

CLASS I (Iª CLASE)

Verbs of the first and second conjugations only; **e** becomes **ie** and **o** becomes **ue** throughout the singular and in the third plural of all present tenses.

pensar *to think*

Pres. Ind.	**pienso, piensas, piensa,** pensamos, penséis, **piensan**
Pres. Subj.	**piense, pienses, piense,** pensemos, penséis, **piensen**
Imperat.	**piensa,** pensad

volver *to return, turn*

Pres. Ind.	**vuelvo, vuelves, vuelve,** volvemos, volvéis, **vuelven**
Pres. Subj.	**vuelva, vuelvas, vuelva,** volvamos, volváis, **vuelvan**
Imperat.	**vuelve,** volved

CLASS II (II^a CLASE)

Verbs of the third conjugation only; **e** becomes **ie, o** becomes **ue,** as in Class I; **e** becomes **i, o** becomes **u** in the third person singular and plural of the preterit indicative, in the first and second persons plural of the present subjunctive, throughout the imperfect and future subjunctive, and in the present participle.

sentir *to feel, regret*

Pres. Ind.	**siento, sientes, siente,** sentimos, sentís, **sienten**
Pret. Ind.	sentí, sentiste, **sintió,** sentimos, sentisteis, **sintieron**
Pres. Subj.	**sienta, sientas, sienta, sintamos, sintáis, sientan**

Imperf. Subj. { (s form) **sintiese,** etc.
{ (r form) **sintiera,** etc.

Fut. Subj.	**sintiere,** etc.
Imperat.	**siente,** sentid
Pres. Part.	**sintiendo**

dormir *to sleep*

Pres. Ind.	**duermo, duermes, duerme,** dormimos, dormís, **duermen**
Pret. Ind.	dormí, dormiste, **durmió,** dormimos, dormisteis, **durmieron**
Pres. Subj.	**duerma, duermas, duerma, durmamos, durmáis, duerman**

Imperf. Subj. { (s form) **durmiese,** etc.
{ (r form) **durmiera,** etc.

Fut. Subj.	**durmiere,** etc.
Imperat.	**duerme,** dormid
Pres. Part.	**durmiendo**

CLASS III (III^a CLASE)

Verbs of the third conjugation only; **e** becomes **i** (there are no **o** verbs) in all forms that had any radical change in Class II.

pedir *to ask (for)*

Pres. Ind.	**pido, pides, pide,** pedimos, pedís, **piden**
Pret. Ind.	pedí, pediste, **pidió,** pedimos, pedisteis, **pidieron**
Pres. Subj.	**pida, pidas, pida, pidamos pidáis, pidan**

Imperf. Subj. { (s form) **pidiese,** etc.
{ (r form) **pidiera,** etc.

Fut. Subj.	**pidiere,** etc.
Imperat.	**pide,** pedid
Pres. Part.	**pidiendo**

ORTHOGRAPHIC-CHANGING VERBS
(VERBOS CON CAMBIO ORTOGRAFICO)

Verbs of the first conjugation ending in **car, gar, guar,** and **zar** have the following changes before **e** (that is, in the first person singular preterit indicative and throughout the present subjunctive):

c to **qu**	**sacar** *to take out* **saqué,** sacaste, etc. **saque, saques,** etc.
g to **gu**	**pagar** *to pay for* **pagué,** pagaste, etc. **pague, pagues,** etc.
gu to **gü**	**averiguar** *to ascertain* **averigüé,** averiguaste, etc. **averigüe, averigües,** etc.
z to **c**	**empezar** *to begin* **empecé,** empezaste, etc. **empiece, empieces,** etc.

Verbs of the second and third conjugation ending in **cer** and **cir, ger** and **gir, guir,** and **quir** have the following changes before **o** and **a** (that is, in the first person singular present indicative and throughout the present subjunctive):

c to **z** (if the ending **cer** or **cir** is preceded by a consonant)

> **vencer** *to conquer*
> **venzo,** vences, etc.
> **venza, venzas,** etc.
>
> **esparcir** *to scatter*
> **esparzo,** esparces, etc.
> **esparza, esparzas,** etc.

c to **zc** (if the ending **cer** or **cir** is preceded by a vowel)

> **conocer** *to know*
> **conozco,** conoces, etc.
> **conozca, conozcas,** etc.

g to **j**

> **coger** *to catch*
> **cojo,** coges, etc.
> **coja, cojas,** etc.
>
> **dirigir** *to direct*
> **dirijo,** diriges, etc.
> **dirija, dirijas,** etc.

gu to **g**	**distinguir** *to distinguish*
	distingo, distingues, etc.
	distinga, distingas, etc.
qu to **c**	**delinquir** *to be delinquent*
	delinco, delinques, etc.
	delinca, delincas, etc.

Verbs whose stem ends in a vowel change unaccented **i** between two vowels to **y** (that is, in the third person singular and plural preterit indicative, throughout the imperfect and future subjunctive, and in the present participle):

leer *to read*	leí, leíste, **leyó, leyeron**
	leyese, etc.
	leyera, etc.
	leyendo

Verbs ending in **uir** in which the **u** is sounded insert **y** before all vowels except **i** throughout all present tenses:

incluir *to include*	**incluyo, incluyes, incluye,** incluimos,
	incluís, **incluyen**
	incluya, etc.

Some verbs ending in **iar** and **uar** bear the written accent on **i** and **u** throughout the singular and the third person plural of all present tenses:

enviar *to send*	**envío, envías,** etc.
	envíe, envíes, etc.
	envía (imper.)
continuar *to continue*	**continúo, continúas,** etc.
	continúe, continúes, etc.
	continúa (imper.)

Verbs ending in **eír,** in changing stem **e** to **i,** drop the **i** of endings beginning with **ie** or **io:**

reír *to laugh*	**río, ríes,** etc.
	reí, reíste, **rio,** etc.
	riese, etc.
	riera, etc.
	riere, etc.
	riendo

Verbs whose stem ends in **ll** or **ñ** drop the **i** of endings beginning with **ie** and **io.** Likewise, irregular preterits with stems ending in **j** drop **i** of endings beginning with **ie** and **io:**

bullir *to boil*

bulló, bulleron
bullese, etc.
bullera, etc.
bullere, etc.
bullendo

reñir *to scold, quarrel*

riñó, riñeron
riñese, etc.
riñera, etc.
riñer etc.
riñendo

decir *to say*

dijeron
dijese, etc.
dijera, etc.
dijere, etc.

Other verbs like **decir** are **traer** *(to bring)* and compounds of **ducir,** such as **conducir** *(to conduct).*

Some verbs are both radical-changing and orthographic-changing:

comenzar *to begin*

comienzo
comience

colgar *to hang*

cuelgo
cuelgue

IRREGULAR VERBS
(VERBOS IRREGULARES)

Only those moods and tenses that have irregularities are given here.

Verbs that are irregular in the past participle only are: **abrir** *(to open)* **abierto; cubrir** *(to cover)* **cubierto; escribir** *(to write)* **escrito;** and **romper** *(to break)* **roto.**

andar *to go, walk*

Pret.	**anduve, anduviste, anduvo, anduvimos, anduvisteis, anduvieron**
Imperf. Subj.	{ (s form) **anduviese,** etc. { (r form) **anduviera,** etc.
Fut. Subj.	**anduviere**

asir *to seize*

Pres. Ind.	**asgo, ases, ase, asimos, asís, asen**
Pres. Subj.	**asga, asgas, asga, asgamos, asgáis, asgan**

Appendix

caber *to be contained in*

Pres. Ind.	**quepo, cabes, cabe, cabemos, cabéis, caben**
Pret. Ind.	**cupe, cupiste, cupo, cupimos, cupisteis, cupieron**
Fut. Ind.	**cabré, cabrás, cabrá, cabremos, cabréis, cabrán**
Cond. Ind.	**cabría, cabrías, cabría, cabríamos, cabríais, cabrían**
Pres. Subj.	**quepa, quepas, quepa, quepamos, quepáis, quepan**
Imperf. Subj.	{ (s form) **cupiese,** etc. { (r form) **cupiera,** etc.
Fut. Subj.	**cupiere,** etc.

caer *to fall*

Pres. Ind.	**caigo, caes, cae, caemos, caéis, caen**
Pret. Ind.	**caí, caíste, cayó, caímos, caísteis, cayeron**
Pres. Subj.	**caiga, caigas,** etc.
Imperf. Subj.	{ (s form) **cayese,** etc. { (r form) **cayera,** etc.
Fut. Subj.	**cayere,** etc.
Past Part.	**caído**

conducir *to conduct*

Pres. Ind.	**conduzco, conduces, conduce, conducimos, conducís, conducen**
Pret. Ind.	**conduje, condujiste, condujo, condujimos, condujisteis, condujeron**
Pres. Subj.	**conduzca, conduzcas, conduzca, conduzcamos, conduzcáis, conduzcan**
Imperf. Subj.	{ (s form) **condujese,** etc. { (r form) **condujera,** etc.
Fut. Subj.	**condujere,** etc.

dar *to give*

Pres. Ind.	**doy, das, da, damos, dais, dan**
Pret. Ind.	**di, diste, dio, dimos, disteis, dieron**
Pres. Subj.	**dé, des, dé, demos, deis, den**
Imperf. Subj.	{ (s form) **diese,** etc. { (r form) **diera,** etc.
Fut. Subj.	**diere,** etc.

decir *to say, tell*

Pres. Ind.	**digo, dices, dice, decimos, decís, dicen**
Pret. Ind.	**dije, dijiste, dijo, dijimos, dijisteis, dijeron**
Fut. Ind.	**diré, dirás, dirá, diremos, diréis, dirán**
Cond.	**diría, dirías, diría, diríamos, diríais, dirían**
Pres. Subj.	**diga, digas, diga, digamos, digáis, digan**
Imperf. Subj.	{ (s form) **dijese,** etc. { (r form) **dijera,** etc.

Fut. Subj.	**dijere**, etc.
Imperative	**di, decid**
Past Part.	**dicho**
Pres. Part.	**diciendo**

errar *to err*

Pres. Ind.	**yerro, yerras, yerra, erramos, erráis, yerran**
Pres. Subj.	**yerre, yerres, yerre, erremos, erréis, yerren**
Imperative	**yerra, errad**

estar *to be*

Pres. Ind.	**estoy, estás, está, estamos, estáis, están**
Pret. Ind.	**estuve, estuviste, estuvo, estuvimos, estuvisteis, estuvieron**
Pres. Subj.	**esté, estés, esté, estemos, estéis, estén**
Imperf. Subj.	{ (s form) **estuviese**, etc. { (r form) **estuviera**, etc.
Fut. Subj.	**estuviere**, etc.
Imperative	**está, estad**

haber *to have (impers., to be)*

Pres. Ind.	**he, has, ha,** (impers., **hay), hemos, habéis, han**
Pret. Ind.	**hube, hubiste, hubo, hubimos, hubisteis, hubieron**
Fut. Ind.	**habré, habrás, habrá, habremos, habréis, habrán**
Cond.	**habría, habrías, habría, habríamos, habríais, habrían**
Pres. Subj.	**haya, hayas, haya, hayamos, hayáis, hayan**
Imperf. Subj.	{ (s form) **hubiese**, etc. { (r form) **hubiera**, etc.
Fut. Subj.	**hubiere**, etc.

hacer *to do, make*

Pres. Ind.	**hago, haces, hace, hacemos, hacéis, hacen**
Pret. Ind.	**hice, hiciste, hizo, hicimos, hicisteis, hicieron**
Fut. Ind.	**haré, harás, hará, haremos, haréis, harán**
Cond.	**haría, harías, haría, haríamos, haríais, harían**
Pres. Subj.	**haga, hagas, haga, hagamos, hagáis, hagan**
Imperf. Subj.	{ (s form) **hiciese**, etc. { (r form) **hiciera**, etc.
Fut. Subj.	**hiciere**, etc.
Imperative	**haz, haced**
Past Part.	**hecho**

ir *to go*

Pres. Ind.	**voy, vas, va, vamos, vais, van**
Imperf. Ind.	**iba, ibas, iba, íbamos, ibais, iban**
Pret. Ind.	**fui, fuiste, fue, fuimos, fuisteis, fueron**
Pres. Subj.	**vaya, vayas, vaya, vayamos, vayáis, vayan**

Imperf. Subj.	{ (s form) **fuese,** etc.
	{ (r form) **fuera,** etc.
Fut. Subj.	**fuere,** etc.
Imperative	**ve, id**
Pres. Part.	**yendo**

jugar *to play*

Pres. Ind.	**juego, juegas, juega, jugamos, jugáis, juegan**
Pret. Ind.	**jugué, jugaste, jugó, jugamos, jugasteis, jugaron**
Pres. Subj.	**juegue, juegues, juegue, juguemos, juguéis, jueguen juega, jugad**

oír *to hear*

Pres. Ind.	**oigo, oyes, oye, oímos, oís, oyen**
Pret. Ind.	**oí, oíste, oyó, oímos, oísteis, oyeron**
Pres. Subj.	**oiga, oigas, oiga, oigamos, oigáis, oigan**
Imperf. Subj.	{ (s form) **oyese,** etc.
	{ (r form) **oyera,** etc.
Fut. Subj.	**oyere,** etc.
Imperative	**oye, oíd**
Past Part.	**oído**

oler *to smell*

Pres. Ind.	**huelo, hueles, huele, olemos, oléis, huelen**
Pres. Subj.	**huela, huelas, huela, olamos, oláis, huelan**
Imperative	**huele, oled**

poder *to be able*

Pres. Ind.	**puedo, puedes, puede, podemos, podéis, pueden**
Pret. Ind.	**pude, pudiste, pudo, pudimos, pudisteis, pudieron**
Fut. Ind.	**podré, podrás, podrá, podremos, podréis, podrán**
Cond.	**podría, podrías, podría, podríamos, podríais, podrían**
Pres. Subj.	**pueda, puedas, pueda, podamos, podáis, puedan**
Imperf. Subj.	{ (s form) **pudiese,** etc.
	{ (r form) **pudiera,** etc.
Fut. Subj.	**pudiere,** etc.
Pres. Part.	**pudiendo**

poner *to put, place*

Pres. Ind.	**pongo, pones, pone, ponemos, ponéis, ponen**
Pret. Ind.	**puse, pusiste, puso, pusimos, pusisteis, pusieron**
Fut. Ind.	**pondré, pondrás, pondrá, pondremos, pondréis, pondrán**
Cond.	**pondría, pondrías, pondría, pondríamos, pondríais, pondrían**
Pres. Subj.	**ponga, pongas, ponga, pongamos, pongáis, pongan**
Imperf. Subj.	{ (s form) **pusiese,** etc.
	{ (r form) **pusiera,** etc.

Fut. Subj.	**pusiere,** etc.
Imperative	**pon, poned**
Past Part.	**puesto**

querer *to wish:*

Pres. Ind.	**quiero, quieres, quiere, queremos, queréis, quieren**
Pret. Ind.	**quise, quisiste, quiso, quisimos, quisisteis, quisieron**
Fut. Ind.	**querré,** etc.
Cond.	**querría,** etc.
Pres. Subj.	**quiera, quieras, quiera, queramos, queráis, quieran**
Imperf. Subj.	{ (s form) **quisiese,** etc. { (r form) **quisiera,** etc.
Fut. Subj.	**quisiere,** etc.
Imperative	**quiere, quered**

saber *to know*

Pres. Ind.	**sé, sabes, sabe, sabemos, sabéis, saben**
Pret. Ind.	**supe, supiste, supo, supimos, supisteis, supieron**
Fut. Ind.	**sabré,** etc.
Cond.	**sabría,** etc.
Pres. Subj.	**sepa, sepas,** etc.
Imperf. Subj.	{ (s form) **supiese,** etc. { (r form) **supiera,** etc.
Fut. Subj.	**supiere,** etc.

salir *to go out*

Pres. Ind.	**salgo sales, sale, salimos, salís, salen**
Fut. Ind.	**saldré,** etc.
Cond.	**saldría,** etc.
Pres. Subj.	**salga, salgas, salga, salgamos, salgáis, salgan**
Imperative	**sal, salid**

ser *to be*

Pres. Ind.	**soy, eres, es, somos, sois, son**
Imperf. Ind.	**era, eras, era, éramos, erais, eran**
Pret. Ind.	**fui, fuiste, fue, fuimos, fuisteis, fueron**
Pres. Subj.	**sea, seas, sea, seamos, seáis, sean**
Imperf. Subj.	{ (s form) **fuese,** etc. { (r form) **fuera,** etc.
Fut. Subj.	**fuere,** etc.
Imperative	**sé, sed**

tener *to have*

Pres. Ind.	**tengo, tienes, tiene, tenemos, tenéis, tienen**
Pret. Ind.	**tuve, tuviste, tuvo, tuvimos, tuvisteis, tuvieron**
Fut. Ind.	**tendré,** etc.
Cond.	**tendría,** etc.

Pres. Subj.	**tenga, tengas, tenga, tengamos, tengáis, tengan**
Imperf. Subj.	{ (s form) **tuviese,** etc. (r form) **tuviera,** etc.
Fut. Subj.	**tuviere,** etc.
Imperative	**ten, tened**

traer *to bring*

Pres. Ind.	**traigo, traes, trae, traemos, traéis, traen**
Pret. Ind.	**traje, trajiste, trajo, trajimos, trajisteis, trajeron**
Pres. Subj.	**traiga, traigas, traiga, traigamos, traigáis, traigan**
Imperf. Subj.	{ (s form) **trajese,** etc. (r form) **trajera,** etc.
Fut. Subj.	**trajere,** etc.

valer *to be worth*

Pres. Ind.	**valgo, vales, vale, valemos, valéis, valen**
Fut. Ind.	**valdré,** etc.
Cond.	**valdría,** etc.
Pres. Subj.	**valga, valgas,** etc.
Imperative	**val, valed**

venir *to come*

Pres. Ind.	**vengo, vienes, viene, venimos, venís, vienen**
Pret. Ind.	**vine, viniste, vino, vinimos, vinisteis, vinieron**
Fut. Ind.	**vendré,** etc.
Cond.	**vendría,** etc.
Pres. Subj.	**venga, vengas,** etc.
Imperf. Subj.	{ (s form) **viniese,** etc. (r form) **viniera,** etc.
Fut. Subj.	**viniere,** etc.
Imperative	**ven, venid**
Pres. Part.	**viniendo**

ver *to see*

Pres. Ind.	**veo, ves, ve, vemos, veis, ven**
Imperf. Ind.	**veía, veías, veía, veíamos, veíais, veían**
Pres. Subj.	**vea, veas,** etc.
Past Part.	**visto**

Vocabularies

• ABBREVIATIONS

adj.	adjective
adv.	adverb
Am.	Spanish-American
demon. pron.	demonstrative pronoun
dir. obj.	direct object
f.	feminine
fam. obj. pron.	familiar object pronoun
impers.	impersonal
indir. obj.	indirect object
inf.	infinitive
m.	masculine
n.	neuter
obj. of prep.	object of a preposition
obj. pron.	object pronoun
pl.	plural
prep.	preposition
reflex. pron.	reflexive pronoun
rel. pron.	relative pronoun

• SPANISH—ENGLISH

a to, at; of; __ **menudo** often; __ **propósito** by the way; __ **que** until
abanico *m.* fan
abierto open, opened
abogado *m.* lawyer
abrazar to embrace
abrigo *m.* coat
abrir to open; __**se el apetito** to whet one's appetite
abuela *f.* grandmother
abuelo *m.* grandfather; __**s** grandparents
acá here
acabar to end, finish; __ **de** to have just
accidente *m.* accident
aceptar to accept
acera *f.* sidewalk
acerca de about, concerning
acercarse a to approach
acompañar to accompany
aconsejar to advise
acordar (ue) to remind, remember; __**se (ue) (de)** to remember
acostarse (ue) to go to bed, lie down
actitud *f.* attitude
actividad *f.* activity
actriz *f.* actress
actual present
acuerdo *m.* agreement, accord; **de __ con** in accord with; **estar de __** to agree, be in agreement
adecuado adequate
adelante forward; **de aquí en __** henceforth
además moreover, besides; __ **de** in addition to, besides
adicional additional
adiós good-bye
adjetivo *m.* adjective
admirablemente admirably
adornar to adorn
adorno *m.* adornment
adquirir to acquire
adversario *m.* adversary
aeropuerto *m.* airport
aficionado: ser __ a to be fond of
afirmativo affirmative
afortunado fortunate
afueras *f. pl.* outskirts
agencia *f.* agency; __ **de turismo** tourist agency
agente *m.* agent
agradable agreeable, pleasant
agradecer to thank; __**le a uno** to be grateful to one for
agradecimiento *m.* gratitude, thanks

agua *f.* water
aguacero *m.* shower
águila *f.* eagle
ahora now; __ **mismo** right now
ahorrar to save
aire *m.* air; **al __ libre** in the open air
ala *f.* wing
Alberto *m.* Albert
alcanzar to catch up to, overtake
alcázar *m.* palace
alcoba *f.* bedroom
alegrar to gladden; __**se (de)** to be happy (about), rejoice (in)
alegre happy
alegría *f.* joy, cheer, gladness
alejarse (de) to go away (from)
algo something, somewhat, rather
alguien someone, somebody; anybody, anyone
alguno, –a, –os, –as someone, somebody; anyone, anybody; some, any; **alguna que otra vez** sometimes
Alicia *f.* Alice
alistarse to enlist
almacén *m.* department store
almorzar (ue) to lunch, have lunch
almuerzo *m.* lunch; **a la hora del __** at lunchtime
alrededor de around
alto high, tall; **en __** upright, upward; **lo __** the top; **altas horas** late hours
altruísta *m. or f.* altruist
altura *f.* height, altitude
alumbrar to illuminate
alumna *f.* student
alumno *m.* student
allá there, over there
allí there; **de __ en adelante** thereafter
amable kind
amarillo yellow
ambiente *m.* ambient, atmosphere
ameno pleasant
amigo *m.* friend
amplio wide
ancho wide
andaluz Andalusian
andar to walk, run *(of a machine)*
anillo *m.* ring
animadamente animatedly
anoche last night
anteayer day before yesterday
antemano: de __ beforehand
anteojos *m. pl.* eyeglasses
anterior previous
antes before; __**(de) que** before; **lo __ posible** as soon as possible

anticipación: con __ in advance
antiguo old
Antonio *m.* Anthony
año *m.* year; **al** __ a year; **todo el** __ all year; **el** __ **pasado** last year; **el** __ **que viene** next year
aparte aside
apéndice *m.* appendix
apetito *m.* appetite; **abrirse el** __ to whet one's appetite; **un** __ **canino** a ravenous appetite
aplauso *m.* applause
aplicado industrious
apoyar to support
aprender to learn
aprovechar to profit by, benefit from
apunte *m.* note
apuro *m.* worry, need, fix
aquel, aquella, aquellos, aquellas that (over yonder), those; former
aquí here; __ **tienes tu casa** make yourself at home; **de** __ **en adelante** hereafter; **por** __ here, around here
árbol *m.* tree
arbusto *m.* shrub
armar to mount, pitch
armario *m.* closet
arreglar to arrange
arriba up, above
arroz *m.* rice; __ **con pollo** chicken with rice
arte *m. or f.* art
artículo *m.* article
artista *m. or f.* artist
asamblea *f.* assembly
ascensor *m.* elevator
así so, thus
asignatura *f.* course, subject
asistencia *f.* attendance
asistir a to attend
asombrar to surprise, astonish
aspecto *m.* aspect; **tener el** __ **muy triste** to look very sad
atacar to attack
ataque *m.* attack
atender (ie) to tend, attend; to wait on customers
atleta *m. or f.* athlete
atravesar (ie) to cross
aun still, even
aún still, yet
ausencia *f.* absence
ausentarse to be absent (*away*)
ausente absent
autobús *m.* bus
automático automatic
automóvil *m.* auto
autor *m.* author
avenida *f.* avenue
averiguar to ascertain

avión *m.* plane; **en** __ by plane
¡ay! alas!
ayer yesterday
ayuda *f.* help
ayudar to help
ayuntamiento *m.* city hall
azúcar *m.* sugar
azul blue

bachillerato *m.* high school degree
bailar to dance
baile *m.* dance
bajar to go down, descend; take down; get out
bajo low, short; *prep.* beneath, under
balcón *m.* balcony
banco *m.* bank, bench
banda *f.* band
bandera *f.* flag
banderilla *f.* *barbed dart with banderole*
banderillero *m.* *bullfighter who thrusts banderillas into neck or shoulders of bull*
banquete *m.* banquet
baño *m.* bath; **cuarto de** __ bathroom; **traje de** __ bathing suit
barato cheap
barco *m.* boat
barrer to sweep
barrio *m.* suburb, district
bastante sufficient; rather
bastar to be sufficient, enough
baúl *m.* truck; **hacer el** __ to pack the trunk
Beatriz *f.* Beatrice
beber to drink
beca *f.* fellowship
béisbol *m.* baseball
bello beautiful
bendecir to bless
beneficio *m.* benefit
Bernardo *m.* Bernard
biblioteca *f.* library
bicicleta *f.* bicycle
bien well; **está** __ okay, all right; __ **venido** welcome
billete *m.* ticket, bill
blanco white
blusa *f.* blouse
boca *f.* mouth
boda *f.* wedding
boleto *m.* ticket
bolsa *f.* purse
bonito pretty
bordo: a __ aboard
bosque *m.* forest
botella *f.* bottle
botellita *f.* small bottle
botija *f.* earthen jug
botones *m.* bellboy

breve brief, short
brillantina *f.* brillantine
bromista *m. or f.* joker
bueno good
bufanda *f.* scarf
buscar to look for

caballero *m.* gentleman
caballo *m.* horse; **ir a** __ to ride horseback
caber to fit, be contained in
cabeza *f.* head; **dolor de** __ headache
cada each, every
caer to fall; **ya caigo** now I understand
café *m.* coffee
caja *f.* box
calcetín *m.* sock
caliente warm, hot
calmar to calm
calor *m.* heat; **hacer** __ to be warm
(*weather*)
caluroso warm, hot
calzoncillo *m.* undershort
callar to quiet; __se to be quiet
calle *f.* street
cama *f.* bed; **hacer la** __ to make the
bed
camarero *m.* waiter
cambiar to change, exchange
cambio *m.* change
caminar to walk
camino *m.* road
camioneta *f.* station wagon
camisa *f.* shirt
camiseta *f.* undershirt
campo *m.* country, field
canario *m.* canary
canción *f.* song
canino: un apetito __ a ravenous appetite
cansar to tire; __se to grow tired
cantar to sing
canto *m.* singing, song
capeador *m.* *bullfighter who waves cape
before bull*
capear *to wave or flourish the cape at the
bull*
capitán *m.* captain
capítulo *m.* chapter
cara *f.* face
¡caracoles! confound it!
¡caramba! confound it!
carcajadas: reír a __ to burst out laughing
cárcel *f.* jail
Carlos *m.* Charles
Carlota *f.* Charlotte
carne *f.* meat
carnicería *f.* butcher store
caro dear, expensive

carrera *f.* course, career; boulevard
carretera *f.* highway
carrito *m.* cart
carta *f.* letter; **a la** __ à la carte
cartel *m.* sign
cartera *f.* brief case, billfold, wallet
cartero *m.* letter carrier
casa *f.* house; **a** __ home; __ **de campo**
country house; __ **de correos** post
office; **en** __ at home; **aquí tienes
tu** __ make yourself at home
casar to marry off; __se **(con)** to marry
caserío *m.* country house
casi almost
casilla de teléfono *f.* telephone booth
caso *m.* case
catarro *m.* cold
catedrático *m.* college professor
catre *m.* cot
causa *f.* cause; **a** __ **de** because of
caza *f.* hunting
cazar to hunt
celebrar to celebrate; __se to take place
célebre celebrated
celos *m. pl.* jealousy; **dar** __ to make
jealous; **tener** __ to be jealous
cena *f.* supper
cenar to eat supper
centavo *m.* cent
centro *m.* center; downtown
cepillar to brush
cerca near(by); __ **de** near
cercano neighboring, nearby
cerrar (ie) to close
certamen *m.* contest
cervecería *f.* brewery
cerveza *f.* beer
cesta *f.* basket
ciencia *f.* science; __ **política** political
science
cien(to) one hundred; **diez por** __ ten
per cent
cigarrillo *m.* cigarette
cinco five
cincuenta fifty
cine *m.* movies
cinematográfico movie
cinta *f.* ribbon
cinturón *m.* belt
circo *m.* circus
cita *f.* date, appointment
ciudad *f.* city
claro clear; of course; __ **está** it is evident; __ **que sí** of course
clase *f.* class, kind; **trabajo de** __ class
work
clásico classical
clima *m.* climate
cobrador *m.* conductor
cocina *f.* kitchen, cooking

cocinar to cook
cocinera *f.* cook
coche *m.* car; en ___ by car
codo *m.* elbow; **hasta los ___s** up to the elbows
coger to catch; ___ **del brazo** to catch by the arm
cojín *m.* cushion
cola *f.* queue *(line of people)*
colchón *m.* mattress
colectivo *m.* bus
colgado hanging
colgar **(ue)** to hang (up)
colina *f.* hill
colmo *m.* overflow, limit; **esto es el ___** this is the limit
colocar to place
comandante *m.* commander
comedia *f.* play, comedy
comedor *m.* dining room
comentar to comment on
comentario *m.* comment
comenzar **(ie)** to begin
comer to eat; ___**se** to eat up; **cosas de ___** things to eat; **dar de ___** to feed
comerciante *m.* merchant
comida *f.* meal, dinner
comité *m.* committee
como as, like; ___ **si** as if; **¡___ no!** of course!
¿cómo? how?
cómodo comfortable
compañero *m.* companion; ___ **de cuarto** room mate
compañía *f.* company
competir to compete
complementario complementary, supplementary
completar to complete
completo complete
composición *f.* composition
compra *f.* purchase; **ir de ___s** to go shopping
comprador *m.* buyer
comprar to buy
comprender to understand; to comprise
con with; ___ **tal que** provided that; ___**migo** with me; ___**tigo** with you; ___**sigo** with (him)self, (her)self, (it)self, (one)self
concepto *m.* concept
concierto *m.* concert
condición *f.* condition, status
condicional *m.* conditional *(tense)*
conducir to conduct; drive
conejo *m.* rabbit
conferencia *f.* lecture
confesar **(ie)** to confess
confianza *f.* confidence
congreso *m.* convention, congress

conmemorar to commemorate
conmigo with me
conocer to know, be acquainted with, meet; ___**se** to meet
conocido well known
conocimiento *m.* knowledge
conseguir to get, obtain; to succeed in
consejero *m.* adviser
consejo *m.* advice *(often used in the plural)*
consentir **(ie, i) (en)** to consent (to)
consigo with (one)self, (him)self, (her)self, (them)selves
consiguiente: por ___ consequently
constitución *f.* constitution
construir to construct
contar **(ue)** to tell, relate; count; ___ **con** to rely on
contemplar to contemplate
contener to contain
contento content, happy
contestar to answer
continuar to continue
contra against
contrario contrary
contribuir to contribute
convencer to convince
convenir to be fitting, suit
conversación *f.* conversation
conversador *m.* "chatter box", conversationalist
conversar to converse
corbata *f.* tie
cordialidad *f.* cordiality; **con ___** cordially
cordillera *f.* mountain range
coro *m.* choir, chorus
corona *f.* crown
correcto correct
correo: casa de ___s post office
correr to run
corrida **(de toros)** *f.* bull fights
cortaplumas *m.* penknife
corto short
cosa *f.* thing
cosecha *f.* crop
coser to sew
costar **(ue)** to cost
costumbre *f.* custom; **como de ___** as usual; **de ___** as usual
creer to believe; **creo que sí** I think so; **___ ¡Ya lo creo!** I should say so!
criada *f.* servant
criado *m.* servant
cristal *m.* windowpane
Cristina *f.* Christine
cruz *f.* cross; ___ **roja** Red Cross
cruzar to cross
cuaderno *m.* notebook; ___ **de apuntes** memorandum book

cuadra *f.* block
cuadro *m.* picture, painting
¿cuál? which? which one?
cualquier(a) any
cuanto all that; **en __** as soon as, when; **__ más . . . tanto más** the more . . . the more; **¿cuánto?** how much?; **¿cuántos?** how many?; **¿cuánto tiempo hace?** how long ago?
cuarto *m.* room; *adj.* fourth; **__ de baño** bathroom
cuatro four
cubierto meal of the day; regular dinner; **__ de** covered with
cubrir to cover
cuello *m.* neck
cuenta *f.* account, bill; **darse __ de** to realize
cuento *m.* story
cuerno *m.* horn
cueva *f.* cave
cuidado *m.* care; **¡cuidado!** take care! **con __** carefully; **tener __** to be careful
cuidar to take care (of)
cultura *f.* culture
cura *f.* cure; *m.* priest
curso *m.* course; **seguir __s** to take courses
cuyo whose

chaleco *m.* vest
chaqueta *f.* jacket, coat
charlar to chat
cheque *m.* check
chica *f.* girl
chico small; *m.* boy; **los __s** the children
chileno Chilean
chimenea *f.* chimney, fireplace
chiste *m.* joke
chófer *m.* chauffeur
choque *m.* collision
chuzos: llover a __ to rain pitchforks

dañado damaged
dar to give; **__ con** to come across; **__ de comer** to feed; **__ un paseo** to take a walk; **__se cuenta de** to realize; **me da lo mismo** it's all the same to me; **__se la mano** to shake hands; **__ una película** to show a picture
datar to date
de of, from, by; **__ modo que** so (that)
debajo de under, beneath, below
deber to owe, ought; **__ de** *plus inf.* must *(indicating probability)*
decano *m.* dean

decidir to decide
decir to say, tell; **__se a sí mismo** to talk to oneself; **es __** that is to say; **querer __** to mean
decisión *f.* decision
decoración *f.* decoration
dedicarse to devote oneself
defender (ie) to defend
definido definite
dejar to leave, let, allow; **__ de** to stop; **no __ de** not to fail to
delante de in front of
deletrear to spell
delgado thin
delito *m.* crime
demasiado too much
democracia *f.* democracy
dentro within, inside
departamento *m.* department
depender de to depend on
dependienta *f.* clerk
dependiente *m.* clerk
deporte *m.* sport
depositar to deposit
derecha: a la __ at (to) the right
derecho right; straight ahead
desayunarse to eat breakfast
desayuno *m.* breakfast
descansar to rest
descolgar (ue) to take down
describir to describe
descubrir to discover
descuento *m.* discount
desde from; since; **__ luego** of course
desear to desire, wish
desfile *m.* parade
desgraciadamente unfortunately
desierto *m.* desert; *adj.* deserted
desilusionado disillusioned
despacio slowly
despacho *m.* office
despedida *f.* farewell; **fiesta de __** going away party
despedir (i) to dismiss; **__se (i) de** to take leave of, say good-bye to
despertador *m.* alarm clock
despertar (ie) to awaken; **__se** wake up
después afterwards; **__ de** after; **__ que** after
destapar to uncork
destrozar to destroy
desván *m.* attic
detener(se) to stop
detrás (de) behind, after; **por __** in back, behind
devolver (ue) to return, give back
día *m.* day; **al __ siguiente** on the following day; **hoy __** nowadays; **por __** per day; **todo el __** all day; **todos**

los __s every day; **buenos** __s good day, good morning

diablo *m.* devil

diálogo *m.* dialogue

diccionario *m.* dictionary

dicha *f.* happiness

Diego *m.* James

diente *m.* tooth

diez ten

diferencia *f.* difference

difícil difficult

dificultad *f.* difficulty

¡diga! hello!

diligencia: con __ diligently

diligentemente diligently

dinero *m.* money

Dios God; **¡por __!** Good Heavens! For Heaven's sake!

diputado *m.* deputy

dirección *f.* address

dirigir to direct

disco *m.* record

disculparse (por) to apologize (for)

discurso *m.* speech

discusión *f.* discussion; argument

discutir to discuss

Disneylandia *f.* Disneyland

distar to be far, distant

distinto different

divertido amusing

divertirse (ie, i) to enjoy oneself, have a good time

doblar to turn

doce twelve

docena *f.* dozen; **la __** a dozen

doctorado *m.* doctor's degree, doctorate

documento *m.* document

dólar *m.* dollar

doler (ue) to ache

dolor *m.* pain; __ **de cabeza** headache

domingo *m.* Sunday

donde where

¿dónde? where?

doña *f. Spanish title used before Christian names of married women or widows*

dormir (ue, u) to sleep; __ **como un tronco** to sleep like a log; __**se** to fall asleep, to sleep

dormitorio *m.* dormitory

dos two

dramatización *f.* dramatization

droguería *f.* drug store

ducha *f.* shower

duda *f.* doubt; **sin __** doubtless

dudar to doubt

dulce sweet; __**s** *m. pl.* candy, sweets

durante during

durar to last

durazno *m.* peach

e and

economía *f.* economy, economics

económico economic, financial

echar to throw, cast away; __ **piropos** to flatter

edad *f.* age; **tener más __** to be older

edición *f.* edition

edificio *m.* edifice, building

Eduardo *m.* Edward

educación *f.* education

ejemplar *m.* copy

ejemplo *m.* example; **por __** for example

ejercicio *m.* exercise

ejército *m.* army

el the, the one

él he, him, it *(m.)*

elegir (i) to elect

Elena *f.* Helen

ella she, her, it *(f.)*

ello it *(n.)*

ellos, −as they, them

embajador *m.* ambassador

emoción *f.* emotion

empezar (ie) to begin

empleado *m.* employee

emplear to employ, use

empleo *m.* job, employment

empujar to push

en in, at, on; __ **cuanto** as soon as

enamorado in love

enamorarse de to fall in love with

enano *m.* dwarf

encaje *m.* lace

encantar to enchant

encargado in charge

encargarse de to take charge of

encender (ie) to light

encima de on top of

encontrar (ue) to find; meet; __**se con** to meet

enemigo *m.* enemy

enero *m.* January

enfermedad *f.* illness

enfermera *f.* nurse

enfermo sick, ill

engañar to deceive

engordar to get fat

enorme enormous

Enrique *m.* Henry

ensalada *f.* salad

ensayo *m.* essay

enseñanza *f.* teaching

enseñar to teach

entender (ie) to understand; **bien entendido** I understand

enterarse de to find out about, learn of, be informed of

entonces then; **en aquel __** at that time

entrada *f.* entrance, admission
entrar (en) to enter
entre between, among; **_ tanto** meanwhile
entregar to deliver, hand over
entretener to entertain
entretenimiento *m.* entertainment
entrevista *f.* interview
entusiasmado enthusiastic
entusiasmo *m.* enthusiasm
enviar to send
época *f.* epoch, time; **en esa _** at that time
equipaje *m.* baggage
equipo *m.* team, equipment
equivocarse to be mistaken
Ernesto *m.* Ernest
escaparate *m.* show window
escaparse to escape
escena *f.* scene
escenario *m.* stage
escoger to choose
escolar *adj.* school
escribir to write
escritor *m.* writer
escuchar to listen (to)
escudero *m.* squire
escuela *f.* school; **_ secundaria** high school; **_ superior** high school
ese *adj.* that
ése *pron.* that one; the former
esforzarse to exert oneself
esfuerzo *m.* effort
eso *pron.* that; **a _ de** at about; **por _** therefore
España *f.* Spain
español *m.* Spanish
esparcir to scatter
especial special
especialización *f.* specialization
especializarse to specialize
especie *f.* kind
espejo *m.* mirror
esperar to hope, wait (for); **_se** to wait
espontáneo spontaneous
esposa *f.* wife
esposo *m.* husband
esquí *m.* ski
esquiar to ski
esquina *f.* corner
establecer to establish
estación *f.* season; station
Estados Unidos *m. pl.* United States
estancia *f.* stay
estante *m.* shelf
estar to be; **está bien** okay, all right
este *adj.* this
éste *pron.* this (one); the latter
Esteban *m.* Stephen

estilo *m.* style; **por el _** of the kind, like that
estimular to stimulate
estómago *m.* stomach
estorbo *m.* hindrance
estrella *f.* star
estudiante *m.* student
estudiantil *adj.* student
estudiar to study
estudio *m.* studio
estudioso studious
estupendo stupendous
estúpido stupid
Europa *f.* Europe
evitar to avoid
exactamente exactly
exagerar to exaggerate
examen *m.* examination
excepto except
excursión *f.* trip, outing
excusa *f.* excuse
existir to exist
experiencia *f.* experience
explicar to explain
explorador *m.* explorer
explotar to exploit
exposición *f.* exhibit
expresar to express
expresión *f.* expression
extranjero foreign
extrañar to surprise
extraordinario extraordinary
extremo *m.* end, side

fabricación *f.* make
fácil easy; **es _** it is easy
fácilmente easily
facturar to check
faena *f.* task; windup *(in bullfighting)*
falda *f.* skirt
falta *f.* mistake; **sin _** without fail; **hacer _** to lack
faltar to be lacking, lack; need, miss
familia *f.* family
famoso famous
farol *m.* light; lantern
fase *f.* phase
favor *m.* favor; **_ de** please; **por _** please; **hacer el _ de** please
favorito favorite
fecha *f.* date
Federico *m.* Frederick
felicitaciones *f. pl.* congratulations
felicitar to congratulate
Felipe *m.* Phillip
feria *f.* fair
fiebre *f.* fever
fiesta *f.* fiesta, festival
figura *f.* figure

figurarse to imagine
fijarse (en) to notice
filosofía *f.* philosophy
fin *m.* end; a __es de at the end of;
al __ finally; con el __ de for the purpose of; por __ finally
finalmente finally
finca *f.* farm
firmar to sign
flor *f.* flower
fondo *m.* background
forma *f.* form
formación *f.* formation
formar to form
fortuna *f.* fortune, luck
foto *f.* photo
fotografía *f.* photograph
fracaso *m.* failure
francamente frankly
francés French
Francia *f.* France
frase *f.* sentence, phrase
fraternidad *f.* fraternity
freno *m.* brake
frente a in front of
fresa *f.* strawberry
fresco cool; hacer __ to be cool
(*weather*); tomar el __ to get some
fresh air
frío *m.* cold; hacer __ to be cold
(*weather*)
frontera *f.* border
fruta *f.* fruit
fuego *m.* fire
fuente *f.* fountain
fuera de outside (of)
fuerte strong
fumar to smoke
función *f.* performance
funda *f.* pillow case
fundación *f.* foundation
fundar to found
fusilar to shoot
fútbol *m.* football; jugar al __ to play
football
futuro *m.* future

gabán *m.* overcoat
gallina *f.* hen
gana *f.* desire; de buena __ gladly;
tener __s de to feel like
ganar to win
ganga *f.* bargain
garaje *m.* garage
garganta *f.* throat
gasolina *f.* gasoline
gasolinera *f.* gas station
gastar to spend
gasto *m.* expense

gata *f.* cat
gaucho *m.* cowboy
generoso generous
gente *f.* people
gerente *m.* manager
gira *f.* tour
glorioso glorious
gobernador *m.* governor
gobierno *m.* government
golondrina *f.* swallow
gordo stout; el premio __ first prize
gozar (de) to enjoy
grabar to record (*a sound, a song, a
phonograph record*)
gracia *f.* joke; ¡qué __! how funny!
gracias thanks
grada *f.* step
grado *m.* degree
graduarse to graduate
gramática *f.* grammar
gran(de) great, large
gripe *f.* grippe
gritar to shout
grupo *m.* group
guante *m.* glove
guardainfante *m.* farthingale
guardar to keep; __ cama to stay in
bed; __ silencio to keep silent
guisante *m.* pea
gustar to like, be pleasing (to)
gusto *m.* taste; pleasure; con mucho __
gladly, with much pleasure; mucho
__ en conocerte glad to meet you;
tener mucho __ en to be pleased to

haber to have; __ de to be to; __ que
(*impersonal*) one must; hay (*imp.*)
there is (are); ¿qué hay? what's up?
habitación *f.* room
hablar to speak
hablador(a) talkative
hacer to do, make; __ calor to be warm;
__ el papel to play the part; __ falta
to lack, need; __ fresco to be cool
(fresh); __ un viaje to take a trip; __
frío to be cold
hacia toward
hacienda *f.* farm, ranch
hacha *f.* ax
hambre *f.* hunger; tener __ to be
hungry
hamburguesa *f.* hamburger
hasta (que) until, up (to); even; __ la
vista until we meet again; __ luego
see you later; __ pronto see you soon
he: __ aquí here is; __lo aquí here it is
hechura *f.* workmanship
hermana *f.* sister

hermano *m.* brother; **__s** brothers, brothers and sisters
hermoso beautiful
hermosura *f.* beauty
hielo *m.* ice
hija *f.* daughter
hijo *m.* son; **__s** children, sons
hispánico Hispanic
Hispanoamérica *f.* Hispanic America
historia *f.* history
histórico historic(al)
hoja *f.* leaf
hola hello
holandés Dutch
holgazán (a) lazy
hombre *m.* man; **¡__!** man alive!
hombro *m.* shoulder
honesto modest, decent
honrar to honor
hora *f.* hour, time; **¿a qué __** at what time?; **(a) la __ de la comida** (at) dinner time; **altas __s** late hours
horario *m.* timetable, schedule
hospedar to lodge
hoy today; **__ día** nowadays
huaraches *m. pl.* *(Am.)* sandals
hueso *m.* bone; **mojado hasta los __s** soaked to the skin
huésped *m.* guest
huevo *m.* egg; **poner __s** to lay eggs
huir to flee
humo *m.* smoke

igualmente the same to you; likewise; the pleasure is mine
imaginarse to imagine
imitar to imitate
impacientarse por to become impatient to
impermeable *m.* raincoat
importancia *f.* importance
importante important
importar to matter, be important
imposible impossible
incendio *m.* fire
incluir to include
incluso including
inconveniente *m.* objection; **tener __ (de)** to have an objection (to)
incorporarse to sit up
indicar to indicate
indio *m.* Indian
indiscreto indiscreet
industria *f.* industry
infierno *m.* hell
informalidad *f.* informality
ingenio *m.* talent, creative faculty; skill
inglés English
ingresar to enter, become a member
inmediatamente immediately

inscribirse to register
insistir to insist
insulto *m.* insult
inteligencia *f.* intelligence
inteligente intelligent
intención *f.* intention; **tener la __ de** to intend
interés *m.* interest; **tener __ (en)** to be interested (in)
interesante interesting
interesar to interest; **__se en** to be interested in
intermedio *m.* intermission
internacional international
interno *m.* intern; **de __** as an intern
interrogativo interrogative
interrumpir to interrupt
intervenir to take part
inundar to flood
investigar to investigate
invierno *m.* winter
invitación *f.* invitation
invitado *m.* guest
invitar to invite
ir to go; **__ de compras** to go shopping; **__se** to go (away); **¡qué va!** of course not!
Italia *f.* Italy
izquierdo left

jabón *m.* soap
jai alai *a Spanish game of Basque origin similar to handball*
jamás ever, never, not . . . ever
jamón *m.* ham
jardín *m.* garden
jefe *m.* chief
jira *f.* tour
Jorge *m.* George
joropo *m.* *Venezuelan dance*
José *m.* Joseph
Josefina *f.* Josephine
joven young; **el __** the young man; **la __** the young lady; **los __es** the youths
Juan *m.* John
Juana *f.* Jane
Juanita *f.* Jane
Judit *f.* Judith
jueves *m.* Thursday
jugador *m.* player
jugar (ue) to play; **__ al béisbol** to play baseball; **__ al fútbol** to play football
jugo *m.* juice
juguete *m.* toy
junio *m.* June
juntar to gather
junto joined, united, together; **__ a** next to
justicia *f.* justice

kilo *m.* kilo (kilogram)
kiosko *m.* kiosk, stand

la the; her; you *(f.);* it *(f.)*
laboratorio *m.* laboratory
lado *m.* side; **al otro __** on the other side
ladrón *m.* thief
lago *m.* lake
lamentar to lament, be sorry
lana *f.* wool
lancha *f.* launch
lanza *f.* lance
lápiz *m.* pencil
largo long; **vestida de __** in a formal dress
lástima *f.* pity
lavandería *f.* laundry
lavar to wash; **__ en seco** to dry clean; **__se** to wash oneself
le him; to him, to her, to you
lección *f.* lesson
lectura *f.* reading
leche *f.* milk
lechuga *f.* lettuce
leer to read
legumbre *f.* vegetable
lejos far; **__ de** far from; **a lo __** in the distance
lengua *f.* language
lentamente slowly
lenteja *f.* lentil
lentísimamente most slowly
lento slow
leña *f.* firewood
levantar to raise, lift; **__se** to get up
ley *f.* law
libertad *f.* liberty
libertar to free
libra *f.* pound
libre free
librería *f.* book store
libro *m.* book
límite *m.* limit
limonada *f.* lemonade
limosna *f.* alms
limpiar to clean
limpieza *f.* cleaning
lindo pretty, fine
línea *f.* line
lisonjero *m.* flatterer
lista *f.* list, menu
listo ready, alert, prepared
literatura *f.* literature
lo it; how; **__ que** that which, what
localidad *f.* seat
Londres London
luego then, later, next; **desde __** of course

lugar *m.* place; **en primer __** in the first place; **tener __** to take place
Luis *m.* Louis
Louisa *f.* Louise
lujo: de __ luxurious
luna *f.* moon; **__ de miel** honeymoon
lunes *m.* Monday; **el __ pasado** last Monday
luz *f.* light

llama *f.* flame
llamar to call, call on; **__ a la puerta** to knock at the door; **__se** to be called
llanta *f.* tire
llave *f.* key
llegada *f.* arrival
llegar to arrive; **__ a ser** to get to be, become
llenar to fill
llevar to carry, take, be, bear, wear; **__se** to carry off, take away
llover (ue) to rain; **__ a chuzos** to rain pitchforks
lluvia *f.* rain; **días de __** rainy days

madre *f.* ·mother
maduro ripe, mature
maestro *m.* teacher
magnífico magnificent
mal badly
maleta *f.* valise; **hacer las __s** to pack the bags
malo bad; ill; **hacer mal tiempo** to be bad weather; **lo __** the bad part
mamá mother
mandar to send, order
manejar to drive
manera *f.* manner, way; **de ninguna __** by no means; **de otra __** otherwise
manifestación *f.* demonstration
mano *f.* hand
mantequilla *f.* butter
manzana *f.* apple
mañana tomorrow; *(f.)* morning; **__ por la __** tomorrow morning; **hasta __** see you tomorrow; **pasado __** day after tomorrow; **todas las __s** every morning
mapa *m.* map
maquillaje *m.* make up
máquina *f.* machine, engine; **__ de escribir** typewriter
mar *m.* sea
marcha: ponerse en __ to start
marcharse to go away, leave
Margarita *f.* Margaret
María *f.* Mary
marido *m.* husband
marina *f.* navy
marqués *m.* marquis
Marta *f.* Martha

más more, most; **¿qué __?** what else?
matador *m.* killer of bulls
matar to kill
Mateo *m.* Matthew
materia *f.* subject
Matilde *f.* Matilda
matricular(se) to register, enroll
Maximiliano *m.* Maximilian
mayordomo *m.* majordomo
mayoría *f.* majority
media *f.* stocking
medicina *f.* medicine
médico *m.* doctor
medida *f.* measure; **hecho a la __** made to order; **a __ que** while, as
medio half
mediodía midday; **al __** at noon
mejor better, best
mejorar to improve, get better
mencionar to mention
menina *f.* maid of honor *(at court)*
menor younger, youngest
menos less, except
mentir (ie, i) to lie
mentira *f.* lie
menudo: a __ often
mercado *m.* market
mercancía *f.* merchandise
merecer to merit, deserve
mes *m.* month; **el __ pasado** last month; **el __ que viene** next month
mesa *f.* table, desk; **poner la __** to set the table
mesera *f.* waitress
meter to put; **__se a** to plunge into; **¿en dónde te has metido?** where have you been?
mexicano Mexican
mi my
mí me
miedo *m.* fear; **tener __ de** to be afraid of
miel *f.* honey; **luna de __** honeymoon
miembro *m.* member
mientras while; **__ tanto** meanwhile
miércoles *m.* Wednesday
Miguel *m.* Michael
mil thousand
milla *f.* mile
minuto *m.* minute; **a los pocos __s** after (in) a few minutes
mío mine, of mine
mirar to look at
misión *f.* mission
mismo self, same; **ahora __** right now; **lo __** the same (thing); **me da lo __** it's all the same to me
moda *f.* fashion
modelo *m.* model
moderno modern

modismo *m.* idiom
modo *m.* mode, manner; **de __ que** so that; **de ningún __** by no means; **de todos __s** in any event
mojado wet; **__ hasta los huesos** soaked to the skin
molestar to bother
momento *m.* moment
moneda *f.* money; coin
monja *f.* nun
montado mounted
montaña *f.* mountain
montar a caballo to go horseback riding
montera *f.* cap
monumento *m.* monument
morir (ue, u) to die
mosca *f.* fly
mostrador *m.* counter
mostrar (ue) to show
motivo *m.* motive; **con __ de** for the purpose of, in order to
mozo *m.* boy, waiter
muchacha *f.* girl
muchacho *m.* boy
mucho much, a great deal
muebles *m. pl.* furniture
muerte *f.* death
mujer *f.* woman, wife
mula *f.* mule
mundo *m.* world; **todo el __** everybody
museo *m.* museum
música *f.* music
muy very

nacimiento *m.* birth
nación *f.* nation
nada nothing, not . . . anything; at all; **ni __ de eso** nor anything like that
nadar to swim
nadie no one, nobody, not any one
naranja *f.* orange
navegante *m.* navigator
Navidad *f.* Christmas
necesario necessary; **lo __** what's necessary, the necessary thing
necesitar to need
negar (ie) to deny
negativo negative
neófito *m.* neophyte
nevar (ie) to snow
ni neither, nor
nido *m.* nest
nieto *m.* grandchild
nieve *f.* snow
ninguno no, none, not any, neither one
niña *f.* child
niño *m.* child
nivel *m.* level
no no, not

noche *f.* night, evening; **esta __** tonight; **por la __** in the evening; **toda la __** all night; **buenas __s** good evening; **todas las __s** every night
nombrar to name
nombre *m.* name
Norteamérica *f.* North America
norteamericano North American
nosotros, –as we, us
nostalgia *f.* nostalgia, homesickness
nota *f.* grade; **sacar buenas __s** to get good grades
notar to note
noticia *f.* news
noticiario *m.* news(reel)
novela *f.* novel
novia *f.* sweetheart
novio *m.* boy friend
nube *f.* cloud
nuestro our
Nueva York New York
nuevamente again
nueve nine
nuevo new; **¿qué hay de __?** what's new?
número *m.* number
nunca never, not . . . ever

o either, or
obedecer to obey
objeto *m.* object
obra *f.* work
observar to observe
obstante: no __ nevertheless
obtener to obtain
océano *m.* ocean
ocio *m.* leisure
ocioso idle
Octavio *m.* Octavius
octubre October
oculista *m. or f.* oculist
ocupado busy
ocurrir to occur
ochenta eighty
ocho eight
oferta *f.* offer
oficial *m.* officer
oficina *f.* office
ofrecer to offer
oír to hear, listen to; **__ decir** to hear it said
ojalá (que) would that, I wish that!
ojo *m.* eye; **¡mucho __!** watch out!
olvidar to forget
olvidarse (de) to forget
ómnibus *m.* bus
once eleven
oponerse a to oppose
oportunidad *f.* opportunity

orden *f.* order *(command);* *m.* order *(of a series)*
ordenar to order
ordinario: de __ ordinarily
organizar to organize
orquesta *f.* orchestra
oscuro dark, black
oso *m.* bear
otoño *m.* autumn, fall
otro other, another
oveja *f.* sheep

Pablo *m.* Paul
Pacífico *m.* Pacific
padre *m.* father; *pl.* parents
paella: __ a la valenciana *f.* Valencian dish: meat, vegetables, and fish cooked with rice
pagar to pay (for)
página *f.* page
país *m.* country
paisaje *m.* landscape
pajar *m.* hay loft
pájaro *m.* bird
palabra *f.* word
palacio *m.* palace
pálido pale
paliza *f.* whipping; **sufrir una __** to get a whipping
pan *m.* bread, loaf of bread
panamericano Pan American
pantalón *m.* trouser
pañuelo *m.* handkerchief
papa *f.* potato
papá *m.* father
papel *m.* paper; role; **hacer el __** to play the part
paquete *m.* package
par *m.* pair
para for, by, in order to, to; **__ que** in order that; **¿__ qué?** why? what for?
paraguas *m.* umbrella
parar(se) to stop
parecer to seem, think; **a mi __** in my opinion; **¿qué te parece?** what do you think of?
pared *f.* wall
pareja *f.* couple
paréntesis *f.* parenthesis
pariente *m.* relative
parque *m.* park; **__ zoológico** zoo
participar to participate
partido *m.* match, game
partir to depart
pasado past, passed, last; **__ mañana** day after tomorrow
pasajero *m.* passenger
pasar to pass, spend, enter, happen, come in

pasearse to take a walk
paseo *m.* walk; **dar un** — to take a walk
pasillo *m.* corridor, hall
pastel *m.* pie, pastry
pastilla *f.* bar
pastor *m.* shepherd
patinar to skate
patrona *f.* landlady
payaso *m.* clown
paz *f.* peace
pedir (i) to ask (for), order; — **prestado** to borrow
Pedro *m.* Peter
peinarse to comb one's hair
peine *m.* comb
peinilla *f.* small comb
película *f.* picture, movie; **dar una** — to show a picture
pelo *m.* hair
peluquería *f.* barbershop
pena *f.* pain, grief; **valer la** — to be worth while
pensamiento *m.* thought
pensar (ie) to think; — **en** to think of; — *(plus inf.)* to intend
pensión *f.* boarding house ·
peor worse, worst
Pepe *m.* Joe
pequeño small
percha *f.* rack
perder (ie) to lose
perdonar to pardon
perfectamente perfectly
perfecto perfect
periódico *m.* newspaper
periodista *m. or f.* reporter
periquillo *m.* little parrot
permanecer to remain
permitir to permit
pero but
perro *m.* dog
persona *f.* person
pertenecer to belong
pesar: a — **de** in spite of
pescado *m.* fish *(that has been caught)*
pescar to fish, "catch"
peseta *f.* peseta *(Spanish monetary unit)*
peso *f.* *Mexican coin corresponding roughly to the American dollar*
picador *m.* picador *(mounted bullfighter who thrusts a goad into the bull)*
picardía *f.* (a bit of) knavery, mischief
picarón *m.* rascal, sharper
pico *m.* peak
pie *m.* foot
pino *m.* pine tree
pintar to paint
pintor *m.* painter
pintoresco picturesque
pintura *f.* painting, picture

piña *f.* pineapple
piropo *m.* compliment; **echar** —**s** to flatter
piscina *f.* swimming pool
piso *m.* floor
pistola *f.* pistol
pizarra *f.* blackboard
planchar to iron
planta *f.* plant
plata *f.* silver, money
plática *f.* talk, chat
plato *m.* plate, dish
playa *f.* beach
plaza *f.* plaza; — **de toros** bullring
pleno full; **en** — **verano** at the height of the summer
pluma *f.* pen, feather
pluscuamperfecto *m.* pluperfect
pobre poor, without money *(after noun)*; unfortunate *(before noun)*
pobrecito *m.* poor fellow
poco little; —**s** few; **en** — **tiempo** in a short time
poder can, be able; **a más no** — to the utmost; **no** — **más** not to be able to do more, cannot but give up; **no** — **menos de** not to be able to help
poema *m.* poem
poesía *f.* poetry
policía *f.* police
político political
polvo *m.* powder, dust
pollo *m.* chicken; **arroz con** — chicken with rice
poner to put (on); to make; to play; to set; to send; — **huevos** to lay eggs; —**se** to become *(plus adj.)*, to put on; —**se en marcha** to start
por for, by, along, through, of, per; — **aquí** around here; — **ciento** percent; **¿por qué?** why?; **porque** because
porción *f.* portion
porque because
¿por qué? why?
portarse to behave
portugués Portuguese
posible possible
postal *f.* post card
postre *m.* dessert
potencial *m.* conditional
práctica *f.* practice
práctico practical
precio *m.* price
precioso precious
preciso: ser — to be necessary
preferir (ie, i) to prefer
pregunta *f.* question; **hacer una** — to ask a question
preguntar to ask *(a question)*

premio *m.* prize; **el __ gordo** first prize
prender to catch
preocupar to preoccupy, worry; **__se (por)** to worry (about)
preparar to prepare
preparativo *m.* preparation
presencia *f.* presence
presentar to present; **__ un examen** to take an exam
presidente *m.* president
prestado: pedir __ to borrow
prestar to lend
pretérito *m.* preterit; **__ anterior** preterit perfect
prima *f.* cousin
primero first; **en primer lugar** in the first place; **por primera vez** for the first time
primo *m.* cousin
princesa *f.* princess
prisa *f.* haste; **de __** quickly, hurriedly
prisionero *m.* prisoner
privilegiado privileged
probabilidad *f.* probability
probar (ue) to prove
probarse (ue) to try on
problema *m.* problem
producir to produce
profesor *m.* teacher
profesora *f.* teacher
programa *m.* program
prohibir to forbid, prohibit
prometer to promise
pronombre *m.* pronoun
pronto soon, quickly; **tan __ como** as soon as
pronunciar to pronounce, deliver
propina *f.* tip
propio own, same
proponerse to propose
propósito *m.* plan; **a __** by the way
proteger to protect
próximo next
proyección *f.* slide
proyecto *m.* project
prueba *f.* proof, test
publicar to publish
pueblecito *m.* small town
pueblo *m.* people, town
pues well, since, as
puesto *m.* position; **__ que** since
pulsera *f.* bracelet
puma *f.* puma, cougar
punto *m.* point; **en __** exactly, on the dot; **estar a __ de** to be on the point of

que that, what, which, who; than
¿qué? what? which? **¡__!** how! what! what a! **¿__ tal?** how are you? **¡__ va!** of course not; **¿__ más?** what else?

quedar(se) to stay, remain, be; **__se con** to take
quehacer *m.* chore
querer to wish, want; to love; to try *(in preterit tense)*; to refuse *(in negative preterit)*; **__ decir** to mean
querido dear
¿quién? who?; **¿de __?** whose?
química *f.* chemistry
quince fifteen; **__ días** two weeks
quinto fifth
quitar to remove, take *(away from)*; **__se** to take off

ramillete *m.* bouquet
rápido rapid, fast
rato *m.* while
raza *f.* race
razón *f.* reason; **tener __** to be right
real royal
recado *m.* message
receptor *m.* receiver
receptoría *f.* (reception) desk
receta *f.* prescription
recibir to receive
recibo *m.* receipt
recién recent; **__ llegado** newly arrived; **__ venido** *m.* newcomer
recientemente recently
recitar to recite
recoger to pick up
reconocer to recognize
recordar (ue) to remember, remind, recall
recuerdo *m.* souvenir
reemplazar to replace, substitute
referirse (ie, i) to refer
refrán *m.* proverb, saying
refrenar to curb, check, restrain
refresco *m.* refreshment
regalar to give
regalo *m.* gift
regatear to haggle
regla *f.* rule; **por __ general** as a general rule
regresar to return
rehusar to refuse
reina *f.* queen
reír to laugh; **__ a carcajadas** to burst out laughing; **__se de** to laugh at
reloj *m.* watch
remar to row
remedio *m.* remedy, help; **no hay __** it can't be helped
rendición *f.* surrender
rendido tired, worn out
renombre *m.* renown
renta *f.* rent
repasar to review

repaso *m.* review
repetir (i) to repeat
representante *m.* representative
representar to represent, perform
requisito *m.* requisite
residencia *f.* dormitory
resolver (ue) to solve
respeto *m.* respect
restorán *m.* restaurant
resultado *m.* result
resultar to prove to be, turn out to be
retirarse to retire, withdraw
reunión *f.* meeting
reunir to gather, raise (money); __se
to meet
revista *f.* magazine
revolución *f.* revolution
revuelto scrambled
rey *m.* king; reyes *m. pl.* king and
queen
riachuelo *m.* streamlet
Ricardo *m.* Richard
rico rich
rincón *m.* corner
río *m.* river
robar to rob, steal
Roberto *m.* Robert
robo *m.* robbery
Rodrigo *m.* Roderick
rogar (ue) to beg
rojo red
romper to break, tear
ropa *f.* clothing; __ interior underwear
rosa *f.* rose
roto broken, torn
rucio *m.* silver-gray
ruido *m.* noise
rumbo a in the direction of
ruso Russian
ruta *f.* route

sábado *m.* Saturday
sábana *f.* sheet
saber to know, know how, learn; to
find out *(in preterit)*
sabroso tasty
sacar to take out; __ buenas notas to
get good grades; __ la cabeza por la
ventanilla to stick one's head out the
window
sala *f.* living room
salir to leave, come out, go out; __ bien
en el examen to pass the exam;
__ mal en el examen to fail the exam
salón *m.* room, hall; __ de baile ball-
room
salsa *f.* dressing
saltar to jump; __ a la vista to come
into view, to be obvious
salud *f.* health

saludable healthful
saludar to greet
salvavidas *m.* lifeguard
san(to) saint
sangre *f.* blood
sarape *m.* blanket
sarcásticamente sarcastically
sarniento *m.* itching
sastrería *f.* tailor shop
satisfecho satisfied
se one, oneself, yourself, himself, herself, itself, themselves
secar to dry
sección *f.* section
seco dry; lavado en __ dry cleaned
secretaria *f.* secretary
secundario secondary; escuela secundaria high school
sed *f.* thirst; tener __ to be thirsty
seda *f.* silk
seguida: en __ at once
seguir (i) to continue, follow; __ cursos
to take courses
según according to (what)
segundo *m.* second
seguro sure
seis six
selección *f.* selection
sello *m.* stamp
semana *f.* week; a la __ weekly; la __
pasada last week; la __ que viene
next week; por __ per week; todas
las __ every week
semestre *m.* semester
sencillo simple, easy
sendero *m.* path
sentado seated, sitting
sentar (ie) to seat; fit, become; __se to
sit down
sentir (ie, i) to regret, be sorry; to feel;
__se to feel
señalar to point out
señor *m.* Mr., gentleman, sir
señora *f.* Mrs., madam, lady
señorita *f.* Miss, young lady
separar to separate, reserve
septiembre September
séptimo seventh
ser to be; llegar a __ to become; __ que
to be the fact
serio serious
serpiente *f.* serpent
servicio *m.* service
servilleta *f.* napkin
servir (i) to serve; ¿en qué puedo servirle? what can I do for you?; ¿para
qué sirve? what's it good for?
sesenta sixty
sesión *f.* session
setenta seventy

si if
sí yes; indeed; yourself, himself, herself, oneself
siempre always
sierra *f.* sierra, jagged mountain range
siete seven
siglo *m.* century
significado *m.* significance
siguiente following
silencio *m.* silence; **guardar __** to keep silent
silla *f.* chair
simpático friendly, nice
sin without; **__ que** without; **__ duda** without doubt
sinfónico symphonic
sino but, except; **__ que** but
sinopsis *f.* synopsis
sinvergüenza *m. or f.* rascal
sitio *m.* site, place
situación *f.* situation
smoking *m.* tuxedo
sobra: de __ more than enough
sobre *m.* envelope; *prep.* on, above; about, concerning; **__ todo** above all, especially; **__ manera** exceedingly, beyond measure
sobresaliente distinguished *(in an examination)*
sobrina *f.* niece
sobrino *m.* nephew
sociedad *f.* society
socio *m.* member
sol *m.* sun; **hacer (haber) __** to be sunny
soldado *m.* soldier
solicitar to solicit, ask for
solo alone, lonely
sólo only
sombra *f.* shadow; **a la __ de** in the shade of
sombrerera *f.* hatbox
sombrerería *f.* hat shop
sombrero *m.* hat
sonar (ue) to sound, ring
sopa *f.* soup
sororidad *f.* sorority
sorprender to surprise
sorpresa *f.* surprise
sospechar to suspect
su your, his, her, its, their
suavizar to ease
subir to go up, ascend, bring up, come up, get into, get ahead
subjuntivo *m.* subjunctive
sublevación *f.* uprising
subrayar to underline
suceder to happen
sucio soiled
Sud América *f.* South America
sueldo *m.* salary

suelo *m.* ground, floor
suerte *f.* luck
sufrir to suffer
sugerencia *f.* suggestion
sugerir (ie, i) to suggest
sujeto *m.* subject
supermercado *m.* supermarket
suponer to suppose
sustantivo *m.* noun
sustituir to substitute
susto *m.* fright, scare
suyo his, hers, its, yours, theirs

tal such(a); **con __ que** provided that; **¿__ qué?** how are you? how was?
taller *m.* studio
también also
tampoco neither, not . . . either
tanto, -a so much; **por lo tanto** therefore
tantos, -as so many
tardar en to be long in
tarde *f.* afternoon; **por la __** in the afternoon; **buenas __s** good afternoon; **todas las __s** every afternoon; *adv.* late; **más __** later
tarea *f.* task
tarjeta *f.* card; **__ postal** postcard
tauromaquia *f.* art of bullfighting
taza *f.* cup
te you, to you
té *m.* tea
teatral theatrical
teatro *m.* theater
tejado *m.* roof
Tejas Texas
tela *f.* cloth
telefonear to telephone
teléfono *m.* telephone
telegrama *m.* telegram; **poner un __** to send a telegram
tema *m.* theme
temblar to shake
temer to fear
temperatura *f.* temperature
temporada *f.* season
temprano early
tender to stretch out
tener to have; **__ celos** to be jealous; **__ hambre** to be hungry; **__ inconveniente (de)** to have an objection (to); **__ lugar** to take place; **__ miedo** to be afraid; **__ que** to have to; **__ razón** to be right
tenis *m.* tennis
Teodoro *m.* Theodore
tercero third
terminar to end, finish
terraza *f.* terrace
terremoto *m.* earthquake

tertulia *f.* evening party

tía *f.* aunt

tiempo *m.* time; tense; weather; **a __** on (in) time; **en poco __** in a short time; **hacer mal __** to be bad weather

tienda *f.* shop, store; tent

tierra *f.* land, earth

tintorería *f.* dry cleaning establishment

tío *m.* uncle; **__s** aunt and uncle

tirar to throw

título *m.* title

toalla *f.* towel

tocadiscos *m.* record player

tocar to touch; to play *(an instrument)*

todo all, everything; **__ el año** all year; **__ el mundo** everybody; **__ el día** all day; **__s los días** every day

tomar to take; **__ el fresco** to get some fresh air

Tomás *m.* Thomas

tomate *m.* tomato

torear to fight bulls

toreo *m.* bull fight(ing)

torero *m.* bullfighter

toril *m.* bullpen

toro *m.* bull

torre *f.* tower

tortilla *f.* *(Am.)* corn meal cake

trabajador hardworking

trabajar to work

trabajo *m.* work; **__ de clase** classroom work

traducir to translate

traer to bring

tráfico *m.* traffic

trago *m.* swallow, swig

traje *m.* suit, costume

tránsito *m.* traffic

transporte *m.* transportation

tranvía *m.* streetcar

trasladarse to move

trasquilado shorn

tratar to handle; deal with; treat; **__ de** to treat of, deal with; to try to *(plus inf.)*; **__se de** to be a question of

treinta thirty

tremendo, –da tremendous

tren *m.* train

tres three

trigo *m.* wheat

triste sad

tronco *m.* trunk *(of a tree)*; **dormir como un __** to sleep like a log

tu you

turismo *m.* tourism; **agencia de __** tourist agency

turista *m. or f.* tourist

tuyo yours, of yours

¡uf! whew!

úlcera *f.* ulcer

último last, latest

único only, sole; **lo __** the only thing; **los __s** the only ones

unido united

universidad *f.* university

universitario *adj.* university

un(o) one, a, an; **unos** some, a few, several

usar to use

usted you; **__es** you *(pl.)*; *(abbreviated* **Ud., Uds., Vd., Vds., V., VV.)**

usualmente usually

útil useful

uva *f.* grape

vaca *f.* cow

vacaciones *f. pl.* vacation(s); **estar de __** to be on vacation

vaivén *m.* motion

valenciano Valencian

valer to be worth; **__ la pena** to be worth while

valeroso valient

valija *f.* valise

valioso valuable

valle *m.* valley

vano vain

vapor *m.* steamship; **por __** by steamship

varios various, several

vaso *m.* glass

veinte twenty

veintidós twenty-two

veintitrés twenty-three

velocidad *f.* speed

vencedor *m.* conqueror

vencer to conquer

vendedor *m.* seller

vender to sell

Venecia Venice

venezolano Venezuelan

venir to come

ventaja *f.* advantage

ventana *f.* window

ver to see; **a __** let's see

verano *m.* summer; **el __ que viene** next summer

verbo *m.* verb

verdad *f.* truth; **¿__?** true? isn't it so?

verdadero true, real

vergüenza *f.* shame

verso *m.* verse

vestido *m.* dress

vestir (i) to dress; **__se de** to dress in, wear

vez *f.* time; **alguna que otra __** sometimes; **en __ de** in place of; **otra __** again; **por primera __** for the first time; **una __** once; **una __ por semana** once a week; **muchas veces** often

viajar to travel

viaje *m.* trip; **hacer un** __ to take a trip
vibración *f.* vibration
vida *f.* life
vidrio *m.* glass
viejo old
viento *m.* wind
viernes *m.* Friday
vino *m.* wine
visita *f.* visit
visitar to visit
víspera *f.* eve, day before
vista *f.* view; **hasta la** __ until we meet again
viuda *f.* widow
vivir to live

vocabulario *m.* vocabulary
volar (ue) to fly
volver (ue) to return
vuelo *m.* flight
vuelta *f.* change; **dar una** __ to take a walk

y and
ya already; __ **que** since
yo I

zapato *m.* shoe
zigzaguear to zigzag
zoológico zoological; **parque** __ zoo

• ENGLISH–SPANISH

a un, una
able: to be __ poder (ue)
absent ausente
ache doler (ue)
accompany acompañar
according to según
account: on __ **of** por
addition: in __ además
advise aconsejar
afraid: to be __ temer, tener miedo
after después de *(prep.)*; después que *(conj.)*
afternoon tarde *f.;* **this** __ esta tarde
afterwards después
again otra vez
age edad *f.*
aged viejo
ago: a week __ hace ocho días, hace una semana; **an hour** __ hace una hora; **fifteen minutes** __ hace quince minutos; **three years** __ hace tres años; **two days** __ hace dos días
agree convenir en, estar de acuerdo con
airplane avión *m.*
all todo; **at** __ alguno *(after a negative)*, nada *(after a negative);* __ **day** todo el día; __ **that** todo lo que, cuanto
also también
always siempre
amaze asombrar
American norteamericano
Andalusian andaluz
angry enfadado; **to become** __ enfadarse, ponerse enfadado
another otro

answer contestar, responder; contestación, respuesta *f.*
any algun(o), cualquier(a); ningun(o) *(after a negative);* __ **one (body),** alguien, alguno, nadie *(after a negative)*
anyone alguien, nadie *(with negative)*
anything nada *(with negative)*
appointment cita *f.*
approach acercarse (a)
argue argüir, disputar
arm brazo *m.*
around alrededor de; a eso de *(time);* __ **here** por aquí
arrange arreglar
arrive llegar
art arte *m. or f.*
artist artista *m. or f.*
as como; **as . . . as** tan . . . como; __ **soon** __ luego que, tan pronto como; __ **much** __ tanto como; __ **many** tantos como; __ **if** como si; __ **usual** (como) de costumbre
ask preguntar *(question);* pedir (i) *(request)*
at a, en; __ **a distance** a lo lejos; __ **once** en seguida; __ **that moment** en aquel momento; __ **all** alguno *(after a negative);* nada *(after a negative);* __ **about** *(referring to time)* a eso de; __ **that time** en aquel entonces
athlete atleta *m. or f.*
attend asistir (a)
aunt tía *f.;* __ **and uncle** tíos *m. pl.*
author autor *m.*
avenue avenida *f.*
Aztec azteca

bad mal(o)
be ser, estar; **to __ to** haber de (*plus inf.*); **to __ in favor of** estar por; **to __ sure** estar seguro
beach playa *f.*
beautiful bonito, hermoso
because porque; **__ of** por, a causa de
become ponerse (*plus adj.*); llegar a ser (*plus noun*)
bed cama *f.*; **to go to __** acostarse (ue); **to put to __** acostar (ue); **in __** en la cama
before antes de (*prep.*); antes que (*conj.*)
begin empezar (ie) a
behalf: on __ of por, en nombre de
behind detrás (de)
believe creer
besides además de
best mejor; **the __ thing** lo mejor
between entre
big grande
bill cuenta *f.*
blackboard pizarra *f.*
blind ciego
blond rubio *m.*; **__e** rubia *f.*
board pizarra *f.*
book libro *m.*
border frontera *f.*
boring cansado, aburrido
born: be __ nacer
boy muchacho *m.*
Brazil Brasil *m.*
bread pan *m.*
break romper(se)
bring traer; **__ down** bajar; **__ up** subir
broken roto; **__ down** descompuesto
brother hermano *m.*
brunette morena
build construir
building edificio *m.*
bus colectivo, autobús
businessman hombre de negocios *m.*
but pero, sino (que)
buy comprar
by por, de, para

call llamar
can *v.* poder (ue)
capital capital *f.* (*of a country*); capital *m.* (*money*)
car coche *m.*
card postal *f.*; tarjeta *f.*
carefully cuidadosamente, con cuidado
carelessly descuidadosamente, sin cuidado
catch coger; **__ by the arm** coger del brazo
cathedral catedral *f.*
cent centavo *m.*
ceramics cerámica *f.*

certain cierto
Charles Carlos
cheer alegrar
chief jefe *m.*
child niña *f.*; niño *m.*
church iglesia *f.*
city ciudad *f.*
class(room) clase *f.*; **in __** en la clase
clean limpiar
clearly claramente
clerk dependiente *m.*, dependienta *f.*
close cerrar(se) (ie)
coat abrigo *m.*
coffee café *m.*
cold frío; **to be __** tener frío (*persons*); hacer frío (*weather*)
collision choque *m.*
come venir; **__ in** entrar, pasar
complete completar
confess confesar (ie)
consent consentir (ie, i) (en)
construct construir
continue continuar, seguir
contrary contrario
convince convencer
cook cocinero *m.*; cocinera *f.*; *inf.* cocinar
corner rincón *m.* (*inside*); esquina *f.* (*outside*)
cost costar (ue)
council consejo *m.*; **student __** consejo estudiantil
count contar (ue)
country campo *m.*; país *m.*
course curso *m.*; **of __** claro que sí, por supuesto
cousin primo *m.*; prima *f.*
cover (with) cubrir (de)
covered cubierto
cow vaca *f.*
cross atravesar, cruzar
crowd multitud *f.*; gentío *m.*
Cuban cubano

dare atreverse (a)
daughter hija *f.*
day día *m.*; **all __** todo el día; **every __** todos los días; **on the following __** al día siguiente
dead muerto
deceive engañar
decide decidir(se)
dentist dentista *m.*
deserve merecer
desk escritorio *m.*; mesa *f.*
dictionary diccionario *m.*
die morir (ue, u)
difficult difícil
dining room comedor *m.*

dinner comida *f.;* **at __ time** a la hora de la comida
discover descubrir
distance distancia *f.;* **in the __** a lo lejos
distinctly distintamente
do hacer
doctor médico *m.*
document documento *m.*
dollar dólar *m.*
door puerta *f.*
doubt duda *f.;* **without __** sin duda; *inf.* dudar
dress vestido *m.*
drink beber
drive conducir
drop caerse, dejar caer

each cada; **__ other** se
ear oreja *f.;* oído *m.*
earn ganar
easy fácil
eat comer; **__ up** comerse; **__ing** el comer
egg huevo *m.*
either o; **__ . . . or** o . . . o; tampoco *(after a negative)*
elect elegir (i)
end terminar, acabar
enjoy gozar de; **__ oneself** divertirse (ie, i)
enter entrar (en)
entire entero, todo
escape escapar(se)
Europe Europa *f.*
even if aunque
ever jamás, nunca *(after a negative or comparative)*
every cada, todos los; **__body** todos; **__ day** todos los días, cada día; **__thing American** todo lo americano
eye ojo *m.*
example ejemplo *m.;* **for __** por ejemplo
examination examen *m.*
examine examinar
excellent excelente
except excepto
exchange cambiar; **in __ for** por, en cambio de
exhibition exposición, exhibición *f.*
expensive caro
explain explicar
eye ojo *m.*

fail salir mal en; **not to __ to** no dejar de
fair feria *f.*
fall caer
false falso
family familia *f.*
famous famoso
far lejos (de)

farm finca *f.*
fast rápido
fat gordo
father padre *m.*
favor: be in __ of estar por
feed dar de comer
feel sentirse (ie, i)
few pocos, pocas; cuantos, cuantas; unos, unas
fifteen quince
fifth quinto
fill (with) llenar (de)
find encontrar (ue), hallar; **__ out** enterarse de
finish terminar
first primer(o); **in the __ place** en primer lugar; **at __** al principio
fish pez *m. (live);* pescado *m. (out of water)*
five cinco
floor suelo *m.*
fly volar (ue)
folkloric folklórico
foot pie *m.*
for por, para
forbid prohibir
foreigner extranjero *m.*
forest bosque *m.*
forget olvidar(se) (de)
forty cuarenta
fountain fuente *f.*
four cuatro
French francés *m.*
frequently frecuentemente, con frecuencia
fresh fresco
Friday viernes *m.*
fried frito; **__ potatoes** papas fritas
friend amigo *m.;* **__ly** simpático
from de, desde, a
fruit fruta *f.*
funny: how __! ¡qué gracia!
furniture *(piece of furniture)* mueble *m.; otherwise pl.* muebles

game juego *m.;* partida *f.*
generally generalmente
George Jorge
German alemán
get conseguir; **__ good grades** sacar buenas notas; **__ to be** llegar a ser; **__ up** levantarse; **__ (someone) up** levantar; **__ married** casarse
gift regalo *m.*
girl muchacha, chica *f.*
give dar; **__ up** no poder más
glad: be __ (to) alegrarse (de)
go ir; **__ away** irse, marcharse; **__ to bed** acostarse (ue); **__ down(stairs)** bajar; **__ out** salir

God Dios
gold oro *m.;* **to be made of** ___ ser de oro
good buen(o)
grade nota *f.;* **to receive good** ___s sacar buenas notas
grandfather abuelo *m.*
grapefruit toronja *f.*
grass hierba *f.*
gravely gravemente
great grande; **a** ___ **deal** mucho
green verde
greet saludar
group groupo *m.*
gym gimnasio *m.*

half medio
hall pasillo *m.*
hand mano *f.*
handkerchief pañuelo *m.*
handsome guapo
hang colgar (ue)
happen pasar, ocurrir, suceder
happiness felicidad *f.*
happy alegre, contento; **to be** ___ alegrarse (de)
hat sombrero *m.*
have tener; haber *(auxiliary):* ___ **just** acabar de; ___ **time** tener tiempo; ___ **to** tener que *(plus inf.)*
he él
head cabeza *f.;* ___ **for** ir para
hear oír, oír decir
heavy pesado
Helen Elena
help ayudar; **it couldn't be helped** no había remedio
her la *(dir. obj.);* le *(indir. obj.);* ella; su(s), suyo (–a, –os, –as); de ella *(obj. of prep.)*
here aquí; **around** ___ por aquí
high alto
high school escuela superior *f.*
highway carretera *f.*
him le, lo *(dir. obj.);* le *(indir. obj.);* él
his su(s), suyo (–a, –os, –as); de él *(obj. of prep.)*
home (a) casa; **at** ___ en casa
hope esperar
horribly horriblemente
horse caballo *m.;* ___**back riding** montar a caballo
hour hora *f.*
house casa *f.*
how cómo, ¿cómo? ¡cuánto!; ___ **much?** ¿cuánto?; ___ **many?** ¿cuántos?
hundred cien(to)
hungry: to be ___ tener hambre

I yo
ice cream helado *m.*

idea idea *f.*
idol ídolo *m.*
if si
ill enfermo
illusion ilusión *f.*
imagine figurarse, imaginarse
impatient: to be ___ **to** impacientarse por
impressive impresionante
in, into en, a, de *(after a superlative);* ___ **addition (to)** además (de); ___ **time** a tiempo
including incluso
industrious aplicado
inform informar
insist insistir (en), empeñarse (en)
instructor profesor *m.;* profesora *f.*
intelligent inteligente
interesting interesante
interrupt interrumpir
investigation investigación *f.*
invitation invitación *f.*
it él, ella, ello, lo, la *(usually omitted as subject pronoun)*
its su, sus

James Jaime, Diego
Japanese japonés
John Juan
joke chiste *m.*
jump saltar
justice justicia *f.*

kill matar
kind amable
know *(how)* saber; *(be acquainted with)* conocer

lady mujer, señora, *f.;* **young** ___ señorita *f.*
large grande
last último, pasado; ___ **week** la semana pasada; ___ **month** el mes pasado; ___ **year** el año pasado
late tarde; ___**r** más tarde, después; **see you** ___**r** hasta luego
lawyer abogado *m.*
lazy perezoso
learn aprender, saber *(find out)*
least: at ___ por (a) lo menos
leave salir (de) *(intrans.);* dejar *(trans.);* **take** ___ **of** depedirse (i) de
leg pierna *f.*
lesson lección *f.*
let dejar; ___ **us** vamos a *(plus inf.)*
letter carta *f.*
library biblioteca *f.*
lie mentira *f.*
lift levantar
lightly ligeramente

like gustar, querer; **be __** *(resemble)* parecerse a; **look __** *(seem)* parecer; como *(prep.)*
little pequeño, poco; **a __** un poco
live vivir
living: for a __ ganarse el pan
lonely solo, solito
long largo; **__ time** largo rato, mucho tiempo; **for a __ time** hace mucho tiempo; **so __** hasta luego; **no __er** ya no
look: __ at mirar; **__ for** buscar; **__ like** parecerse a
lose perder (ie)
lot: a __ mucho
Louis Luis
love querer, amar
low bajo
lunch almuerzo *m.*
lying tendido

maid criada *f.*
mail correo *m.*
make hacer; **__ money** ganar dinero
man hombre *m.*
manager gerente *m.*
many muchos
market mercado *m.*
married casado
marry casarse; **__ off** casar
Mary María
matter asunto *m.;* **what is the __ with . . . ?** ¿qué tiene . . . ?
maybe tal vez
me me *(obj. pron.);* mí *(after prep.);* **with __** conmigo
meal comida *f.*
mean querer decir; **__while** mientras tanto
means: by all __ de todos modos
meet encontrar (ue), encontrarse (ue) con; conocer
meeting reunión *f.*
member miembro *m.*
message recado *m.*
Mexican mejicano
milk leche *f.*
million millón *m.*
mine mío
minute minuto *m.*
miss señorita *f.*
miss *(inf.)* echar de menos *(feel the absence of);* faltar a *(a meeting, class);* perder *(a moving object)*
mistaken: be __ estar equivocado
mister señor *m.*
moment momento *m.;* **a few __s later** a los pocos momentos
Monday lunes *m.*
money dinero *m.;* plata *f.;* **to make __** ganar dinero

month mes *m.;* **last __** el mes pasado
more más
morning mañana *f.;* **in the __** por la mañana
mother madre *f.*
mountain montaña *f.*
movies cine *m.*
museum museo *m.*
must deber *(obligation);* deber de *(probability)*
my mi

name nombrar; **my __ is** me llamo
nap siesta *f.;* **to take a __** echar una siesta
near cerca de; **__ here** aquí cerca; **__ by** cerca
necessary necesario
need necesitar
neighborhood vecindad *f.*
neither ni, tampoco; **__ . . . nor** ni . . . ni
never nunca, jamás
new nuevo
news noticia(s) *f.*
next: __ year el año que viene; **__ week** la semana que viene
niece sobrina *f.*
night noche *f.;* **last __** anoche
no ninguno *(adj.);* no *(adv.);* **__ one, __body** nadie; **__ longer** ya no
nobody nadie
noise ruido *m.*
none ninguno
not no
notebook cuaderno *m.*
nothing nada
novel novela *f.*
now ahora
number número *m.*
numerous numeroso
nurse nodriza *f.;* enfermera *f.*

objection: to have an __ tener inconveniente
occasion ocasión *f.*
o'clock: to be one __ ser la una
offer ofrecer
office oficina *f.*
often a menudo, muchas veces
old viejo; **older** mayor; **oldest** (el) mayor
on en, sobre, a; **__ the way to** de camino a, camino de
once una vez; **at __** en seguida
one un(o), se; **the __ that** el(la) que; **only __** único
only sólo
open abrir, abierto
opinion opinión *f.*
opportunity oportunidad *f.*

orange naranja *f.*
order pedir (i), ordenar, mandar; **in __ to** para; **in __ that** para que
our nuestro
over por, encima de

page página *f.*
paint pintar
painting pintura *f.*
palace palacio *m.*
Pan American panamericano
paper papel *m.*
parents padres *m. pl.*
park parque *m.*
party tertulia *f.*
pay pagar
peace paz *f.*
pen pluma *f.*
pencil lápiz *m.*
people gente *f.*
perfect perfecto
permit permitir
persuade persuadir
pick up recoger
pistol pistola *f.*
pity lástima *f.*
place lugar *m.;* **in the first __** en primer lugar; **in __ of** por
plane avión *m.*
plate plato *m.*
play jugar *(a game);* tocar *(musical instrument);* comedia *f.*
please gustar; por favor; (haga el) favor de *(plus inf.);* tenga la bondad de *(plus inf.)*
police policía *f.*
poor pobre
Portuguese portugués
possible posible
potato papa *f.*
precisely exactamente
prefer preferir (ie, i)
prepare preparar
present presente *(adj.);* regalo *m.*
president presidente *m.*
pretty bonito
probably probablemente *(or expressed by future or conditional of probability)*
problem problema *m.*
professionally profesionalmente
professor profesor *m.*
promise prometer
provided that con tal que
purchase comprar
purse bolsa *f.*
put poner; **__ on** ponerse; **__ to bed** acostar (ue)

question pregunta *f.*

rack percha *f.*
rain llover (ue)
ranch rancho *m.;* hacienda *f.*
rapidly rápidamente, con rapidez
rather algo
reach llegar a
read leer
realize darse cuenta de
receive recibir; **__ good grades** sacar buenas notas
record disco *m.*
red rojo
regret sentir (ie, i)
regularly regularmente
remember acordarse (ue) de
rent alquilar
research investigación *f.*
residence hall residencia *f.*
rest descansar
return volver (ue), regresar; devolver (ue) *(give back)*
rich rico
right: to be __ tener razón
road camino *m.*
rob robar
robbery robo *m.*
Robert Roberto
room cuarto *m.;* habitación *f.*
Rose Rosa
rose rosa *f.*
row fila *f.*
rule regla *f.*
run correr, ir; andar *(of a machine)*

sad triste; **__ ones** los tristes
salary sueldo *m.*
same mismo
say decir
scene escena *f.*
school escuela *f.*
scream gritar
seat silla, butaca *(orchestra) f.*
see ver
sell vender
send mandar, enviar; **__ a telegram** poner un telegrama
separate separar
serious serio
serve servir (i)
set poner; **__ the table** poner la mesa
seven siete
seventeen diez y siete
seventy setenta
seventy-five setenta y cinco
shave afeitar(se)
she ella
ship vapor *m.*
shirt camisa *f.*
shoe zapato *m.*
short bajo

silk seda *f.*
sign firmar
since puesto que, desde que
sing cantar
sister hermana *f.*
sit (down) sentarse (ie)
skeleton esqueleto *m.*
skirt falda *f.*
skull calavera *f.*
sleep dormir (ue, u); __ing dormido
slender delgado
slow lento
slowly lentamente
small pequeño
smoke fumar
snow nieve *f.*
sock calcetín *m.*
soldier soldado *m.*
some algún(o) *(often not translated in Spanish)*
somebody alguien
something algo
somewhat algo
sonorous sonoro
soon pronto; as __ as tan pronto como, luego que
sorority sororidad *f.*
soup sopa *f.*
Spain España
Spaniard español *m.*
Spanish español
speak hablar
speed velocidad, prisa *f.*
spend gastar; pasar *(vacation)*
spite: in __ of a pesar de
splendid espléndido
spoon cuchara *f.*
standing parado, de pie
statue estatua *f.*
steal robar
stone piedra *f.*
stop parar(se); dejar de
store tienda *f.*
story cuento *m.*
stranger extranjero *m.*
street calle *f.*
stretched out tendido
strong fuerte
student estudiante, alumno *m.*
study estudiar
succeed (in) lograr, conseguir *(plus inf.)*
such tal
support sostener
suppose suponer
sure seguro
surprise sorpresa *f.*
swim nadar

table mesa *f.*
take llevar, tomar, traer; __ a walk dar

un paseo; __ care of cuidar; __ charge of encargarse de; __ down bajar; __ from quitar; __ leave of despedirse (i) de; __ off quitarse; __ out sacar; __ place tener lugar, celebrarse
talk hablar
talkative hablador *m.*
tall alto
taste estar
teach enseñar
teacher profesor *m.*
tear romper, desgarrar
telegram telegrama *m.*
telephone telefonear, llamar por teléfono
television televisión *f.*
tell decir, contar, relatar
ten diez
terrible terrible
Texas Tejas
than que, de, del (de la, de lo, *etc.*) que
that que *(conj. or rel. pron.)*; ese, esa; aquel, aquella; eso, aquello *(demon. pron.)*; el, la, lo *(before* que *or* de); all __ todo lo que, cuanto
the el, la, los, las
theater teatro *m.*
their su, sus
them los, las; les; ellos, ellas; themselves ellos mismos, ellas mismas; se *(reflex. pron.)*
there allí; __ is, are hay; __ was había
they ellos, –as
thin delgado
thing cosa *f.;* the best __ lo mejor
think pensar (ie), creer; __ of pensar en, pensar de *(opinion)*; parecer; don't you __? ¿no le parece?
this este, –a *(dem adj.)*; __ one éste, –a *(dem. pron.)*
those esos, esas; aquellos, aquellas
thousand mil
three tres
through por
ticket boleto *m.*
tie corbata *f.*
time tiempo *m.;* hora *f.;* at dinner __ a la hora de la comida; for a long __ hace mucho tiempo; to have a wonderful __ divertirse mucho; on __ a tiempo
timetable horario *m.*
tired cansado
to a, para, de, en
today hoy
tomorrow mañana
tonight esta noche
top lo alto
torn roto
touch tocar

tourist turista *m. or f.*
tower torre *f.*
town pueblo *m.*
train tren *m.*
travel viajar
tree árbol *m.*
trip viaje *m.*
truck camión *m.*
truth verdad *f.*
try tratar(de)
Tuesday martes *m.;* **last** __ el martes
  pasado
twelve doce
two dos

umbrella paraguas *m.*
unable no poder
uncle tío *m.*
understand comprender, entender (ie)
unfortunately desafortunadamente
United States Estados Unidos *m. pl.*
university universidad *f.*
until hasta
us nos, nosotros
usual usual; **as** __ (como) de costumbre

very muy
view vista *f.*
visit visitar

wait esperar
walk paseo *m.; (inf.)* caminar, andar;
  to take a __ dar un paseo
wallet cartera, billetera *f.*
want querer, desear
warm caliente
wash lavar(se)
watch reloj *m.;* **to** __ mirar
way modo *m.;* manera *f.;* **by** __ **of** por
we nosotros
wear llevar
weather tiempo *m.*
week semana *f.;* **last** __ la semana
  pasada; **next** __ la semana próxima
well bien
what que, lo que *(rel. pron.);* __? ¿qué?,
  ¿cuál?; __ **a!** ¡qué!
when cuando; __? ¿cuándo?
where donde; __? ¿dónde?
whether si

which que, lo que, lo cual; __? ¿qué?,
  ¿cuál?
while rato *m.;* **for a long** __ hace mucho
  tiempo, hace largo rato
whistle silbar
white blanco
who que, quien, el (la) que, el (la) cual;
  __? ¿quién?; **he** __ quien, el que
whose cuyo *(rel. pron.);* __? ¿de
  quién(es)?
why por qué
wife esposa *f.*
will querer; voluntad *f.*
window ventana *f.*
wise sabio
wish desear, querer
with con, de
without sin
woman mujer *f.*
wood madera *f.*
wool lana *f.*
wonder: *sign of probability expressed by
  the future or conditional tenses or their
  compounds*
wonderful: to have a __ **time** divertirse
  (ie, i) mucho
word palabra *f.*
work trabajar; trabajo *m.*
world mundo *m.*
worry apuro *m.;* __ **about** preocuparse
  por
would that ojalá que
write escribir
wrong: to be __ no tener razón

year año *m.;* **last** __ el año pasado;
  next __ el año que viene, el próximo
  año; **to be . . .** __**s old** tener . . . años
yesterday ayer
yet todavía
you usted (Ud., V., Vd.) *sing.;* ustedes
  (Uds., VV., Vds.) *pl.;* tú, *(fam. sing.);*
  vosotros, –as *(fam. pl.);* le, lo, la, los,
  las, les *(obj. pron.);* te, ti *(fam. obj.
  pron.)*
young joven; __ **man** joven m.; __
  woman (lady) señorita *f.*
your su, el (la, los, las) de Vd.; tu(s),
  el tuyo, la tuya, los tuyos, las tuyas

Index

(Numbers refer to pages)

a (preposition) 72
  idiomatic usage with certain verbs
    81–82
  personal 72
absolute construction 234
absolute superlative 142
adjectives 124–129
  absolute superlative 142
  agreement 125
  comparison 137–138
  demonstrative 112–113
  indefinite 92–95
  interrogative 151–153
  irregular comparison 138–139
  of nationality 125
  past participles used as 233
  plural 125
  position 126–127
  possessive 108–110
  relative 156–157
  shortened forms 127–128
  special uses 129
  used as nouns 56
  with **ser** and **estar** 60
adverbs 129–130, 249–250
  absolute superlative 142
  comparison 138–139
  formation 129–130
  indefinite 92–95
  irregular comparison 138–139
  relative 157
affirmative and negative words (pronouns, adjectives, adverbs) 92–95
ago 9
al with infinitive 229
aquí, allí, acá, allá 249
articles, see definite article, indefinite
  article, neuter article
augmentatives 250
aun 250

como si clauses 219
comparison
  of adjectives 137–138
  of adverbs 138–139
  of equality 139
concession, clauses of 213
conditional sentences 216–219
conjunctions 241–242
conocer, compared with **saber** 32
contraction of definite article 45

dative after certain verbs 81–82
days of the week 99
de after a superlative 140
deber 218
definite article 42–44
  contraction 45
  forms 42
  used for possessive 44
  uses 42–44
  with geographic names 43
demonstratives
  adjectives 112–113
  fourth 114
  neuter 115
  pronouns 113–114
diminutives 250
donde, relative adverb 157

estar
  apparent passive with 172–173
  uses 59–60
exclamations 154–155

faltar 80

gran, grande 128
gustar 80

hacer
  causative 198 (footnote)

in idiomatic expressions of time 8–9, 11

imperatives 187
impersonal expressions 200
in after a superlative 140
indefinite words
  adjectives 92–95
  adverbs 92–95
  forms 92–95
  pronouns 92–95
  reflexive 167
  uses 92–95
indefinite article 45–46
  forms 45
  omission 46
  uses 45–46
indicative mood 7–13, 24–27
  compound tenses 27–31
  simple tenses 7–13, 24–27
indirect commands 185
indirect questions 153
infinitive 228
  after prepositions 229
  after verb 230–231, 246
  after verbs of sense perception 230
  perfect 228
  uses 228–229
  without preposition 246
interrogatives 151–153
  as exclamations 154–155
intransitive verbs, indirect object pronouns with 80

months 100

negatives 92–95
neuter **lo**
  as article 47
  as pronoun 77–78
nouns
  abstract 42
  gender 40
  plural 41
  used in general sense 42
numerals
  cardinal 96–97
  ordinal 97–98

ojalá que 186
only 140 (footnote 1)

para 244–245
participles, see past participle, present participle

passive voice 172–173
past participle 231
  irregular 231 (footnote 2)
  uses 232–235
pero and **sino** 242
personal **a** 72
poder 32 (footnote), 218
por 242–244
possessive
  adjectives 108–110
  pronouns 110–111
present participle 231
  irregular 231 (footnote 1)
  uses 231–232
prepositions 242–243, 246–247
  por and **para** 242–245
probability 25, 27, 31
progressive tense 60
pronouns
  demonstrative 113–114
  indefinite 92–95
  interrogative 151–153
  personal 73
  position of direct object, indirect object, and reflexive forms 74–84
  possessive 110–111
  reflexive 167
  relative 156–157
  uses of prepositional forms 82–83
  uses of subject forms 73–74
proviso, clauses of 215
purpose clauses 214

querer 24 (footnote 1), 218
quien 151–153

reciprocal verbs 168
reflexive constructions 167–171
reflexive substitute 173–174
relatives 156–157

saber and **conocer** 32
santo, Santa, San 128
seasons 99
sequence of tenses 202–203
ser 56–58
shortened form of adjective 127–128
sino 242
softened statements 218
subjunctive 181–186, 197–201, 213–219
  in clauses of concession 213
  in **como si** clauses 219
  in conditional sentences 216–219

in dependent clauses 185–186, 197–
200, 213
in independent clauses 181–184
in negative imperatives 187
in relative clauses 201
in softened statements 218
sequence of tenses 202–203
substitutes for the passive 173–174

temporal clauses 213
tense
conditional 26–27
conditional perfect 31
future 24–25
future perfect 31
imperfect 10–11
perfect 27–28
pluperfect 29
present 7–9
present perfect 27–28
preterit 12–13
preterit perfect 30
progressive 60
sequence 202–203

than 140
time 98–99
todavía 250
todo 78 (footnote 1)

vamos a 182 (footnote 1)
verbs
dative after certain 81–82
irregular 263–268
orthographic-changing 261–263
radical-changing 259–260
reciprocal 168
reflexive 167–171
regular 255–259
special meanings in preterit 12, 32
special meaning in reflexive form 169
with and without prepositions 246–
248

would 10

ya 249–250